Uncovering Australia

Uncovering Australia

Archaeology, Indigenous people and the public

Sarah Colley

Smithsonian Institution Press
Washington, D.C.

Published in 2002 in the United States of America
by the Smithsonian Institution Press
in association with Allen & Unwin
83 Alexander Street
Crows Nest NSW 2065
Australia

ISBN: 1–58834–058–9

Library of Congress Control Number: 2002107161

National Library of Australia Cataloguing-in-Publication Data available

Typeset by Midland Typesetters, Maryborough, Victoria, Australia
Printed in Singapore, not at government expense

09 08 07 06 05 04 03 02   5 4 3 2 1

Contents

Preface

Since the 1970s, when fieldwork in Australia began in earnest, archaeologists have unlocked a vast trove of stories about the past which fascinate many Australians. Archaeology relies on studying material evidence—things and places from the past which are often important to non-archaeologists as well. Media reports about the destruction of important archaeological sites by developers, about bottle collectors digging into historic sites, and about Indigenous ancestral remains that continue to be held in museum collections interest more people than just archaeologists. Claims by archaeologists for increasingly earlier dates for human occupation of the continent are front page news. In the early 1970s archaeological evidence suggested a date of 40 000 years ago for the first human settlement. Suggestions are now pushing this date back to 60 000 years ago, or even earlier. Not all archaeologists agree with this, and to some descendants of the earliest inhabitants the dates are irrelevant: they know that their ancestors have always lived here. Yet such dates are important and have been drawn into the political domain to influence the way the public views Indigenous claims.

Professional archaeology in Australia is only about 40 years old. This period has witnessed many changes in Australian society which are reflected in the way Australian archaeologists go about their work. Of particular importance have been the changing roles of Indigenous people in managing their own cultural places, and government control of archaeology through the introduction of planning and heritage legislation.

These aspects have become increasingly apparent to me since I began teaching archaeology. In 1990 I was appointed as a lecturer in Australian archaeology and cultural heritage management at the University of Sydney and began reading widely about the practice of prehistory and archaeology in Australia. I became interested in the way knowledge produced by archaeologists since the 1960s was closely entangled with political and social issues. As I prepared and delivered my lectures I also found that Tasmania featured prominently in the literature, and that Tasmanian case studies were especially useful for introducing students to key theoretical, political and ethical issues relevant to the practice of Australian archaeology more generally.

The original idea

I was first approached by Allen & Unwin in 1996 to write a book about archaeology in Tasmania. In that year an updated edition of Lyndall Ryan's widely acclaimed history of Aboriginal Tasmania, *The Aboriginal Tasmanians*, was published, with the support and assistance of many members of the Tasmanian Aboriginal community. Ryan's book was first published in 1981 and the new edition made passing reference to Tasmanian prehistory and archaeology. So many significant things had happened in this field since 1981 that the publisher felt the topic merited a book in its own right. I met Lyndall Ryan during this time and we talked about archaeology in Tasmania and the courses I'd developed. She suggested my name to the publisher[1] and a project was conceived.

Archaeological research began in earnest in Tasmania from the 1960s onwards. This work soon demonstrated that people had lived there for tens of thousands of years, and were there when the island of Tasmania as we know it today did not yet exist. Low sea levels caused by global climatic changes associated with the last ice age exposed a single landmass consisting of what are now the islands of Tasmania, mainland Australia, New Guinea and the continental shelf in between. Tasmania and Bass Strait were a large peninsula at the southern tip of this landmass. When sea levels rose again about 10 000 years ago, the islands of Tasmania were created. Archaeological and other evidence demonstrates that people living there became isolated from the rest of the world until Abel Tasman sailed to the islands in AD 1642. We presume this isolation came about because the people's boats could not complete the crossing over the wide and stormy waters of Bass Strait between Tasmania and the mainland— although people could and did make sea voyages to closer offshore islands.[2]

Then, during the early 1980s, the Tasmanian Hydro-Electric Commission, backed by the state government, proposed flooding areas around the Franklin River in the south-west. This threatened large tracts of unlogged forest which were highly valued by scientists for their biodiversity and by other members of the public for their unspoilt natural beauty. In the wake of the proposal stone tools and other evidence of human activity were found in an area of thick rainforest where it was previously thought no one had ever lived. Archaeological excavations conducted at Kutikina and Deena Reena caves for an environmental impact study ahead of the proposed dam showed that people were living in the area at least 20 000 years ago. The archaeological value of Kutikina Cave, with its potential to inform about the early prehistory of Australia, became a major argument against dam construction which threatened this and other sites in the region. Archaeologists presented such evidence in the High Court case which eventually ruled against the dam.[3]

Indigenous groups, archaeologists and environmentalists all opposed the flooding of the Franklin in what historian Tom Griffiths described as 'an uneasy shifting alliance'.[4] The Tasmanian Aboriginal Centre (TAC) declared Kutikina Cave a 'sacred site', claiming ownership on behalf of the Tasmanian Aboriginal community. TAC opposition to further excavation strained its relationship with the archaeologists. Environmental conservationists were also suspicious of the archaeologists, accusing them of being 'mind merchants' who were 'disturbing the forest' with invasive technology and science. Archaeologist John Mulvaney, who had become involved in the case, commented that such attitudes arose in part because archaeology showed that people lived in the region long before the dense forests developed. This undermined idealistic notions of a 'timeless Wilderness' favoured by many environmentalists.[5] Griffiths also described 'open antagonism' between the TAC and the Wilderness Society, with Tasmanian Aboriginal Jim Everett complaining that the environmentalists used the existence of Aboriginal sites to argue against the dam, but were unwilling to support Aboriginal land rights claims.

The Franklin Dam case has been well documented elsewhere and is somewhat old news now. Nevertheless it was extremely important in the history of relations between archaeologists, Indigenous people, environmentalists, government and the wider community, not only in Tasmania but elsewhere in Australia, because of the political significance of the issues involved (not least states' rights) and the enormous publicity it generated.

After the dam was stopped, the south-west Tasmanian forests were placed on the World Heritage List by the Commonwealth government.

Between 1987 and 1991 archaeologists from La Trobe University's Department of Archaeology in Melbourne conducted major excavations in the area as part of the Southern Forests Archaeological Project (SFAP).[6] Their major achievement was to locate, excavate, date and conduct detailed archaeological analyses of a series of rock shelter sites, which had been occupied from at least 35 000 years ago. Many sites were abandoned some time before 12 000 years ago, at which time the environment started to change from relatively cool, open country to the dense temperate rainforests which characterise the area today. The protection of these forests was central to the area's nomination to the World Heritage List. The work of the SFAP has great archaeological importance, not least because it documents that people were living at the southern-most part of the Australian continent, in fairly cold and open environmental conditions, by at least 35 000 years ago. This has important implications for scientific understanding of the timing and nature of human settlement of the Australian continent as a whole.[7]

As the Kutikina Cave case showed, relations between archaeologists and Indigenous groups have not always run smoothly. Indeed, an earlier notable dispute arose from the production of Tom Haydon's 1978 documentary *The Last Tasmanian*. The documentary traced the history of British colonisation in Tasmania and its impact on Tasmanian Aborigines, claiming the British had committed genocide in Tasmania by murdering or otherwise causing the death of all the Tasmanian Aborigines. Truganini was described as the last surviving Tasmanian Aboriginal and the last of her 'race'. *The Last Tasmanian* also included interviews with several Indigenous Tasmanians from the Bass Strait islands talking about their history and traditions such as mutton-birding, and in which they also strongly denied their own Indigenous identity. Although the documentary was not just about archaeology, the story was told by two archaeologists (Rhys Jones and Jim Allen), and included footage of Jones conducting library and museum research into Tasmanian Aboriginal history. Jones' archaeological work at Rocky Cape, and his theories about isolation and the decline of precolonial Tasmanian Aboriginal society, featured strongly in the film.[8]

The documentary was greeted with worldwide acclaim but was roundly condemned by Tasmanian Aborigines and their supporters for

denying their existence, their Aboriginality and their rights.[9] Writing in
1983, Tasmanian Aboriginal Ros Langford described how members of the
Tasmanian Aboriginal community felt they had been betrayed by Rhys
Jones and Tom Haydon over the making of the documentary:

> Tom Haydon and Dr Jones approached the Aboriginal community for
> assistance with their work and the making of the film. We were told that
> there would be consultation and sharing of information. We supplied
> them with all of the information required for the film—names, addresses,
> places, contacts and so on. We were promised in return that we would
> see the film, have a say in its editing and generally be involved in the
> view that the film was expressing. That process occurred over a number
> of years. Because of that, many Aboriginals opened their hearts, told
> stories, revealed secrets. We trusted and were betrayed. We weren't con-
> sulted, our stories were edited, a particular line was advanced, and we
> helped portray the story which denied our existence.[10]

The sentiments expressed in *The Last Tasmanian* about the meaning of
Aboriginality in Tasmania are still influential today, even though such
ideas were challenged in 1992 by the Steve Thomas documentary *Black
Man's Houses*. In this documentary, set on Flinders Island in Bass Strait, Thomas
explicitly aimed to address some of what he felt were damaging misconceptions about Tasmanian Aborigines which had been refuelled in the
public mind by *The Last Tasmanian*. The film was made with the support and
collaboration of members of the Tasmanian Aboriginal community who
featured in the documentary and told stories about their Aboriginality,
their history and their lives. Historical archaeology also featured in the
documentary, but this time it was used to support Aboriginal claims to the
Flinders Island site. The documentary was screened on national television
in the early 1990s and won an award from the Australian Film Institute.[11]

A more recent deterioration of relations between archaeologists and
Aboriginal Tasmanians occurred in 1995 when some archaeologists from
La Trobe University became embroiled in a highly publicised dispute with
the Tasmanian Aboriginal Land Council (TALC) about control of, and
access to, excavated materials, many of which were undergoing analysis in
Melbourne. For reasons which are not clear to those not directly involved,
and which have been subject to much often acrimonious argument in the
media and in academic forums, the TALC sought an injunction in the
Australian Federal High Court to force the La Trobe archaeologists to

surrender five archaeological assemblages from excavations in Tasmania. The sites included three of the Southern Forests Archaeological Project sites, one northern Tasmanian site occupied during the last few thousand years, and one contact-period site which had previously been excavated by La Trobe archaeologist Tim Murray.[12] As of October 1995 the materials had been removed from the archaeologists by the court and returned to Tasmania and, according to Murray and Allen, were being held in storage on behalf of the Tasmanian government. From the perspective of certain Australian archaeologists, these events were especially significant because the materials in question were not human remains or secret sacred objects, which usually have particular cultural or religious significance to Indigenous people, but items such as stone tools, food remains, animal bone fragments and soil samples. Communities elsewhere in Australia have usually given consent for archaeologists to study these sorts of items, subject to adequate consultation. The facts of the *TALC v. La Trobe* case are disputed and controversial, but the La Trobe archaeologists were accused of not consulting adequately with the Tasmanian Aboriginal community, of breaking the code of ethics of the Australian Archaeological Association, and of acting illegally with regard to excavation permits. The archaeologists in question have vigorously denied these charges and documented the many ways in which they believe the charges are false. Nevertheless, an atmosphere of particular mistrust was generated.

A different book

These events were still fresh in people's minds in 1996 when I was approached by Allen & Unwin to write the book about archaeology in Tasmania. Everywhere in Australia the government controls the actions of anyone who seeks to disturb important historic places, including archaeologists. To excavate an Aboriginal site in Tasmania requires permission from the TALC before the Tasmanian Parks and Wildlife Service will issue a permit. Permits are not required to write books. Yet I felt I should consult. The history and politics of archaeology in Tasmania are complicated, and much relevant information is not readily available in the public domain. I wished to interview people and gain access to unpublished materials held in local libraries and collections. Given the nature of the subject matter, incorporating Indigenous perspectives was essential.

As the book was about archaeology, and the TALC dealt with Indigenous archaeology in Tasmania, I approached it in the first instance for help. The TALC at first refused, but eventually arranged for me to meet members of the Tasmanian Aboriginal community in Hobart and elsewhere in Tasmania. I also talked to several archaeologists and cultural heritage professionals about my project. As might be expected I got a range of reactions. Some people thought it was worthwhile and interesting and wanted to support it. Others were ambivalent. Some were opposed to it as yet another example of a non-Indigenous researcher, whom people didn't know and had no reason to trust, coming into an Indigenous community expecting people to freely donate their time and effort to something over which they had no control, which had no obvious benefit to the community or to individuals, and had the potential to seriously misrepresent Aboriginal people in a negative way. Some people stated that Aboriginal people in Tasmania should be writing their own books about Aboriginal history and archaeology, and that non-Aboriginal people had said enough on this topic already.

For me the visit to Tasmania was very useful, and I decided to abandon the book. I felt it was pointless to embark on such a project without active input from members of the Tasmanian Aboriginal community. I knew some people were willing to help me—and with time and effort I may have been able to persuade others to allow me to proceed. But I realised that I did not have the resources needed to conduct the level of consultation which would be required. I would have had to rethink the whole project, greatly extending the time frame and the scope. A large research grant would be needed to cover my own expenses and to pay people for their participation. There was no guarantee that such funding would be available. Archaeological research grants in Australia are normally only awarded to conduct excavations and fieldwork—not to write books. I could have gone ahead anyway and written a book based on whatever publicly available information I could find, without the cooperation or support of the TALC. In doing so I would not have written the kind of book I wanted, and I would have risked alienating Aboriginal people in Tasmania. I threw the project into the 'too hard' basket and moved on to other things.

However, as my teaching has shown me, events in Tasmania have much to contribute to a more general overview of the nature of archaeological knowledge in Australia. Issues raised by the practice of archaeology in Tasmania are the same as those which apply elsewhere in Australia. A similar history holds of colonial settlers invading Indigenous land, killing, desecrating, and stealing remains with little regard for Indigenous people's beliefs and feelings for land and ancestors.

The same situation holds of Indigenous people fighting for their rights—essential components of which are the ownership and control of cultural materials and ancestral remains, and the way Indigenous people and their culture are represented. Elsewhere in Australia, too, there are archaeologists who feel aggrieved by Indigenous attempts to control their research, and others who want to work collaboratively, respecting Indigenous people's rights and views. The situation in Tasmania most vividly presents factors operating widely in Australian archaeology. These include the relationship between 'science' and Indigenous rights; community-based action against development which threatens important cultural places; and the role of government and the media in mediating interactions between different interest groups.

This, then, is a book about the practice, politics and ethics of Australian archaeology in general, with some reference to the Tasmanian situation. It places particular emphasis on places significant to Indigenous peoples as these are central to archaeology in Australia. This is a land that has an Indigenous past stretching back beyond 40 000 years and an Indigenous citizenry which is only just getting back ownership of this past. Cultural heritage management has been crucial to this process.

The book aims to present an easily accessible overview to students, interested members of the public, academics in other disciplines and archaeologists overseas. People not actively involved in professional archaeology often have to rely for information on media reports or on a few better known and widely available academic journal articles which, when read in isolation and out of context, cannot provide up-to-date and detailed knowledge about this complicated and frequently controversial subject.

There are other books on Australian archaeology and cultural heritage management which are accessible to a general audience. Most relevant to the subjects discussed here are Josephine Flood's *Archaeology of the Dreamtime* and John Mulvaney and Johan Kamminga's *Prehistory of Australia*. These authors are highly aware of most of the topics I cover here—John Mulvaney in particular has written extensively on similar subjects in different contexts—but both these books concentrate on the 'nuts and bolts' of mainstream Australian prehistory; they avoid extensive discussion of cultural heritage management, ethics and politics.

Michael Pearson and Sharon Sullivan's *Looking after Heritage Places* introduces the reader to the basics of Australian cultural heritage management including, but not restricted to, archaeology and Indigenous places. My own book would have been very hard to write without the existence of such a work. Two books written primarily for high school teachers of ancient history and archaeology—and their students—deal with some ethical and social issues raised in my book and may be of further interest: these are Louise Zarmati and Aedeen Cremin's *Experience Archaeology* and David Frankel's *Remains to be Seen*.

While my own book is aimed at non-specialists and people working outside Australian archaeology, I hope that at least some of it may also be of interest to some Australian archaeologists and cultural heritage managers— even if they feel they know most of it already. In examining and juxtaposing an apparently disparate set of arguments and information, interconnections which are not always immediately obvious start to emerge. This has certainly been my experience in researching and writing this book.

Acknowledgements

Because this book is aimed at a broad audience, textual references have been kept to a minimum. I have tried to strike a balance between acknowledging other people's contributions and providing full bibliographic references and sources of further information, and not cluttering up the pages with too many little numbers. This has generally been achieved by grouping together all the references relating to points in a paragraph in one endnote at or near the end of the relevant paragraph.

In writing this book I wanted to share several years of knowledge and experience gained from teaching Australian archaeology and cultural heritage management at Sydney University. The research and writing was also supported by two Special Studies Programmes from Sydney University in 1996 and 2000 and a 1996 Sabbatical Fellowship at the Australian National University's Humanities Research Centre in Canberra.

Many people have helped me over the last four or five years. As in all projects of this kind there are simply too many to list here, but I am grateful for everyone's contribution. For their help in the early stages of the project I'd like to mention Robyne Bancroft, Prue Gaffey, Angela McGowan and Rob Sim. The book would never have been started without intellectual and other support from Lyndall Ryan. Some people provided information, sent me copies of their work, or gave feedback on early chapter drafts. For such input I'd like to thank: Huw Barton, Alison Betts, Denis Byrne, John Clegg, Leigh Dayton, Hilary du Cros, Brian Egloff, Tony English, Roland Fletcher, David Frankel, Clive Gamble, Lesley Head, Phil Hunt, Nadia Iacono, Tracy Ireland, Ian Jack, Wayne Johnson, Cheryl Jones, Matthew Kelly, Sharon Lane, Isabel McBryde, Ian McNiven, Helen Nicholson, Colin Pardoe, Iain Stuart, Paul Taçon and Peter White. I'd especially like to thank Tessa Corkill and Laila Haglund for information regarding the M2 motorway case, and Judy Field for taking me to Cuddie Springs with her and sharing so much information. Val Attenbrow's support reading drafts and discussing her own writing experiences with me is especially appreciated. Attenbrow's *Investigating Sydney's Aboriginal Past* is in press at the time of writing this.

Five academic readers, some of whom preferred to remain anonymous, provided incisive feedback on an earlier version of the manuscript. All their comments, even the negative ones, were very useful in reframing and redrafting my work and I'm grateful to them for their efforts. For practical assistance with finding references and manuscript editing I wish to thank Aedeen Cremin, Penny Crook and Susan Poetsch. Allen & Unwin editors Mary Rennie, Colette Vella and Karen Penning guided me skilfully through the final stages of editing and book production. John Iremonger has been pivotal to the whole project, as well as being very supportive and accommodating of a large number of delays and changes in direction.

Others have supported me in less obvious but no less essential ways. For this, special thanks to Penelope Allison, Anne Bickford, Frank Colley, Robert Colley, Johan Kamminga, Estelle Lazer, Ingereth Macfarlane, Dana Mider, Yvonne Paul, Alan Subkey, Joanne Thompson and Robin Torrence.

My book is dedicated to the memory of my mother, Muriel Colley.

Sarah Colley
Sydney
January 2002

Archaeology in Australia

The first known archaeological excavation in Australia was at Sydney Cove in AD 1788, when Governor Phillip got his men to dig into an earth mound hoping to find more about the people who had made it. Further sporadic digging into Indigenous sites continued in the nineteenth and early twentieth centuries, mostly by geologists who had discovered bones of extinct animals in deposits that dated to the last ice age. They were looking for evidence of associated human activity, such as stone tools, to see if people also had lived here during the ice age. Before late twentieth-century legislation made their activities illegal, active groups of amateurs also dug into sites to collect Indigenous stone tools.[1]

Nevertheless, archaeology was slow to develop in Australia before the mid-twentieth century. Geologists, failing to find stone tools in direct association with extinct animal bones, stopped looking. Most amateur artefact collectors had little interest in the people who had made the tools they acquired, or in archaeology. Before scientific dating methods such as radiocarbon were invented in the 1950s, and in the absence of written historical records, it was hard if not impossible for researchers to determine the age of artefacts and sites. In Europe and elsewhere the size and shape of prehistoric stone tools vary through time in obvious ways and stone tool typology had become a useful relative dating method from the nineteenth century. No such patterns were apparent in Australia, so this line of research was unproductive.

From the early days of colonisation the newcomers speculated about the origins, antiquity and racial affinities of Australia's Indigenous people. British ideology regarded people in colonised countries across the world as inferior. Racist nineteenth-century theories placed Australian Aborigines at the lowest stage of human evolution—as fossilised survivors of ancient cultures which, unlike Europeans, had failed to grow or change. Scholars and the public alike viewed Indigenous Australians and their cultures as timeless and unchanging.[2] Such attitudes also had a negative impact on the development of Australian archaeology. Using archaeology to study the Aboriginal past was thought by many people to be pointless—while using archaeology to study the remains of colonial settlement as part of Australian history was not considered at all.

In 1929 Norman Tindale and Herbert Hale conducted what is widely regarded as the first proper archaeological excavation in Australia, at the Devon Downs rock shelter in South Australia. Seven years later, in 1936, Fred McCarthy conducted comparable work at the Lapstone Creek rock shelter, at the foot of the Blue Mountains in New South Wales. These excavations are significant for being systematic and scholarly, for employing scientific methods and for the relatively prompt publication of their details. Most importantly, the excavators recorded differences in stone tool types in the successive layers of each site, and these were interpreted as showing change in people's behaviour through time. These studies constitute the first formal scholarly recognition in Australia that archaeology could be used to study change in past Indigenous cultures.[3]

Tindale and McCarthy went on to conduct further excavations and both developed, published and argued for their own schemes of pre-AD 1788 Indigenous stone tool types and what this meant for the continent's human prehistory. Neither Tindale nor McCarthy were professionally trained in archaeology. Both were scholars with wide interests who worked in anthropology and the natural sciences, and both were based in museums—Tindale at Adelaide's South Australian Museum and McCarthy at Sydney's Australian Museum. They both also relied on, and actively encouraged, amateur involvement in their projects, since before the 1960s there was little formal institutional support for archaeological research in Australia.[4]

Major research questions

John Mulvaney is commonly described as being the founder of Australian prehistory. Having completed his undergraduate degree at Melbourne University, he went overseas to study prehistoric archaeology at Cambridge.

On his return in the 1950s he taught the first course in Australian prehistory at an Australian university, in the history department at the University of Melbourne. Economic growth and political changes in the 1960s and 1970s were important for the development and expansion of academic archaeology in and beyond the university system. By 1964 more than a dozen staff and graduate students were employed as Australian prehistorians in universities in Canberra, Sydney and Armidale. More pre-historians were appointed at these and other Australian universities during the 1970s. This allowed the development of important fieldwork-based research and training for new generations of Australian archaeologists. Especially significant was the Department of Prehistory, established as part of the Australian National University's Institute of Advanced Studies (IAS) in Canberra. The IAS received generous research funding from the Commonwealth government, and with no undergraduate teaching respon-sibilities, its staff and research students were able to initiate major fieldwork-based research programmes in prehistoric archaeology in Australia and the Pacific.[5]

The Commonwealth government also supported the study of Aborigi-nal prehistory beyond the universities through the Australian Institute of Aboriginal Studies (AIAS) established in Canberra in 1964. The aim of the AIAS (now the Australian Institute of Aboriginal and Torres Strait Islander Studies) was to promote Aboriginal studies, including prehistory, and to foster cooperation among universities, museums and other institutions.[6]

As in other countries, Australian archaeology has changed and grown through the work of influential individuals, the finding of key sites, the development and application of new methods and techniques—particu-larly radiocarbon dating—and the history of government and institutional support for various types of archaeological scholarship.[7] Australia's status as a now politically independent former British white-settler colony with a minority Indigenous population was also central to the way archaeology developed here. British invasion and colonialism from the eighteenth century onwards, and the changing nature of relations between Indigenous and other Australians, have influenced both the kinds of research archaeol-ogists and the public have been interested in, and the nature of Australian archaeological practice. Many archaeologists appointed to Australian uni-versities in the 1960s and 1970s were trained in the British university system. Others trained in North America, Canada, New Zealand, Africa and elsewhere. So most ideas about archaeology were initially imported into Australia. However, only some overseas theory and practice is directly applicable or useful here and archaeologists have generally modified these to suit local conditions.

As Australian prehistory began to develop as a distinct academic field in the 1960s, archaeologists began addressing a coherent set of questions about Australia's past before AD 1788. New work built closely on that of others and researchers were keen to engage in debate with each other. Few external restrictions were placed on a prehistorian's right to research wherever and whatever they thought was valuable to science or especially interesting. Another major feature of research during this time was the energy and confidence with which it was pursued and presented by what was essentially a cohort of freshly appointed and enthusiastic young staff. This reflected broader trends in Australian society at that time related to economic prosperity and the so-called baby boom generation's confidence in its own abilities and in the future. This confidence was only enhanced by employment growth, job security and ample funds for research. In many ways the 1960s and early 1970s could be described as the golden age of Australian prehistory.[8]

The questions academic prehistorians asked were similar to those which had preoccupied British colonial explorers and settlers since the eighteenth century. Where had Australia's Indigenous people come from? How had they got here and when did they arrive? Had there been one or several waves of human migration? Once here, how quickly had people occupied the whole continent? What was the physical environment like when people arrived and what impact had humans had on it? How and why had people's culture changed through time and in different parts of the continent?

Accurate dates were needed to answer such questions. Researchers such as Tindale and McCarthy had recognised change in the archaeological record, but had not been able to date it. Radiocarbon dating, developed in North America in the 1950s, could provide absolute dates for organic materials like bone, shell and charcoal, which were common in Australian sites. Prehistorians applied this new method to their systematic excavations of Indigenous sites. A major breakthrough came in 1960 when Mulvaney obtained radiocarbon dates from Kenniff Cave rock shelter in central Queensland, which proved people had lived there at least

14 000 years ago during the last ice age. Since then researchers have continued to push the first date of human arrival and settlement of the continent further and further back.

During the 1960s and 1970s, explanations about Australia's human past were given mainly in terms of ecology, technology and population dynamics, reflecting the particular British and North American intellectual heritage of many Australian researchers, and the belief that archaeology was a scientific endeavour, or at least closely linked to the natural sciences and physical anthropology. In association with other sciences, archaeology addressed questions about human evolution, and in Australia prehistorians worked closely with geomorphologists, pollen specialists and other environmental scientists to reconstruct the long-term environmental history of the Australian continent, of which humans were seen as an integral part. Such interests are reflected in the title of a key 1971 publication edited by John Mulvaney and Jack Golson—*Aboriginal Man and Environment in Australia*.[9]

Prehistorians also drew on cultural and social anthropology, and to a much lesser extent on history, in what is known as an ethnographic approach. Contemporary observations of Indigenous life made by settlers, historians and anthropologists were mined for analogies to explain pre-1788 Australia. Some prehistorians conducted their own ethnoarchaeological research, working in contemporary Indigenous communities and recording material outcomes of people's behaviour (for example, mapping the location and features of chipped stone left behind when people made stone tools, or recording the size, shape and composition of hearths and rubbish middens) to help interpret the archaeological record. Several eminent US archaeologists visited Australia in the 1970s and early 1980s to study contemporary Indigenous societies as part of an intellectual project aimed at establishing universally applicable general laws of human behaviour.[10]

Australian prehistory was painted with a broad brush—researchers often extrapolated to the whole continent, or a large region of it, based on finds from a handful of sites or even a single site. During the 1960s and 1970s, this was entirely appropriate as there was a very limited amount of archaeological data against which theories could be tested. So little was known about the prehistory of Australia that any new find could become immediately significant.

Excavations which became very important to the establishment of the discipline of prehistory were conducted at Lake Mungo and the Willandra Lakes area of western New South Wales in the late 1960s and early 1970s. They involved several researchers, mostly from the Australian National University in Canberra. The Willandra Lakes sites consist of scatters of archaeological materials exposed on the ground surface deriving from old camping and burial places along the shores of a now defunct lake system. The sites date from different phases of the last ice age until the recent past. Radiocarbon dating at Willandra Lakes in the mid-1970s placed human settlement of the area back to at least around 36 000 years ago.[11] Such an unexpectedly early scientific date for human presence in Australia was immediately relevant to theories of human evolution and of worldwide interest. Lake Mungo placed Australian prehistory on the world map, whereas before Australia could be dismissed as something of an archaeological backwater. The finds attracted great public interest and the radiocarbon dates entered the rhetoric of politicians and Indigenous land rights activists as proving '40 000 years' of Indigenous occupation.[12]

The Lake Mungo finds were relevant to most of the key questions about Australian prehistory occupying researchers at the time. Public interest in the site encouraged continuing government support for archaeological fieldwork elsewhere in Australia. Numerous other prehistorians also conducted excavations and field recording during the 1960s and 1970s, the results of which have formed the basis of the type of Australian prehistory which has since been summarised in popular overviews and text books.[13]

Some 1960s and 1970s prehistory work stands out as being different from the approaches then generally being taken. In 1976, for example, rather than arguing that environmental change alone dictated people's behaviour, Sandra Bowdler explained changes through time in deposits of shells and fish hooks at a midden site at Bass Point (on the NSW south coast) in terms of gender relations. Bowdler's pioneering interest in gender was not taken up by others in Australia until the 1990s. Other researchers were notable for using archaeology to investigate Indigenous sites from the recent past rather than prehistoric sites. In 1968 Vincent Megaw, for example, excavated shell middens at Kurnell in New South Wales dated to the time of Captain Cook's journey along the east coast of Australia in AD 1770, and reported European as well as Indigenous artefacts. In the Northern Territory Campbell Macknight, Carmel Schrire and Jim Allen excavated sites dated to the period of historically known contact between Indigenous people and visiting Macassan fishermen. The contact archaeology approaches adopted in these studies, which focused on interaction between Indigenous and historically known outsiders, used both documentary and archaeological evidence, and aimed to write history as well as prehistory. They did not, however, generate sustained interest from other researchers, who continued to pursue questions about pre-contact Australia and favour explanations grounded in cultural ecology and related fields.[14]

In the late 1970s and early 1980s Harry Lourandos began publishing a series of papers which represented a radical departure from the accepted wisdom of most 1970s prehistory. His work had an immediate and significant impact on research and theoretical debates in Australian prehistory, in part because, while different, it still addressed key questions of Australian prehistory: the extent to which Indigenous cultures had remained static or changed during the tens of thousands of years before AD 1788, and what had caused change. Lourandos proposed that internal social pressures, involving an 'intensification' of production and/or productivity (in which people modified their behaviour or technology to produce surplus food or other products), explained changes in the Australian archaeological record of the last few thousand years. Compared with much earlier periods during and following the last ice age, the last few thousand years of Australian prehistory seemed to be characterised by a marked growth in the number of archaeological sites, an increase in the range and quantity of materials found in those sites, human expansion into areas of Australia thought to have been previously unoccupied, and a suite of other changes observed by archaeologists.

Lourandos' ideas about intensification as an underlying explanation for such changes contrasted with other explanations based on external factors, such as changes to the environment or natural population growth. His work challenged the basic tenets of cultural ecology and related explanations, and entered the mainstream in that they were challenged in print and at conferences by some of his colleagues. Many other researchers adopted Lourandos' ideas and incorporated them into their own research programmes in the 1980s and 1990s.[15]

Why, then, do archaeologists accept some ideas about the past and reject others? How is it that some approaches to explanation and the kinds of things archaeologists want to know endure for a long time, while other approaches change or are abandoned to be replaced by new ones? These questions are central to the link between archaeological explanation and the broader social and political context within which archaeology is practised. Before discussing these and related issues in the following chapters, it is necessary to first look at the kind of evidence Australian archaeologists are interested in and the way they have interpreted it.

What is the archaeological record?

Archaeology involves careful interpretation of material evidence. Activities which leave no surviving physical traces cannot be studied by archaeologists at all. Material remnants which do survive for archaeologists to study are called the 'archaeological record'. This record is the end product of a series of physical processes, including the actions of archaeologists themselves, which need to be understood to make reliable statements about the past. But what is a reliable statement about the past, and what counts as acceptable evidence? As will be explored in other parts of this book, this depends on the particular theoretical standpoint of the archaeologist.

It is rare in archaeology to find a moment from the past frozen in time and space, as if the archaeologist walked into a room just after the people left, leaving everything behind them. The closest approximations we have to 'frozen moments' are human burials preserved in very cold and dry climates, and underwater wrecks which give us a picture of a ship as it sank. Such sites are uncommon and even then they have usually been subject to at least some decay and disturbance.

The archaeological record also consists of whatever material evidence archaeologists recognise and regard as relevant. As research questions and archaeological methods change through time, so does the archaeological record. Before professional archaeology became established here in the mid-twentieth century, Australia was regarded by most people as having no archaeological record—or at least a very minimal one. And before the development of radiocarbon dating in the 1950s, no one considered that molecules contained in shells and bones from archaeological sites, which can be studied to determine a radiocarbon age, were part of the archaeological record.[16]

Archaeological research into the earliest date of human settlement of Australia illustrates some of the complexities of the archaeological record and the way research questions and other practical matters influence how and what archaeologists record. Most evidence for early dates comes from stone tools buried in soil in rock shelter and cave deposits or in ancient dried out lake beds and other landscape features. Stones with distinctive flaking and shapes which are recognisable as tools provide evidence of human presence. As scientific techniques cannot date these stone tools themselves, archaeologists must rely on dating things found with them, such as sand grains and charcoal in the surrounding soil. The age of the soil provides an approximate date for when the tools were buried.[17]

Tools found in rock shelter and cave sites usually provide more reliable dating evidence than those buried in open sites, which are more prone to disturbance from wind, floods and soil erosion. In shelters and caves, layers build up over time as the roof and walls erode and deposit silt and sand, or even piles of rocks, onto the floor. People visiting and using the shelter leave behind rubbish which also piles up. Many shelters act as a container holding and protecting items for thousands of years. As more material accumulates, the floor moves nearer to the roof. While activities like people digging into the floor to make fires can disturb earlier layers, archaeologists recognise this by paying close attention to changes in soil texture, colour and composition when they excavate, and modifying their interpretations accordingly.

As shelters and caves with deep deposits and stone tools have the greatest potential to answer questions about the date people first arrived in an area, and as this is a question which has interested many prehistorians, there have been many excavations of such sites since the 1960s. Excavation is often by means of deep, narrow holes through the layers of such sites (sometimes jokingly referred to as 'telephone boxes'), rather than wide open-area excavations, as this is the most efficient way to reach the oldest layers at the bottom to take soil samples for dating. The laboratory costs involved in obtaining dates may be high. As the priority of most archaeologists is to date the lowest, earliest layers in a site, the archaeological record for many rock shelter sites consists of dates for the lowest layers, and relatively fewer, or no dates, for higher, younger layers.[18]

The archaeological record is not just what is physically there in the ground. It is equally the notes, photographs, drawings and other recordings made by archaeologists as they excavate and analyse their data, and their later interpretation and synthesis of these data in reports. In Australia, as elsewhere, only a small proportion of archaeological data ever gets analysed and the resulting interpretations and conclusions made widely available to colleagues through publication and other means.[19]

The contribution of ethnography

Archaeologists use historical, recent and contemporary observations of Indigenous Australian life (commonly referred to as 'ethnography') to help them interpret prehistoric archaeological evidence. It is almost impossible to write prehistory from archaeological evidence without at least some reference to such observations. On one level this makes a lot of sense. It seems reasonable that Indigenous people living here at the time of British invasion and colonisation lived in much the same way as their ancestors did. Many traditional items used by Aborigines since AD 1788 are the same or similar to items found buried in archaeological sites, and ethnography is useful for giving names to artefacts and sites and for understanding their basic functions.

David Frankel has discussed the main ways in which prehistorians have used ethnography in Australia. Observations of what people do are particularly useful for understanding site formation processes. For example, some archaeologists have watched Indigenous people making stone tools, butchering animals, collecting and eating shellfish and doing similar practical things, then recorded the material remains left behind to help them recognise such activities in the archaeological record.[20]

Observations of Indigenous life are also useful as a reminder of human diversity and what might have originally been present in a culture but has not survived archaeologically. For example, all historically known and contemporary Indigenous societies use organic materials to make tools, weapons, utensils, ornaments and art. Yet none of these items survive under normal circumstances in archaeological sites. The materials simply rot away. In the past people may have used simple unmodified stone flakes to cut and work wood, leather, bark, plant fibres and myriad other perishable materials. All that survives of such activities are the stone tools themselves and perhaps minute organic traces on the edges of the tools. In such cases archaeological evidence gives a highly limited view of the likely nature of Indigenous material culture before AD 1788. Knowledge of historically recorded recent and contemporary Indigenous societies and cultures reminds the archaeologist of this.

Frankel also comments that accounts of Indigenous life remind archaeologists that *people* were there in prehistory. Some archaeological interpretations can be very abstract, with the major focus on terms, definitions and minor archaeological details. Artefact types or particular rock art styles sometimes seemingly take on a life of their own in the archaeological literature. Australian prehistorians have categorised Indigenous stone tools into types based on attributes such as shape and size, the kind of stone used, manufacturing techniques, geographical distribution and likely function. Prehistorians frequently want to know the earliest dates at which particular tool types or tool production techniques appear in the archaeological record, and the rate at which such phenomena spread across the continent. The outcome of this kind of research has been the production of a large literature about prehistoric stone tools in which archaeologists propose competing models to explain observed long- and short-term variation in the form, function and geographic distribution of different types of stone tools. Most of this discussion is about the stone tools themselves, and much of it is highly obscure to the non-specialist. Only some of it is obviously about Indigenous peoples or their history.[21]

Prehistorians also frequently describe items and phenomena as appearing or disappearing, moving across the continent, distributing themselves in certain ways or undergoing long-term change or stability, without obviously relating this directly to what the people who made and used these things might have been doing. This situation arises precisely because there is only rarely a clear and easily understandable link between what people were doing in the past and the material evidence we are left with. What archaeologists say might be true of the archaeological record itself, but surely the purpose of studying that record is to say something meaningful or interesting about the people who were responsible for such patterns and changes.

Not all archaeologists would agree with this statement. For some researchers, the aim of Australian prehistory is indeed to identify and explain large-scale and long-term patterns in the Australian archaeological record. While these are ultimately considered to reflect human behaviour at some level, they can tell us little or nothing about what people did in the past on a day-to-day basis, or indeed within any humanly meaningful historic time frame. Such issues are at the heart of a major worldwide debate about scales of human behaviour (in time and space) that are observable archaeologically, and the appropriate use of analogies drawn from historical and ethnographic accounts to interpret archaeological data.[22]

Continuity and change

One big problem with using observer accounts of Indigenous life to interpret prehistory is that the past *is* different from the present. We cannot assume that people living in Australia before British invasion necessarily thought or behaved in the same way as, for example, Indigenous people living in northern or central Australia in the late nineteenth or early twentieth centuries, whose culture has frequently been the focus of ethnographic study. Archaeology shows that many material elements of Indigenous people's lives *have* changed through time.[23] For example, archaeologically described tool types such as Bondi points and Pirri points (or southern uniface points) appear then disappear from the archaeological record within the last few thousand years and are not known historically at all.[24] Another well-known example is Rhys Jones' study of the Rocky Cape site in Tasmania where fish bones were found in association with bone points in layers of the site dated before 3500 years ago, but neither have been found in more recent layers. This accords with historical observations that the Tasmanian Aborigines had a taboo against eating scale fish and that they did not use bone points. Archaeological evidence demonstrates a significant difference between eighteenth-century Tasmanian Aborigines and their ancestors living in the same place several thousand years before.[25]

Archaeology also demonstrates that many new elements were added to Indigenous cultures between the time of first human settlement 40 000 years or more ago and the first arrival of European explorers in the seventeenth century. A vast corpus of Indigenous rock art displays numerous changes, elaborations and innovations in both techniques and styles through time. The invention of new stone tool types and manufacturing techniques is apparent in the archaeological record. Many of these tools continued to be used into the historic period.[26] People also developed new and more efficient ways of collecting food, for example by constructing extensive artificial drainage systems and fish traps to harvest eels, and by developing methods to leach poisons from otherwise highly nutritious and abundant cycad plants. Such changes in food harvesting, which are visible in the archaeological record, are thought by some archaeologists to indicate not only the invention of new technologies but also social changes.[27]

It would be unreasonable to expect any society to remain completely static over thousands of years. Today some Indigenous Australians state they have 'the longest surviving culture in the world', meaning that while some elements of their culture have changed, others have remained in place over thousands of years. This combination of continuity and change is evident in the archaeological record, and its extent, cause and significance have been the subject of much debate in Australian prehistory.

Further limits of historical information

Colonial ideology has strongly influenced the way outsiders have portrayed Indigenous Australians as 'primordial' or 'primitive' compared with 'modern' and 'civilised' Europeans.[28] Some European observers present highly romanticised accounts of Indigenous people as 'noble savages' living an idyllic life in peaceful co-existence with their environment until fatally corrupted by the arrival of Europeans. Others portray Indigenous culture as brutal, dangerous and uncivilised, and Indigenous people themselves as ugly, dirty and lazy. Until the mid-twentieth century non-Indigenous Australians commonly thought that it was only a matter of time before Indigenous people and their culture would disappear altogether in the face of competition from superior white culture. Early colonial writers and anthropologists studied Indigenous people as living evidence of a universal human past and therefore emphasised the 'traditional' characteristics of Indigenous societies which were most relevant to such studies.[29]

Historic accounts by definition describe Indigenous societies which had already encountered and been affected by European explorers, British invasion and colonial settlement. Given the profound impact of these events, historical descriptions of Indigenous life may not accurately reflect what life was like before that time. Historic accounts are also quite limited in their geographic coverage and in what they describe. We simply don't have detailed records of every aspect of every Indigenous culture from every part of Australia at the time of first European contact. Much was never recorded before many Indigenous societies and culture were changed forever, and in some cases obliterated, by British invasion. Before then Indigenous people may have lived in far more varied ways than can be surmised from a limited number of historical accounts and more recent ethnographic documentation.

In consequence, archaeologists have tended to extrapolate people's behaviour prior to AD 1788 in many different parts of Australia from information about better documented Indigenous societies in the north, west and inland regions, away from major centres of European occupation and influence. Betty Meehan's comprehensive study of Anbarra women's shell-fishing and other food-collecting activities in Arnhem Land in the Northern Territory in the early 1970s has been used to interpret prehistoric shell midden sites from all over Australia. But even here, as Meehan herself has noted, such reasoning is flawed, as the food-collecting activities she documented in the early 1970s, and their archaeological signature in the form of different types of camp sites, had very specific meanings within the context of Anbarra society and the local environment, and make little direct sense if used elsewhere. Meehan also found that her 1970s data were largely irrelevant to understanding large prehistoric shell mounds in Anbarra country, which were quite different in form, content and location to more recent places, and about which local people had no direct historical knowledge.[30]

Deep and shallow pasts

How Australian prehistorians have dealt with such theoretical issues in their work has often depended on the age of the sites and artefacts they study. A common practice in Australian prehistory has been to divide the Aboriginal past into the Pleistocene (which is often called the 'deep past') and the more recent Holocene periods, although some prehistorians now question the value of such a division. The Pleistocene is the period from before first human settlement of the continent at least 40 000 years ago until around 10 000 years ago. At the end of the Pleistocene world temperatures started to rise, melting glaciers and the polar ice caps. Sea levels began to rise, flooding great areas of land and stabilising at their current levels about 6000 years ago. The period following the Pleistocene is called the Holocene, which continues to the present.[31]

The 'direct historical' approach to using ethnography for archaeological interpretation assumes that such interpretation is most reliable when the historically known society is close in both time and space to the particular archaeological evidence. This contrasts with the 'general comparative' approach in which the archaeology and ethnography (or history) are widely separated in time and space.[32] In general, Australian archaeologists feel most comfortable using historical and anthropological accounts of Indigenous Australian life to assist them in interpreting sites and artefacts dated to the last few thousand years (from the Holocene), rather than much older material, especially that dated to more than 10 000 years ago (in the Pleistocene). This assumes that basic elements of people's lives over the past few thousand years would have been fairly similar to those recorded by Europeans in the last 200 years or so. This certainly seems reasonable for the few decades immediately prior to European contact in the eighteenth century. But how far back in time can such ethnography be pushed? Archaeology—not least Rhys Jones' findings in Rocky Cape— demonstrates that at least some elements of Indigenous culture have changed over the last few thousand years. Few archaeologists would argue that life in Australia tens of thousands of years before the British arrived is likely to be identical to the way Aboriginal people lived in different parts of Australia in the nineteenth century or at other times over the past 200 years.

This debate is not only about the validity and usefulness of 'direct historical' analogy in archaeological interpretation—it is also about the nature of the archaeological record and the kinds of things archaeologists want to know about the past. In investigating questions about early human settlement or people's relationship to the natural environment in the 'deep past', most prehistorians avoid explanations based on ethnography as much as possible. Instead they prefer to rely on general assumptions about human behaviour and interactions with the natural environment drawn from biological and ecological sciences. Explanation is frequently large-scale and long-term—an impersonal and unsocialised past in which populations are described as interacting with environments driven by forces such as population pressure, climatic and environmental change and minimisation of economic or energetic risk. Indeed, the archaeological record from much of the deep past is often only amenable to such explanations. When, for example, the residue of material evidence from several thousand years of human activity is mixed and compressed into a single shallow layer in a rock shelter, it is not possible to interpret such data in terms of the actions of individuals within a time frame measured in individual years or decades.[33]

For those archaeologists who do make heavy use of ethnography to write prehistory which offers some description of human relations (and thus makes direct links between prehistoric archaeological evidence and historically known Indigenous groups), much depends on the nature of the archaeological evidence itself and the age of the site; it is more common for more recent Holocene and contact period sites. Indigenous people themselves have often been keen to embrace such interpretations which extend history into prehistory and emphasise continuity between past and present and the unchanging nature of Indigenous life before British invasion.[34] This is hardly surprising. Colonialist ideology has usually required Indigenous people to defend their cultural rights in terms of continuing tradition, while at the same time denigrating anything which differs from an essentialist view of a timeless, unchanging and 'traditional' Indigenous culture as being 'not really Indigenous' and therefore invalid.[35]

Historical archaeology

Australian archaeology is about much more than the prehistory of Indigenous Australia. Many Australian archaeologists work in overseas countries, and archaeology of the Near East and classical Mediterranean world, often allied to classics and ancient history, was taught in Australian universities long before John Mulvaney and others introduced local prehistory into university curricula.[36] Within Australia, the most significant categories are between prehistory (the archaeology of pre-1788 Aboriginal Australia), historical archaeology (the archaeological study of British colonisation) and maritime archaeology (the study of shipwrecks and places associated with maritime exploration and industries, usually under water). There is also some interest in industrial archaeology. While there are some commonalities between maritime, industrial and historical archaeology, in general maritime archaeology has not involved Indigenous heritage, and until fairly recently most historical archaeologists had little to say about Indigenous history or Indigenous–settler relations under colonialism.

The first research excavations of Australian historic sites were conducted by university-based archaeologists in the 1960s and 1970s. These included Jim Allen's study of the early colonial settlement of Port Essington, Northern Territory, and Judy Birmingham's excavation of an early colonial pottery production site at Irrawang in New South Wales, and at the historic Aboriginal and European site of Wybalenna in Bass Strait, Tasmania.[37] Since then historical archaeology has developed into a major sub-field of Australian archaeology with numerous practitioners, and there is wide popular interest in many historical archaeology projects. However, there have always been far fewer university-based historical archaeologists than prehistorians. Rather, Australian historical archaeology has developed and grown primarily in the context of cultural heritage management. Legislation in several states requires that heritage studies be incorporated into land use planning, and that salvage excavations be conducted ahead of any development work which threatens historic places. Legislation also lays down guidelines for archaeological excavation work. Most historical archaeologists work as consultants on such projects, with a few employed as cultural heritage managers by the Commonwealth and some state governments.[38]

Outside cultural heritage management, a small number of academics and their postgraduate students conduct research in historical archaeology. Many historical archaeology projects, inside and outside the university system, have focused on a specific site and aimed only to record material remains in association with documentary evidence. Fewer projects have compared evidence between sites or involved regional studies aimed at answering broader questions. In general, historical archaeology aims to answer questions about Australia's colonial past which cannot be answered from documentary evidence alone. In other cases the combination of archaeological and documentary evidence allows researchers to write a different kind of history than would result if either type of evidence were considered in isolation.

Historical archaeologists have addressed a range of research questions, including what solutions were devised by British colonists faced with the problems of a new natural and social environment—such as the adaptation of local materials to replace items from home not readily available in the new colony. In the urban setting researchers have been interested in the processes by which early colonial settlements, such as Sydney and

Melbourne, became transformed from small-scale pre-industrial communities into urbanised industrial societies, with particular reference to the development of consumerism related to the growth of mass production of goods. Such work has been strongly influenced by theoretical developments in North American historical archaeology. Broader themes that have been investigated in recent years have been the growth and development of rural landscapes, material evidence for convictism, gender relations, and the history and archaeology of Chinese settlement in Australia.

Maritime and industrial archaeology, which form separate subbranches of Australian historical archaeology, have often concerned themselves with documenting the material remains of particular sites or, in the case of industrial archaeology, recording the history and development of particular industries and manufacturing processes. Given the cultural heritage management context of much Australian historical archaeology, arguments and debates about its proper aims and its relationship to Australian history have been a recurring theme in the literature.[39]

Contact archaeology

Historical archaeology is also important to understanding Indigenous and settler history. British colonisation of Australia was not instantaneous. Preliminary encounters between Indigenous people and European explorers from the seventeenth century were followed by the establishment of the first British settlement at Sydney Cove in AD 1788. From here and other early colonial settlements the newcomers moved in fits and starts across the country, in association with activities such as pastoralism, farming, sealing, whaling, and gold mining. Because most early British settlement was concentrated in the south-east, Indigenous people there suffered the direct impact of invasion and colonialism most severely and earliest.[40]

Elsewhere the colonial frontier expanded more slowly, especially in country of less economic value to Europeans. Much of the arid centre and west of Australia was too dry for extensive British settlement and early contact often occurred along colonial communication routes, such as telegraph and railway lines and associated infrastructure. While pastoralism became important in the tropical north of Australia from the late nineteenth century, the density of European settlement there was also relatively low due to extremes of climate and the remote and rugged nature of the country. In general, Indigenous peoples whose lands were in the centre, north and west of Australia experienced colonialism much later than those in the south and east. Even in the 1970s and 1980s small numbers of Indigenous people were still living in areas of Australia remote from European life.[41] To Indigenous people living in Australia at the time of colonial settlement, whenever and however it occurred, this was an invasion of their land which many of them fought long and hard against.

Archaeological research into Indigenous aspects of Australia's colonial history is usually referred to as 'contact archaeology'. This is a form of historical archaeology which aims to write histories which include Indigenous peoples as well as colonial settlers and other outsiders, and focuses on cross-cultural interaction. Such studies have become more common since the 1990s. Not all contact archaeology is about the British. For example, there has been much research interest in contact between Macassan trepang (sea slug) fishermen from Indonesia and Indigenous people along the north Australian coast in the eighteenth and nineteenth centuries.[42]

Archaeologists researching contact archaeology need to establish what Indigenous societies were like immediately before the arrival of outsiders, to document subsequent continuity and change. Here contact archaeologists face similar problems to prehistorians. Issues raised by reconstructing the nature of Indigenous societies at the boundary of Australian prehistory and historical archaeology have barely been canvassed in the archaeological literature, primarily because interest in such studies is relatively recent.[43] The time frames in which archaeologists write prehistory are generally much longer and cruder than those in which they write history. Archaeological remains from colonial Australia can often be discussed in decades, or even individual years, rather than the centuries, millennia or tens of millennia of Australian prehistory. Therefore the kinds of things that might be said about continuity and change in prehistory are fundamentally different from what can be said about the historic period. Like all historical archaeology, the interplay between documentary and material evidence allows researchers to write a different kind of history than might result from the use of either type of evidence alone.[44] The moving frontier of colonial settlement means that the history of some Indigenous people from the late eighteenth century onwards can be studied using the methods and theories of historical archaeology. Yet in other parts of the country, which were still beyond the frontier at this time and for which documentary evidence is not available until a much later date if at all, Indigenous life needs to be studied using the methods and theories of prehistory.

An early and important example of contact archaeology conducted by a historical archaeologist was Judy Birmingham's study of the history and archaeology of Aboriginal–European contact at Wybalenna on Flinders Island in Bass Strait. Birmingham focused on Indigenous resistance to, and acceptance of, dominant European ideology, and the attempts of George Augustus Robinson to 'civilise' Indigenous Tasmanians in his care. Her excavations were conducted between 1969 and 1971, but the results and analysis were only published in 1992.[45]

Birmingham's project began following an invitation to conduct salvage excavations at Wybalenna in 1969, after amateurs had disturbed the foundations of a terrace of cottages which had housed Indigenous people. As she comments in her 1992 publication, at the time there was no legal requirement that she consult with anyone. Birmingham did not need to ask the TALC or any other members of the Tasmanian Aboriginal community for permission to excavate the site, although there were some Aboriginal people present on the dig.[46]

Because Birmingham's work had not been published at the time, Steve Thomas made only brief reference to the Wybalenna excavations in his 1992 documentary *Black Man's Houses*, which used the Flinders Island site to examine Indigenous identity and history in Tasmania.[47] Indigenous involvement in Thomas' documentary is in stark contrast to Birmingham's project. The main focus of the documentary was on the historic Flinders Island cemetery in which several hundred Indigenous people who had died at the settlement were buried. At the start of the documentary, the cemetery was overgrown and the location of the individual graves was not marked. Members of the Tasmanian Aboriginal community sought the assistance of archaeologist Don Ranson, who is shown in the film working with them conducting a resistivity survey of the cemetery to locate the position of graves under the ground surface. The technique measures differences in the electrical resistance of underground soil features and enables archaeologists to locate buried graves, pits, ditches and other features of possible interest without having to excavate first.[48] The results of the survey were matched with a historical map of the cemetery on which George Augustus Robinson had marked the names of those buried in each plot. This enabled people to place markers on the graves to commemorate their ancestors. In this case, local Indigenous people had asked Don Ranson to help them. The stated purpose of the work was to assist people 'reclaim the history' of the site. The methods used did not involve any excavation or physical disturbance of the ground.

Archaeological values of places

Discussion so far about the nature of the archaeological record, the use of historical and ethnographic information, and the different kinds of prehistory and history produced by researchers depending on their theoretical approach, demonstrates that far from being about 'digging up facts', archaeology involves careful interpretation of evidence. Different archaeologists can produce very different types of prehistory and history, and argument and debate are a normal and expected part of the production of archaeological knowledge in an academic context.

This chapter also demonstrates that despite disagreements, archaeologists have been responsible for drawing public attention to many places and artefacts from Australia's past and have given them value. Many members of the public, including many Indigenous Australians, are interested in, and have welcomed and accepted, the scientific, historic and archaeological values ascribed to places and objects by archaeologists. Other Australians regard these values quite differently and reject, disregard or query them. When archaeology enters the cultural heritage management process, and when archaeologists interact with the public in other ways, the validity and usefulness of archaeological knowledge often comes under scrutiny and in many cases is challenged. Such issues will be explored in the following chapters.

2

The rise and rise of cultural heritage management

Archaeology is rarely politically neutral and can be used by governments and politicians for their own ends. According to Bruce Trigger, archaeologists often study places important to their country's national history, whether real or imagined. Such places are symbols of national identity, and the way archaeologists interpret them is strongly linked to nationalism, colonialism and, in some cases, imperialism.[1]

The importance of governments to archaeology has increased dramatically in the twentieth century. Governments now commonly fund archaeological research and university training for archaeologists and legislate to promote the conservation of national historic places. By late 1999, the governments of 158 countries had signed the UNESCO World Heritage Convention, and 89 governments had signed an international agreement to stop the trade in illegal antiquities.[2]

Trigger and others have shown the varying ways in which political power structures influence archaeology and how the kind of archaeology practised in different countries is shaped by elements of their history and their economic and political status in the world. In extreme instances, dictatorial governments and their leaders have forced archaeologists to interpret the past strictly in ways which supported their own political ambitions, as in the cases of Nazi Germany and the former white colonial regime in Zimbabwe.[3] Most political influence on archaeology is more subtle and comes from forces inside and outside government.[4]

In Australia, nationhood and nationalism have both contributed to and drawn on archaeology. Denis Byrne has discussed how the concept of 'national heritage' has been central to the practice of archaeology in Australia since the 1970s, and how successive Australian governments have appropriated the great time depth of Indigenous occupation of the Australian continent as part of a nationalist project. Byrne argues that this has been done in a colonialist way, which has presented and continues to present contemporary Indigenous people and their culture as invisible and 'unauthentic', thus denying them cultural and other rights. Tracy Ireland also has linked particular notions of Australian nationalism expressed, for example, in ideas about the land as hostile and empty of Aborigines, the bush as the essence of Australia and the landscape as feminine, to the history and practice of Australian historical archaeology. According to both Byrne and Ireland, particular notions of Australian nationalism have arisen as part of Australia's colonial history. Governments have perpetuated some ideas about Australia's past and discouraged others particularly through their involvement in cultural heritage management. Yet in Australia archaeologists have still been able to provide critiques of such ideas and to pursue different kinds of archaeological research which don't necessarily conform to colonialist ideologies.[5] While governments frequently exert strong influence over the management and interpretation of cultural places within their jurisdiction, they can never fully control the past. Other stakeholders can be equally important.

Stakeholders in place

The Australian government's involvement in archaeology revolves primarily around the management of conflicting values associated with places and objects which are important to people's history and identity.

Excavation and other archaeological techniques can be physically invasive and can have an irreversible physical impact on places and objects. What archaeologists say about the past may contradict other people's values and beliefs. Many places that Australian archaeologists call 'prehistoric' sites have spiritual and religious importance to Indigenous people as part of a living culture. This is especially so for burial grounds— places many non-Indigenous people also feel strongly about—but it applies to other sites as well.[6] Even the words used to describe places and things can be contentious. An archaeologist's 'site' may be an Indigenous Australian's 'spiritual place'. 'Fossils' or 'human skeletons' are the remains of someone's relatives or ancestors. In recognition of this possible diversity of meanings, cultural heritage managers in Australia have adopted the term 'cultural place' to describe locations which have associated cultural values.

The same place can hold different meanings and values to a range of stakeholders. For example, an Indigenous rock art site may have scientific value to an archaeologist as an opportunity to gain new knowledge about the prehistory of Australia. The same place may have spiritual significance to its traditional owners because it was created by ancestral beings. Stories associated with the art might also be important for transmitting knowledge to younger community members and maintaining cultural identity. The place may also provide tangible evidence of an Indigenous community's link with land and be relevant to a land rights claim. For similar reasons non-Indigenous landowners may feel negatively about a place which they perceive as a possible threat to their own rights to the land. Should conflict result, the art site could become a symbol of political struggle to a much wider group of Australians.

Other groups may have more mundane interests. Tour operators may value the art as a source of income, while to the tourist it is a place of entertainment, education, boredom or misunderstanding.[7] A local teacher may use the art site as somewhere to take students as part of the curriculum. To an artist the site may be a source of inspiration; to local people, a pleasant place for a picnic. The site may also represent an obstacle to proposed development and therefore be valuable to environmentalists as a means of stopping such development. To a journalist the site may be a good subject for a story, especially if conflict arises over its meaning and value.

With such a range of potential interests, Australian governments, over the last three decades, have introduced legislation, infrastructure and policies to deal with conflicts over cultural places. This has resulted in increased government decision-making about the future of cultural places, and close government involvement in archaeology through the practice of cultural heritage management.[8]

Heritage legislation and policy in Australia

Australia is a federation of six states, and two internal and seven external territories. As the Australian Constitution gives primary responsibility for land management to state governments, state laws and policy are more relevant to archaeology and cultural heritage management on a daily basis than those which originate in Canberra. Nevertheless, the Common-wealth government has considerable power and influence, not least because the states rely on Commonwealth funding.

For archaeologists the situation is messy, because the Commonwealth, the states and internal territory governments have developed their own legislation and policy on cultural heritage management, including archae-ology. This varies in its aims and provisions, and in the level of protection afforded to cultural places. Government policies outside the immediate area of heritage (especially in schools education and cultural tourism), and power struggles between Commonwealth and state governments, also impinge on archaeology and heritage.[9]

Helen Parrott outlines basic legal techniques which, singly or in combination, have been used to fulfil cultural heritage policy objectives in Australia. For example, much heritage legislation (using the 'penal tech-nique') makes it illegal to destroy or damage cultural places under certain circumstances, and imposes penalties such as fines or prohibitions on further development activity. The 'administrative-regulatory technique', which sets up guidelines and procedures and assists people to comply with them, is also common. Using this technique, developers may be obliged to assess the impact of their development proposal on cultural places, and archaeologists must apply for an excavation permit. Other techniques are available, but less commonly applied.[10]

The main types of Australian heritage legislation are discussed by Michael Pearson and Sharon Sullivan in their book *Looking After Heritage Places*. Aboriginal and historic sites protection Acts (also called relics, heritage, sites or historic conservation Acts) protect certain classes of cultural place, as defined in each Act. Most cover either Indigenous or non-Indigenous places, but seldom both. Notification Acts involve com-piling registers of cultural places which are assessed against significance criteria. Sometimes listing confers legal protection; sometimes the regis-ters are simple management tools. Land or site management Acts establish government and statutory level conservation and management services, such as Parks and Wildlife Services and Historic Houses Trusts, which are responsible for cultural places on the land they manage. Planning legisla-tion throughout Australia controls pollution and other environmental impacts and regulates land use and building development. Much of this involves cultural places and archaeology.[11]

Bald statements about the basic provisions of a piece of heritage legislation provide no more than an indication of its general intentions. As Parrott discusses, how legislation is applied in practice is much more important. This depends on the financial, administrative and technical support made available for its implementation, policies and procedures developed by public servants to make the law workable, and other factors like the state of the economy and which political party is in power. A newly elected government which disagrees with the aims of a piece of legislation it has inherited from the previous administration can render it ineffective through resource starvation or administrative change. This avoids having to repeal or amend the existing law which can be costly, lengthy and even politically risky. Parrott also notes that legislation and policy are dynamic entities which must change and grow to remain effective.[12]

What emerges from all this are complex, overlapping and sometimes contradictory sets of legislation, policies and procedures about cultural places, archaeology, Indigenous affairs, land management and environmental protection, all of which can be subject to frequent change. Much policy review happens internally. Information is often only made public at specific stages in the process, if and when the government feels that wider consultation is useful. By whatever means, heritage professionals and archaeologists are required to keep themselves up to date with changes in legislation and policy relevant to their own work. What they need to know depends largely on which states or territories they work in. In cases of dispute or major ambiguity, legal advice may have to be sought.[13]

Heritage and the Commonwealth government

The Commonwealth government is responsible for shaping national policy on heritage management, advising other government agencies on heritage matters and assisting with problems which arise when state or territory heritage legislation fails or proves inadequate. The Commonwealth government oversees the import and export of heritage items, and signs international agreements on heritage protection, provisions of which are binding on states. It controls taxes and can provide tax incentives to promote heritage conservation. Commonwealth government education and research policies impact on university-based archaeology across Australia. Most importantly, the Commonwealth government has major responsibility for Indigenous affairs, with significant implications for archaeology and cultural heritage management.[14]

Most cultural heritage matters fall under the environment portfolio. Existing legislation derives ultimately from the 1970s and Labor Prime Minister Gough Whitlam's vision for Australian heritage. Since then, while successive governments of various political persuasions have amended and introduced new laws, most changes have been in keeping with Whitlam's basic ideals—in rhetoric if not always in practice.

Australia signed the World Heritage Convention in 1974, and the Commonwealth subsequently introduced national legislation to protect and manage Australian places on the World Heritage List considered to have 'outstanding universal cultural and natural value to humankind'. While most of Australia's current World Heritage places are listed for their environmental values, also important are their cultural values, archaeological value included.[15] The *Australian Heritage Commission Act 1975* set up a national list of significant Indigenous, historic and natural places (the Register of the National Estate) and structures and procedures to facilitate their promotion and protection. Other Commonwealth legislation deals with historic shipwrecks, illegal export of heritage items, and the management of heritage places owned by the Commonwealth government itself. Most of these laws impact on archaeology because archaeological value is included in Commonwealth cultural significance criteria.[16]

Following the 1967 referendum which granted the Commonwealth government major powers over Indigenous affairs instead of the states, successive Commonwealth governments have introduced legislation in this area, some of which is relevant to archaeology.[17] Most important has been the *Aboriginal and Torres Strait Islander Heritage Protection Act* introduced by the Labor government in 1984. Administered by the Aboriginal and Torres Strait Islander Commission (ATSIC), this Act protects Indigenous places, objects and ancestral remains from both physical and spiritual threat (i.e. desecration) in cases where state legislation fails.[18] Since the 1980s, this Act has been used by Indigenous people to pressure archaeologists and museums to return ancestral remains for reburial. It was also central to the 1990s Hindmarsh Island affair, when Indigenous people used it to challenge a proposed bridge development at Hindmarsh Island in South Australia, claiming the proposal threatened an important but secret women's place. A Royal Commission set up by the South Australian government overturned the Commonwealth government's decision to halt the development, and dismissed the Aboriginal women's claims as fabricated and inauthentic. The case attracted wide public and media interest and caused political furore.[19] Following this, the present Howard government initiated a major review of the provisions of the *Aboriginal and Torres Strait Islander Heritage Protection Act* in 1995, and in 1998 introduced the Aboriginal and Torres Strait Islander Heritage Protection Bill to replace the existing Act. This is currently before parliament.

In fact, since coming to power in 1996, Prime Minister John Howard's Liberal–National government has initiated a major overhaul of Commonwealth cultural heritage responsibilities.[20] A major aim of the Howard government's proposed changes to both the *Aboriginal and Torres Strait Islander Heritage Protection Act 1984* and the *Australian Heritage Commission Act 1975* which the government is also reviewing, is to devolve some Commonwealth responsibility back to the states. At this stage the likely impact of such changes on Australian archaeology is uncertain.[21]

State and territory heritage legislation
State and territory governments have major responsibility for day-to-day management of cultural places under their own legislation, which varies greatly in its provisions. In all states and territories laws protecting Indigenous heritage were introduced much earlier than those protecting non-Indigenous (mainly European) places. The way Indigenous heritage is protected differs from state to state depending on broader attitudes towards Indigenous people and their culture. For example, states in southeastern Australia (i.e. New South Wales, Victoria, Tasmania) introduced legislation in the 1960s and 1970s to protect what were then regarded as Aboriginal 'relics' of interest to archaeologists for studying prehistory. Very specific and varying definitions of what constitutes a 'relic' under each Act are included in the legislation. Contemporary Aboriginal people were widely thought to have 'lost' their culture through assimilation into mainstream Australian society and their views were not considered relevant. In Western Australia and the Northern Territory (where legislation protecting Aboriginal sacred sites was introduced in 1955), Indigenous people's continuing links with their land, culture and languages are more obvious. Here heritage protection was targeted primarily at places of traditional significance to Indigenous people, including natural landscape

features with no material evidence of occupation or use. Such places have limited or no research value to archaeologists.²²

Some states and territories have separate Acts for Indigenous, non-Indigenous and natural heritage protection; others combine different kinds of heritage under the same Act. This can create ambiguity, uncertainty and overlap in areas of government responsibility. Indigenous sites from the colonial period can also fall between the cracks. By law particular places belong to a landowner, but the government (local, state or Common-wealth, depending on circumstances) controls what may or may not be legally done to places with cultural significance. Legally, Indigenous objects excavated from archaeological sites are owned by the relevant state government, and archaeologists are required to lodge their excavated finds with a museum for long-term storage. Normally, Indigenous communities have no automatic legal right to such material. However, many Australian museums now have policies of returning human skeletal remains and other cultural objects held in their collections to Indigenous communities.

A cursory look at three state situations shows the complexities. In Victoria the two most relevant pieces of legislation are the Victorian *Heritage Act 1995* (administered by Heritage Victoria), which protects non-Indigenous historic sites and shipwrecks, and the *Archaeological and Aborigi-nal Relics Preservation Act 1972* (administered by Aboriginal Affairs Victoria), which protects Indigenous heritage places and items in the state. Indig-enous heritage in Victoria falls under a unique legislative structure which combines the relevant state Act with the Commonwealth *Aboriginal and Torres Strait Islander Heritage Protection Act 1984*. In cases of conflict, the Com-monwealth legislation takes precedence. The Department of Natural Resources and the Environment, which includes Parks Victoria, is respon-sible for managing environmental protection, including historic places within Victoria's national parks.

In the Northern Territory, the Northern Territory Aboriginal Areas Pro-tection Authority administers the *Aboriginal Sacred Sites Act 1989*, which aims to both protect and prevent the desecration of sacred sites. The Heritage Advisory Council to the Department of Lands, Planning and the Environ-ment assists with the management and protection of other heritage places and objects under the territory's *Heritage Conservation Act 1991*. The *Museum and Art Galleries Act 1999*, which also concerns some aspects of heritage, is admin-istered by Museums and Art Galleries of the Northern Territory.

New South Wales has three major pieces of cultural heritage legislation. The *National Parks and Wildlife Act 1974* protects Indigenous 'relics' (as defined under the Act) under the auspices of the NSW National Parks and Wildlife Service (NPWS). The Act, and subsequent amendments, also gives the NPWS responsibility for historic places (Indigenous and non-Indigenous) located on NPWS land. The NSW *Heritage Act 1977* was introduced specifically to protect non-Indigenous heritage, although it can protect Indigenous heritage in some circumstances. This Act is administered by the NSW Heritage Office serving the NSW Heritage Council, which advises the Minister for Urban Affairs and Planning.[23] The *Environmental Planning and Assessment Act 1979* controls land use planning, primarily through local government. Other NSW legislation governs cultural heritage management in some national parks, the management of significant historic houses as museums, and the lodgement in Sydney's Australian Museum of objects excavated by archaeologists from Indigenous cultural places.

These are merely simplified examples of the major pieces of heritage legislation and relevant government agencies in three states. Every other state and internal territory has its own laws and policies with its own different but similarly convoluted system of administration. To complicate matters further, legislation in all states is also subject to periodic review and change.[24]

Managing heritage and culture

One of the central concepts in the heritage legislation we have discussed is that of a 'relic'. The 'relic' is a concept linked to English and European traditions of antiquarianism and interest in the tangible remains of the past.[25] However, the concepts and terms used in the context of cultural heritage management have quite a mixed origin.

Cultural 'resources' and cultural 'heritage'

Ideas about 'cultural resource management' started to appear widely in North American literature from the 1970s and were subsequently adopted in Australia. Michael Schiffer and George Gumerman's influential volume, *Conservation Archaeology: A Guide for Cultural Resource Management Studies* (1977), defined and discussed cultural resources as 'materials, which may include archaeological sites, isolated artifacts, features, historic records, modern individuals and communities, and even biotic provinces and paleontological specimens'. Such scarce and non-renewable resources were considered worthy of conservation and, in some cases, total preservation. A major aim of managing such resources was to determine 'the least loss of information concerning past lifeways'.[26]

Some Australian archaeologists still refer to cultural 'resources', but most now prefer the term 'cultural heritage management'. For example, in Sharon Sullivan and Sandra Bowdler's key book, *Site Surveys and Significance Assessment in Australian Archaeology* (1984), the term 'cultural *resource* management' is widely used, including by Sullivan. Yet, writing in 1996 about her long involvement in Australian archaeology ('Reflexions of 27 Years'), Sullivan uses only the term 'cultural *heritage* management', even when discussing the 1970s. This is more than just a matter of semantics. As originally conceived, 'cultural resources' were usually limited to physical places and objects (e.g. sites and artefacts) and the values ascribed to them were narrowly academic or scientific and primarily about the past. 'Cultural heritage' has a much broader meaning than either 'cultural resources' or 'relics'.

What is heritage?

Tim Bonyhady notes that contrary to popular mythology the term 'heritage' was not invented in the 1960s and 1970s. The expression dates to at least the thirteenth century in Europe, and has been used in Australia on and off since the 1870s in a variety of ways. Gough Whitlam (Labor prime minister of Australia 1972–75) is also credited with having introduced the term 'the national estate' into Australia. Bonyhady notes that Whitlam in fact re-introduced the term, which also has a much longer and changing history of use.[27] As it is currently used in Australia, 'heritage' includes not only tangible or material places and objects, but also intangible things associated with them which are essential to why people value them. Intangible heritage includes ideas, feelings, memories, history, identity and spirituality. 'Heritage' is also often used to describe languages, art, designs, dances, stories, even food and drink. The concept need not even be associated with an actual place or object, although there may be an implied place such as a 'nation' or a 'homeland'. 'Heritage' can also be associated with an important person or event. It is even used by advertisers to sell products such as house paint, men's cologne (*Heritage* by Guerlain) and air travel (Qantas airlines), because of the feelings and ideas the term invokes.

Western societies, including in Australia, often split heritage into different types. In particular, humanly produced cultural heritage (e.g. buildings, artworks) is often separated from natural or environmental heritage (e.g. landscape, plants, animals). Such an approach makes less sense to Indigenous and many non-Western societies. To Indigenous people in Australia, the cultural and natural values of places are often closely intertwined. And, indeed, on closer examination, there is rarely a clear and easy divide between natural and cultural heritage. Where does such a division place gardens and other humanly modified landscapes, for example, or domesticated plants and animals, many of which have heritage value? Even the concept of 'wilderness' as a wholly natural environment untouched by people is often a fabrication. Very few pristine 'wilderness' areas actually exist. Much of the Australian landscape, which Europeans initially viewed as wild and untamed by people, was in fact a product of long-term burning regimes by Indigenous people. Even the south-west Tasmanian rainforest 'wilderness' areas, as archaeologists have demonstrated, have not existed untouched by people forever.[28]

Australian heritage managers are very aware of problems which can arise when heritage is inappropriately divided into cultural and natural components and they are attempting to resolve them. For Indigenous places at least, the divide between cultural and natural heritage management is likely to break down even more over the next few years in response to more direct Indigenous input.[29] The notions of 'cultural landscapes' and 'landscape archaeology', which are currently very topical, go some way towards breaking down the cultural/natural divide. However, the division of heritage into cultural and natural components is deeply embedded in most Australian and international legislation, policy, organisational structures, and in the way people think about and discuss the topic. There are also instances where it is pragmatic to split heritage into cultural and natural. Harry Allen, discussing the management of Kakadu National Park, comments that while the culture/nature divide is inappropriate for Indigenous people's own views of the land, it still remains appropriate to the way scientific research is conducted.[30]

Archaeology itself is primarily concerned with things and places made by people (i.e. cultural heritage). Therefore, most of the following discussion is about cultural heritage management, while recognising problems inherent in the use of this term.

Meanings, things and significance assessment
The notion of heritage, as it is commonly used in Australia, includes components of people's identity, psychological well-being or systems of belief.
Tangible heritage things (places and objects) represent, symbolise,
embody or are in some way associated with such intangibles. It is these
intangible values which make places and objects important; they have no,
intrinsic value of their own.

How and why people ascribe meaning, value or significance to material
places and things, and the relationship between the material and the culture,
are questions which have long vexed anthropologists and archaeologists.
The issue is complex because what material things mean to people depends
on their perceptions, and these can and do change.[31] When academics
struggle with such ideas they do so primarily for philosophical reasons, to
clarify and improve the theories by which they make statements about past
or present societies and cultures. It is not entirely fair to say that such
debates are of little consequence to anyone other than academics themselves, because statements made by academics can, and often do, have real-
world consequences. Cultural heritage managers have to deal with very
similar theoretical issues, for different but often very immediate and pressing
reasons. For example, a historic building or the habitat of an endangered
species may be threatened with destruction by a freeway construction. What
is more important: the freeway or the building? How many million dollars is
the habitat of an endangered species worth? Who should decide these
issues? What should the decision-making process be?

In cultural heritage management, the process of making such decisions
hinges on assessing the significance of heritage. The central importance of
significance assessment to cultural heritage management was well stated
by Sandra Bowdler in 1984, and still holds true today:

> In all areas of heritage management, the assessment of significance is held
> to be the central, most important and most immediate task . . . An assess-
> ment of the significance of a place or site is necessary to decide what
> should be done with it, and if some form of conservation/preservation is
> indicated, a clear statement of significance should indicate **how** that con-
> servation or preservation should be carried out . . . [emphasis in original][32]

Government heritage agencies have developed criteria to assist cultural
heritage managers with their central task of assessing the significance of

places and objects. A key Australian heritage management document has been developed by the Australian Committee of the International Council on Monuments and Sites (ICOMOS), an organisation linked to UNESCO which promotes the conservation of places of cultural significance. The *Australia ICOMOS Charter for the Conservation of Places of Cultural Significance*, otherwise known as the Burra Charter, sets out principles of best practice for the conservation and restoration of cultural places in Australia, including archaeological sites.[33] Peter Marquis-Kyle and Meredith Walker outline the major ideas embodied by the Burra Charter as follows:

- place is important;
- understand the significance of place;
- understand the fabric;
- significance should guide decisions;
- do as much as necessary and as little as possible;
- keep records; and
- do everything in logical order.[34]

Central to the tenets of the Burra Charter is its definition of 'cultural significance' as being 'aesthetic, historic, scientific or social value for past, present or future generations' (Article 1.2).

The principles and definitions of the Burra Charter have been widely influential in Australian heritage management. Only projects which conform to Burra Charter guidelines are eligible for government heritage funding, and some heritage legislation closely follows the Burra Charter's definitions of places of cultural significance. Assessing cultural significance in terms of the broad categories expressed in the Burra Charter (aesthetic, historic, scientific and social) is common practice.

Government departments have further refined and developed their own systems for assessing the heritage value of places under their jurisdiction. The Australian Heritage Commission, for example, developed eight major 'Criteria for the Register of the National Estate'. These include statements about a place's importance in the course or pattern of Australia's natural or cultural history; its potential to yield information that will contribute to a wider understanding of Australia's natural or cultural heritage; and its associations with a particular community or cultural group for social, cultural or spiritual reasons. The NSW Heritage Office's 1996 guidelines on heritage assessment define four major significance criteria (aesthetic, historical, technical/research and social), two principal degree criteria (representativeness and rarity) and a range of other criteria (e.g. intactness, seminal, climactic) which apply primarily to styles of architecture.[35]

The Burra Charter and similar guidelines for assessing significance are very general and open to interpretation. The process of assessing significance is far from simple. Most problematic is the notion of social value, as in many cases other values (aesthetic, historic, scientific) can be viewed as particular types of social value.[36] The Burra Charter itself was designed primarily to aid the preservation and management of European historic buildings (often known as 'the built environment'). Its strong emphasis on *fabric* and its somewhat Eurocentric view of cultural places have long been recognised as inappropriate for dealing with many Indigenous and non-Western places. Accordingly the Burra Charter was revised in 1997. The new version places less emphasis on fabric, acknowledges that places can be associated with conflicting values, and recognises that Indigenous people and other cultural groups have special rights in their own cultural places which must be considered.[37]

Archaeology is included in the Burra Charter guidelines as a type of scientific significance. What is involved in assessing archaeological significance? Bowdler proposes that archaeological significance should be assessed according to *timely and specific research questions*. In association with Anne Bickford, Bowdler provides further basic criteria:

1) Can this site contribute knowledge which no other site can?
2) Can this site contribute knowledge which no other resource, such as documents or oral history or previous research, can?
3) Is this knowledge relevant to specific or general questions about human history or behaviour or some other substantive subject?[38]

This is all well and good—except that research questions change and future research cannot be easily predicted. Assessing archaeological and other types of significance listed in the Burra Charter is not that simple. Particular problems are raised when archaeological consultants have to assess archaeological significance because sites fall under threat from development proposals. Legislation only requires that developers pay for the study of those sites which happen to fall inside the area of their proposed development or which it can be argued will be negatively impacted on by their development. This highly piecemeal approach can make it hard to assess the archaeological significance of individual sites. For example, one criterion of archaeological significance is rarity. Yet if little or nothing is known about the kinds of other sites in a region, including those which lie outside areas threatened by the development, how can the consultants decide if an individual site they find is rare and unusual or, in fact, very similar to many others?

A major theoretical problem is that nearly all archaeological sites have the potential to contribute some knowledge to some archaeological research question. How, then, does a consultant decide what a timely research question is? Who can or should decide whether one type of research question is more important or significant than another? In the absence of peer review in the cultural heritage management context, this is often left to the individual consultant or government heritage manager to decide.

Assessment work of this kind often results in a range of management problems for archaeology. Since the 1980s a number of consultant archaeologists have worked in the Cumberland Plain area west of Sydney. One of these is Jo McDonald, who has discussed how continuing expansion of the city has resulted in the ad hoc but large-scale destruction of hundreds of Indigenous archaeological sites, mostly comprising open stone artefact scatters. Many of these sites have been recorded as part of the assessment process but, as McDonald comments, problems arise because of a lack of any regional strategy for managing archaeological sites, poorly developed understanding of the nature and significance of the region's archaeology because of the piecemeal way it has been studied, and the 'relentless pressure on the archaeological resource'.[39]

Fabric and the conservation ethic

Bowdler's statement about significance assessment also makes reference to another central tenet of cultural heritage management—that culture and heritage retain their value by being conserved or preserved. This is the 'conservation ethic' which holds that cultural resources are valuable because they are finite and non-renewable. Once destroyed they can never be replaced. Heritage managers therefore have an ethical responsibility to ensure that such resources are preserved if possible, and if destruction is inevitable, that decisions are made in a considered and responsible way. Such ideas are incorporated into documents like the Burra Charter and much heritage legislation.

Another fundamental principle of the Burra Charter is that cultural resources (or heritage) are the property of past, present and future generations. No one can own them as such, but each generation holds heritage in stewardship. The present generation has a moral responsibility to look after the resources or heritage they inherited from past generations to preserve them for future generations.

This places primary emphasis on tangible or material heritage and is closely linked to the practice of archaeology, which values heritage mainly for scientific or academic reasons, and which studies things and places to yield information about human behaviour and history. Archaeological concepts are central to much heritage management practice because archaeologists were a major lobby group which put pressure on Western governments in the 1960s and 1970s to introduce legislation to prevent the mass destruction of historic sites and artefacts by large-scale development. Archaeological values and archaeological ways of thinking are thus embodied in much cultural heritage legislation, and many cultural heritage managers have been trained in archaeology.[40]

Indeed, some archaeologists involved in the management of cultural places describe what they do as 'archaeological heritage management'. For example, British archaeologist and heritage manager Henry Cleere has edited two very influential and important works on the subject called *Approaches to the Archaeological Heritage* (1984) and *Archaeological Heritage Management in the Modern World* (1989). Both books present case studies about a range of cultural heritage management issues in different countries, including Australia. Yet cultural and archaeological heritage management are not the same. Cultural heritage management need not involve any archaeology at all, although it often does. In places such as the United States, Canada, New Zealand and Australia, government heritage agencies have been forced, primarily by Indigenous people, to acknowledge the social importance of Indigenous places and objects, and to recognise that archaeology can rarely be considered in isolation from other values.

As already noted, Australian heritage managers must currently take into account aesthetic, historic and social significance, as well as scientific significance, when making decisions about what should be done with heritage places and objects. Denis Byrne and Jonathon Mane-Wheoki, among others, discuss how the notion of needing to conserve the material heritage, or fabric, of a place to retain its value is a peculiarly and very recent Western notion.[41] In Australia the most obvious situation where Western notions of good conservation practice are problematic is the re-painting or re-grooving of Indigenous rock art, where images are renewed as part of continuity of cultural tradition, thereby (in a traditional Indigenous sense) retaining their social significance. Yet in Western conservation terms, re-grooving or re-painting destroys the existing fabric of the place and flies in the face of good practice.

Byrne provides another example in the Confucius Temple at Qufu, Jiangsu Province, China, which has been constantly rebuilt over hundreds of years. While the rebuilding destroyed the previous 'fabric', this was irrelevant to the heritage value of the temple, which not only was more about the spirit of the place itself but which people actually felt and continue to feel was enhanced by constant changes and additions to the building. Another example is the traditional Maori house in New Zealand which was regarded as a living, organic being. Once the house came to the end of its natural life it was abandoned and left to rot away as part of traditional practice. Yet official conservation practices in New Zealand have resulted in examples of such houses being excavated by archaeologists and preserved in museums.

There are also many examples in Western society where altering the fabric of a place is regarded as enhancing, rather than detracting from, its value. Churches and cathedrals are often rebuilt and restored, while home-owners modernise their houses to enhance their value. Yet Western heritage management philosophy, through documents like the original Burra Charter, promotes particular historic or scientific values associated with fabric as being more important than other elements of place.

Management practices
A subject which has received very little direct attention, in the archaeological literature at least, is the concept that heritage should be *managed* at all, rather than being looked after, studied, treasured, left to fade and rot away, sold for a profit or destroyed. The term 'management' presumes no particular outcome—any of the above could result from it. Cultural heritage management is often described in the literature as a process or

a series of steps which need to be undertaken in a particular order, involving certain actions and outcomes, to achieve goals supposedly set by politicians and society under the influence of stakeholders and interest groups.

The strategic planning terminology used by government heritage organisations is also telling. Mission statements in their corporate plans usually lay out very general goals, along the line of 'preserving cultural heritage', 'educating the public' and so on. They then set out specific objectives and strategies for achieving these goals. All this implies a certain degree of mechanistic neutrality on behalf of the people employed by the government to carry out these tasks. It is supposedly the job of public servants to facilitate the management process, not to dictate the outcomes. As anyone who has ever watched an episode of 'Yes Minister' will know, the reality is often very different. The way government departments are structured and organised, and the models of management through which they operate, are clearly important both to the way heritage is perceived and what happens to it.

The organisational structures and modus operandi of non-government organisations (e.g. state branches of the National Trust of Australia, local history societies, industry associations) and other groups involved in the heritage management process also impact on the process and outcomes of heritage management. Large consulting and development companies are likely to be able to deal more effectively with government than many Indigenous community organisations and similar groups, because they have more appropriate management resources and structures and they often 'talk the same language'. A key and related point here is that often it is not so much the resource or heritage that is being managed as people and their actions. This whole topic merits closer and more explicit attention by both Australian academics and heritage managers.[42]

Into the breach

Since the 'golden days' of Australian archaeology in the 1960s and 1970s, university-based archaeologists have seen more and more of their colleagues move into the area of cultural heritage management. Archaeology, like all research, costs money and only certain types of projects are attractive to private sponsors. Fieldwork can be expensive due to transport and accommodation costs for crew and equipment. Excavated materials often need conservation, curation and further transport. Specialist services (radiocarbon dating, pollen analysis) and post-excavation artefact identification require additional funding. Excavation, which the public commonly equates with 'doing archaeology', may be only a small part of a major archaeological research project. Time and resources are also needed for project management, post-excavation recording and analysis of the materials, library research, report writing and publication.[43]

In the 1960s and 1970s there was generous government support for universities and research from which archaeology benefited. The government funded new jobs in research, teaching, and technical and administrative support for prehistory and archaeology, in research institutes (such as the Australian Institute of Aboriginal Studies, the Australian National University's Institute of Advanced Studies), university departments and some museums. Australian archaeologists also supplemented their research with funding from non-government sources such as the Nuffield and Wenner-Gren Foundations.[44]

Since the 1980s successive governments have been increasingly reluctant to spend taxpayers' money on research which, rightly or wrongly, is perceived to have little direct financial benefit to society. The Commonwealth government takes a pro-active role in shaping the kinds of research it thinks will benefit Australia, for example by policy directives which identify key research areas of national importance or themes which the government thinks are appropriate for it to support. Such policy directives influence the awarding of Commonwealth government research grants through its funding bodies. The government also controls funding to universities for their operating costs. Some of this is based on notions of 'research performance', which is measured by indicators such as the number of publications produced by academics each year and numbers of postgraduate research students who complete their degrees. The emergence of mass higher education in Australia and elsewhere has also involved slashed government funding, increased reliance on outside money from industry and student fees, job losses, restructuring and large increases in student numbers. In 2002 the future of Australian universities and government funding for archaeological research are more uncertain than even a decade ago.[45]

The major source of government funding for archaeological research is the Australian Research Council (currently a statutory advisory body to the Minister for Education, Science and Training).[46] Grants are awarded on a competitive basis. Funding applications are subject to intense scrutiny by peer review panels. Criteria and budget guidelines must be strictly adhered to, outcomes clearly specified, and if researchers fail to perform adequately they endanger future support. While greater accountability is no bad thing, a major result has been much tighter control over the kinds of research that gets done. Archaeologists, like other researchers, now spend more and more time chasing research money and providing justification to their institutions and the government for what they are doing, and less time actually doing research. This places especially heavy pressure on archaeologists employed on short-term contracts by universities and museums, where continuing employment is highly uncertain. Many move to cultural heritage management which can offer better pay and job prospects, or leave archaeology entirely.

Heritage legislation created new areas of employment for archaeologists graduating from Australian universities from the 1970s onwards. Given the importance of heritage management, most archaeological practice occurs in this context today. Some jobs for archaeologists exist in state and Commonwealth government departments which have responsibility for heritage. The work involved typically includes the administration associated with managing archaeological sites and materials under relevant legislation, policy development, providing advice to the public and other government agencies, public education, research and perhaps some archaeological fieldwork. More archaeologists work in cultural heritage management as private consultants who contract their services to developers and government agencies for a range of heritage planning and management jobs arising from legislative requirements. Their work might include conducting field-based and archival research to document and assess the significance of archaeological sites in a particular area to assist with future land use planning, or developing a detailed archaeological management plan for a site which an agency wishes to conserve.

Consultants are most frequently hired under environmental planning legislation to assess the likely impact of development proposals on archaeological sites. Such work typically involves documentary and archival research, community consultation and public education as well as archaeo-logical fieldwork. Fieldwork might involve survey (to locate and record sites), salvage excavation (necessary when sites would otherwise be physically destroyed by development) and monitoring (see below). Post-excavation recording and analysis of excavated artefacts, bones and other finds is also often undertaken. Heritage agencies increasingly require tangible research outcomes or other public benefits such as education materials from such work. Archaeological consultants spend a lot of their time writing reports for clients and government departments, explaining the work and justifying their recommendations.

Compromise

Developers are not in the business of archaeology. Most want the assess-ment work done as quickly as possible so they can proceed with their project. It is not in the developer's interest for the consultant archaeologist to find anything likely to derail or hold up a development and cost more money. If a developer is a large organisation which can potentially provide consulting archaeologists with more work in the future, it is not in the con-sultant's interests to cause the developer too many problems. If a consultant is perceived to be too stringent, or too expensive, an unethical developer can simply employ someone else next time they need similar work done. It is the job of government heritage agencies to oversee this process and to minimise dubious and unethical practice. The Code of Ethics of the Aus-tralian Association of Consulting Archaeologists also aims to tackle such issues. However, consultant archaeologists are often placed under strong commercial pressure to compromise their professional standards.[47]

Even when the developers want to do the right thing, archaeological consultants frequently have to complete archaeological research and field-work in very short time frames to limit costs or because not enough time is left between when the client contacts the archaeologist and the date construction or mining is due to commence. In some cases clients have unrealistic expectations of what a consultant can achieve given the time frame and budget and the scope of the work. Such problems can be com-pounded because work is awarded on the basis of competitive tendering. This can lead to situations where standards of work are easily compro-mised, especially if the consultant is inexperienced. If a very large area needs to be surveyed, there may be insufficient time and money available to physically inspect all of it. The sampling strategy adopted may result in fewer sites and artefacts being located and fewer details about them being recorded than most archaeologists would consider desirable for research purposes.

All archaeological survey, recording and excavation involve sampling of some kind, whatever the rationale for the project. It is physically impossible for any archaeologist to observe and record *everything* which may be significant about a place or object. This stems in part from the nature of the archaeological record which is not a fixed entity, but is also contingent on the questions the archaeologist wants to answer, and a number of other factors.[48]

The kinds of material archaeologists usually study are often obscured by thick and impenetrable vegetation or are buried under land surfaces. This is particularly the case with smaller sites with no standing or large structures associated with them, such as stone tool scatters. Locating such sites in forests presents archaeologists with particular problems for which specific methodologies have had to be developed.[49] On the other hand, open areas have their disadvantages too. In the Cumberland Plain and Hunter Valley areas of New South Wales, for example, where large-scale development and mining has required a lot of archaeological assessment work in recent years, the cover is generally thick pasture over homogenous terrain. This makes it hard to predict the likely location of stone tool scatters and similar sites on the basis of landscape features alone.[50]

If the full extent and significance of archaeological remains cannot be determined from surface survey work alone, the consultant may need to recommend test excavations to assist in locating sites and assessing their archaeological significance. The main issue here is that if an archaeologist fails to locate something important during site survey and test excavation, once destroyed the place is gone forever. Furthermore, the 'relics' legislation which applies in some states technically protects even a few stone artefacts. The consultant has been employed by the client to assist them to comply with such legislation and must take reasonable steps to locate and identify as many 'relics' as feasible. Consultant archaeologists must carry the responsibilities of complying with legislation, salvaging material before destruction and working to the developer's satisfaction.

When sites are considered to have little or low archaeological significance, the consultant will recommend that no further action is needed and the proposed development work can proceed. If the relevant government heritage agency is satisfied with the consultant's report, and other aspects of heritage value are not an issue, it will give the developer permission to destroy the archaeological evidence. For Indigenous places, such permission usually requires relevant community consultation. In some states community consultation is now also required for non-Indigenous places involving human burials or for particularly significant places. This does not mean that the community has the final say—it simply means it needs to be asked for its opinion.

If a site is deemed to have archaeological significance the consultant may recommend that the development be stopped. However, it is very rare for a development proposal to be completely blocked because of potential damage to a cultural place.[51] The most common outcome is to require the developer to modify its proposal to reduce the likely impact, for example by building around something rather than digging right through it. If this is not possible or practicable, particularly for large-area ventures such as coal mining, a common compromise is to require the developer to employ archaeologists to record and excavate the places before allowing the development to proceed.

Salvage work and monitoring
Excavation undertaken when places come under threat is often called salvage or rescue work. Salvage work is not always due to development. Natural processes such as erosion and flooding frequently threaten cultural places, especially in unstable dunes along the coast and in arid inland areas, and the government agency responsible may need to take steps to stabilise sites or conduct salvage excavation. For example, Jeanette Hope has described a large-scale project of this kind aimed at conserving Indigenous burials in the Murray-Darling Basin in western New South Wales.[52] More usually, however, the threat *is* from development, and salvage work is conducted to record and collect as much information as possible before the place is destroyed forever. This conjures up images of desperate archaeologists, trowels in hand, working at breakneck speed in front of the rapidly advancing jaws of earth-moving machines. Archaeologists are also employed to 'monitor' or to observe development work as it proceeds. If

any previously unlocated sites or 'relics' are uncovered, work can stop and further action can be taken.

This is a far from ideal arrangement. By the time an earth-moving machine uncovers an archaeological site it is already partially destroyed, thus defeating any conservation outcome. The archaeologist may have to stand for hours in front of large, noisy and dangerous machinery looking out for archaeological 'relics'. If they find anything they must order the machine driver to stop. Many construction site managers and workers are happy to comply with archaeologists, whom they regard as just another requirement of the development process. However, such attitudes are not universal. Archaeologists can be regarded as a nuisance and with suspicion by some members of the development industry. Employing archaeologists, and especially Indigenous archaeologists, to save Indigenous places from destruction is regarded as a waste of money, just holding up development work and likely to lead to land claims against the land owner or developer.

Unsympathetic development workers can engage archaeologists in a constant 'battle of wills' by refusing to stop machinery or change the work programme to salvage archaeological finds. From the developers' perspective it is very inefficient to have to change plans at the last minute or halt machinery while archaeologists investigate sites. Any unexpected delay costs money. Project managers want certainty about the development process at a much earlier stage, so that once given the green light, construction can proceed with minimal interruption.

Effects of cultural heritage management on Australian archaeology

The creation of a whole new branch of applied archaeology operating largely outside the university system has inevitably caused changes to, and rifts in, the profession. Seemingly large amounts of money can be made by archaeologists whose mediocre academic qualifications would never get them even a low-ranked university or museum job—yet the research value of much of this archaeology was, and still is, questionable. In 1986 Sandra Bowdler, writing about consulting archaeology in Tasmania, argued that the aim of Australian prehistory was to answer relevant research questions which would tell archaeologists things about the past which they did not already know. In her opinion, as most cultural heritage management archaeology did not conform to this definition, its value was very limited.[53]

Despite Bowdler's comments, the boundaries between areas of archaeological practice are not so clear cut. The direct commercialisation of what some consulting archaeologists do and the public responsibilities of and power vested in archaeologists employed as public servants create a range of ethical and practical issues which are clearly less applicable to archaeologists employed by universities and museums, if at all. Yet some university- and museum-based archaeologists also engage in consultancy practice. And the work of consultants and heritage managers does produce archaeological research outcomes in many cases. Archaeologists working outside the university system frequently provide professional training opportunities for students and recent graduates. Indeed, cultural heritage management has changed the way Australian archaeology as a whole is practised.

Field methods
A major impact of archaeology conducted for cultural heritage management purposes has been on field methods. For obvious reasons, in cultural heritage management surface survey is more common than extensive excavation, especially for Indigenous sites. The size and shape of survey areas, too, are dictated primarily by the needs of the management process rather than by what is ideal for research. This situation has encouraged archaeologists to develop predictive models for locating sites making use of developments in computer and related technologies such as geographic information systems (GIS), satellite imagery, and electronic surveying and mapping. Expertise in such methods, developed in the context of cultural heritage management, has therefore been more readily available for application on research projects conducted from the universities and museums.

Philosophy and practice
It is also simply untrue that all cultural heritage management archaeology is intellectually worthless, and that consultants and cultural heritage managers never publish anything. Archaeology's entanglement with cultural heritage management has engaged Australian archaeologists in a far wider series of debates and areas of theory than might otherwise have been the case. This has fostered much theoretical and applied

archaeological research, discussion of which fills the pages of many academic journals. Government departments and agencies, as well as private companies, have funded many major archaeological projects with high research value, which have also produced high-quality publications and other useful outcomes.[54]

Nevertheless, research outcomes from consulting projects are often severely restricted by constraints of time and money. This is particularly so for salvage excavations, which are based on the idea that a place can be effectively saved by careful and detailed recording of archaeological information during excavation. According to this logic, it doesn't really matter if the place itself is physically destroyed as long as all data are recorded. Information and artefacts can be lodged with a museum or relevant Indigenous community and are available for archaeologists to study at their leisure. While this sounds like a win-win situation, things are not quite so simple.

The government cannot stop developers from destroying most archaeological sites; economic growth requires development and the extraction of natural resources. Instead, as a compromise, developers are forced to pay for salvage excavation. Money for such work can be viewed as a kind of cultural tax on the development industry. But destroying a place in this way fails to acknowledge anything other than its scientific or archaeological value. It is also physically impossible to record everything about a place and its environmental context. All fieldwork requires the archaeologist to make decisions about what to record and how to record it. The 'archaeological record' has no independent existence outside the theories and interpretations of the archaeologist (see Chapter 1). As a pragmatic response to an insoluble problem, archaeologists have developed standard systems for recording kinds of archaeological data which are widely considered to be most useful for answering a range of current research questions. Yet nobody can predict exactly what kinds of information will and won't be useful to future research. For this reason heritage agencies often require that at least some of the resource be left undisturbed for future research, rather than allowing the whole site to be salvaged. Of course this is not always practical, especially where very large-scale operations such as mining and forestry threaten small and scattered sites.

Developers usually pay for the basic recording and excavation of a place which will otherwise be destroyed by their activities. However, it is much harder to make the developer pay for time-consuming and expensive post-excavation analysis of the finds and for publication. Consequently, salvage excavation has resulted in the collection of increasingly large amounts of data and archaeological materials which remain unstudied, or studied only in a highly superficial way. Data and collections need to be stored and crated and someone has to pay for this. Museums, on which this responsibility usually falls, are increasingly underfunded and many are reluctant or simply unable to continue holding large collections of archaeological materials which never or rarely get used by researchers or the public. Sydney's Australian Museum, for example, now charges deposition fees, but these really only cover the cost of initial processing and not the longer term storage costs.[55]

Research and publication

A series of issues arises from the way some cultural heritage management philosophy classifies archaeology as a set of standardised techniques which can and should be applied primarily to assist in determining the significance of a place to aid in its conservation. Archaeological excavation, which inevitably has physical impact, sits uneasily within heritage guidelines like the Burra Charter, emphasising conservation and minimal interference with fabric. This seemingly prohibits excavation conducted for research alone. However, as the Burra Charter and similar documents also regard archaeology as part of the possible scientific value of a place, research excavation is permitted when this 'adds substantially to a scientific body of knowledge', provided this is 'consistent with the conservation policy for the place'.[56] This is somewhat contradictory.

There are other problems. Heritage legislation has resulted in an explosive increase in known sites, especially Indigenous sites. The standard of archaeological information recording for many of these is woefully inadequate compared with that expected of an academic research project. Yet some recording is perhaps marginally better than none, especially if sites get destroyed by development anyway. Most consulting archaeology never gets peer reviewed (except in some cases, by government heritage managers) or published in academic literature. While there are exceptions, most work results in a few copies of an unpublished report. This 'grey literature' is held by clients, relevant statutory authorities and Indigenous communities, and is not widely accessible. Most consulting archaeology reports cannot be borrowed through the library system, making them especially hard to obtain interstate. Problems of access to information and the dissemination of results have been exacerbated in recent years by the introduction of fees to use reports held by some government departments. In cases involving Indigenous sacred sites and ancestral remains, there may be very tight restrictions on access to data records generally. Indigenous concerns about intellectual property rights also seem likely to further restrict the use of cultural information held in registers in the future.[57]

As we have noted, developers are often reluctant to pay consultants to complete the time-consuming and (at standard consulting rates) expensive job of conducting meaningful research on excavated materials and writing up results for publication in academic journals. Yet doing research is regarded by many archaeologists as being more intellectually rewarding than simply conducting salvage excavation and making basic finds catalogues. In large multi-stage development projects the client may contract different archaeologists to undertake different stages of the work. Some archaeologists feel this also compromises the intellectual value of their work. They may have invested considerable expertise in researching and formulating the design of a project, which is then taken over by another consultant who may be under no obligation even to acknowledge the original intellectual contribution. Similarly, the consultant taking over may inherit something they feel is unworkable or to which they are otherwise unsympathetic. Such problems arise in part because cultural heritage management regards archaeologists as artisans or technicians paid to apply standardised techniques, where any archaeologist is interchangeable with another, and the developer who pays for work owns any intellectual property rights—even though their core business has nothing to do with research at all.

This is very different from the situation for university and some museum-based archaeologists who are not only expected to conduct research as part of their job, but are paid a salary to do so. University staff and their students are therefore often better equipped to undertake research resulting from projects initiated by consultants than are the consultants themselves, who must move on to new jobs to earn a living. Collaborative research between university-based and consulting archaeologists provides one solution to such problems and can work well provided there is adequate consultation and acknowledgement of the intellectual and other contributions of all parties.[58]

Professionalism

Who can claim to be a real archaeologist? What qualifications are required? To whom or what are real archaeologists responsible? Such questions arise when archaeologists are paid for their expertise as part of the cultural heritage management process. For example, when a developer or anyone else hires an archaeologist to advise it about its obligations under heritage legislation, the developer needs to know that the archaeologist is properly qualified to provide good advice and will provide this service in an appropriate and effective manner. Such issues are about professionalism.

Before Australian prehistory was first taught in Australian universities from the 1960s onwards, there was no formal training process for archaeologists in this country, and no group of similarly qualified people with shared knowledge and values to develop and defend archaeological standards. During the 1960s and early 1970s a group of scholars who regarded themselves as professionals, including Fred McCarthy and John Mulvaney, campaigned for the introduction of legislation to protect Aboriginal sites from damage caused by the public. Mulvaney was scathing in his condemnation of 'scientific vandalism' by artefact collectors and fossickers digging into Aboriginal sites to remove objects for their private collections with complete disregard for the loss of archaeological information they caused. He complained of 'a rash of such pillaging by envious and selfish collectors' and about the defacement of Aboriginal rock art sites by photographers chalking in designs to get a better picture. The proposed remedy was more effective legislation and public education.[59]

Before legislation came into effect anyone could dig into or damage cultural places for any reason, provided the land owner agreed. After legislation, amateurs were squeezed out. The only people allowed to purposefully dig into cultural places were archaeologists in the pursuit of legitimate archaeological knowledge. The government then began to regulate some aspects of Australian archaeology by controlling the issue of excavation and field survey permits. Professionalism in Australian archaeology is therefore about academic standards, university training and government regulation.

Excavation permits, research designs and government regulation
Who gets an archaeological excavation permit? Most heritage legislation does not specify. Some Acts require the appointment of professional advisory committees on such matters, but their composition and modus operandi are not specified. It is common practice for the public servants who administer the law to decide which archaeologists and which projects get permission to excavate. Most government departments will only issue an archaeological excavation permit to someone with a university degree in archaeology. However, in some cases it is possible for someone with no archaeology degree to obtain a permit provided they can demonstrate a satisfactory track record of competence in archaeological fieldwork.

Archaeological excavation involves many tasks for which care, patience and the ability to follow instructions are more essential than formal university qualifications. Many digs could not run without the participation of amateur volunteers. Motivated people can acquire extensive excavation skills entirely outside the university system by learning on the job. Some practising archaeologists have worked their way up from volunteer to paid site assistant, trench supervisor, assistant director and even excavation director. They are much better qualified to run a dig than a newly graduated archaeology student with very limited practical experience.

In deciding whether to issue an excavation permit, heritage agencies also require a research design justifying the need for the work and outlining approaches, methods and likely outcomes. Someone with extensive on-the-job training may be a highly skilled archaeological technician, but only a university degree can equip an archaeologist with the necessary theoretical knowledge, research and other skills to design, present and implement an acceptable research proposal—in theory at least. In practice, professional archaeology is regulated by an informal combination of government heritage agencies vetting fieldwork permit applications, and universities training students to acceptable academic standards.

Government departments have developed guidelines outlining minimum standards for research designs, methodology and other aspects of archaeological fieldwork practice (including community concerns and rights), usually after some consultation with the wider profession. However, these guidelines are not comprehensive and many are inadequate, unworkable or otherwise unacceptable.[60] Archaeology is not simply a set of standard techniques which can be applied to a set of universally accepted research questions to produce knowledge and understanding about the past, which everyone regards as equally interesting, valid or useful. Archaeologists disagree with each other about the kinds of things they want to know about the past, and the most appropriate theories and techniques for addressing different research questions. This raises the matter of whether, in the common absence of a broad peer review process, individuals employed by government departments should have the power arbitrarily to dictate acceptable aims and methods to other archaeologists, especially when they may have fewer university qualifications and less archaeological experience than the consultant or academic whose proposal they vet. More than a few angry academic and consulting archaeologists whose research proposals have been queried or rejected by government-employed heritage managers have raised questions about political or bureaucratic control of research agendas.

Closely linked to this issue is the requirement that archaeologists wishing to conduct research on Indigenous places first consult and obtain permission from relevant Indigenous communities before the government will issue an archaeological excavation permit. Archaeologists wishing to access national parks or other government-controlled land to locate and record Indigenous sites may also need a research permit, even if their actions will have no physical impact. Government departments sometimes also require consultation with non-Indigenous community interests (e.g. for study of human burials and graves or where a place is especially controversial).

These requirements to consult have had a major impact on archaeological fieldwork practice. The recent history of archaeological research on Indigenous sites in Tasmania provides a good example of this. Although legislation to protect Aboriginal sites and 'relics' was introduced in Tasmania in 1970 and 1975, in the mid-1970s the Tasmanian government did not recognise the existence of a present-day Indigenous community, preferring to refer to Tasmanian Aborigines as 'descendants', and the legislation made little provision for consulting with them. It was not until the 1980s that the political situation in Tasmania changed and the Tasmanian Parks and Wildlife Service (PWS), as the agency responsible for implementing the legislation, began to require as a matter of policy that archaeologists consult with Indigenous people about their work. Since 1992 it has been PWS practice to require archaeologists to seek formal consent from the Tasmanian Aboriginal Land Council (TALC) on all permits to conduct archaeological research. For archaeologists, this has made conducting research excavations in Tasmania difficult, especially if they want to move excavated materials out of Tasmania for analysis. Discussing the situation in 1996, Tasmanian-based cultural heritage manager Angela McGowan noted that the last permit to be issued for excavation or removal from the state for research purposes was in 1993. Since the Tasmanian PWS started referring applications for archaeological excavation permits to the TALC, only two research applications have been supported. Other than these, excavation permits have only been approved by the TALC in the context of cultural heritage management, where Indigenous places were threatened by developments and construction work.[61]

Training and professionalism
While the government does not dictate the subject matter of an archaeology degree, recent changes to universities have had an inevitable impact on what students learn.[62] Fewer staff and resources and larger class sizes have forced many universities to rethink their teaching methods and curriculum content. Under current funding models students have become customers. Courses that attract large numbers are favoured over those which, because they are more specialised and less popular, are no longer deemed to be financially viable. Staff must often choose between maintaining a broad range of content or providing students with opportunities to develop in-depth understanding of a much smaller range of subjects. Archaeology courses which describe 'lost civilisations' or human evolution in an exciting and entertaining way are usually more popular with the customers than those which focus on the intricacies of Indigenous stone tool typology or on historical archaeological ceramic fabric forms. No university course can, or ever could, provide every student with in-depth knowledge of every aspect of archaeological practice and theory. Choices have always had to be made. In any case, the majority of students who study archaeology at university will never work in the profession. There are not enough jobs, and many students are simply not interested in becoming practitioners.

There is no such thing as an apprentice archaeologist. Cultural heritage managers and consulting archaeologists have no formal input into either the content or form of a university degree in archaeology, nor need they take any responsibility for training and educating students. Yet members of the Australian archaeology profession complain that students who leave university wanting to enter the profession often have substandard practical and professional skills and inadequate detailed knowledge about relevant archaeological sites and materials.

Specialist postgraduate courses in cultural heritage management (including some archaeology) offer a partial solution to providing professional training in universities, but graduates can still emerge with inadequate understanding of archaeology itself. In recognition of such realities, some consulting companies and government heritage agencies have responded positively by offering on-the-job training to graduates with good honours degrees in archaeology to assist them develop their professional careers.[63]

An obvious solution to problems raised by professionalism would be for the whole archaeology discipline (academics, consultants and heritage managers) to regulate themselves. This has never been achieved. While archaeology in Australia, as elsewhere, has many elements of professionalism it is not the same as medicine, dentistry, law and other true professions where practitioners need to be licensed in a way that is linked to a regulated training programme and formal government accreditation. Wider public interests in archaeology and cultural places, and a range of views about the nature of archaeological knowledge, preclude archaeology from ever achieving this kind of professionalisation, even if this were desirable.

Professional organisations

Even though Australian archaeology is not strictly a profession, this has not stopped archaeologists calling themselves professionals and forming their own associations. Australia ICOMOS, discussed earlier in this chapter, is a professional body whose members include heritage architects, urban planners, historians, engineers, builders, heritage managers and archaeologists. Membership requires relevant academic and professional qualifications and demonstrated expertise. The organisation draws its strength and influence from the diversity of its members and its affiliation to UNESCO (as one of 60 national ICOMOS committees worldwide). From the perspective of Australian archaeology, ICOMOS represents too broad a range of professional interests, some of which are incompatible with archaeology.

The Australian Archaeological Association (AAA) and the Australasian Society of Historical Archaeology (ASHA) mainly facilitate the exchange and dissemination of information about research and cultural heritage management by publishing newsletters, journals and monographs, maintaining websites, and running conferences. They also act as lobby groups for Australian archaeology. Membership of AAA and ASHA is open to anyone who pays an annual subscription. No qualifications or expertise in archaeology are required and anyone can attend their conferences, although voting at the annual general meeting is restricted to paid-up members.

In contrast, membership of the Australian Association of Consulting Archaeologists Incorporated (AACAI) is restricted to archaeologists who have requisite academic qualifications and experience in Australian archaeology and cultural heritage management. AACAI was formed in 1979 by a group of mainly Sydney-based consulting archaeologists. It is now a well-established Australia-wide organisation with branches in most states and over a hundred members. However AACAI does not represent Australian archaeologists as a whole. Its main concerns are those relating to consulting archaeology. The stated aims of the organisation are to establish, maintain and encourage adherence to professional standards and ethics (to be achieved by a code of ethics), and to maintain a national register of consultant archaeologists. There are three categories of membership. Full membership is restricted to experienced archaeologists who work full time as archaeological consultants and whose applications are assessed by a membership committee as meeting a range of criteria set down by the Association.[64]

The Australian Institute of Professional Archaeologists (AIPA) has more recently been established by mainly Melbourne-based archaeologists. Unlike AACAI, AIPA aims to be widely representative of the archaeology profession as a whole. It offers various categories of membership based on a mixture of formal university qualifications in archaeology, professional, field and laboratory experience (which can include maritime archaeology and work conducted outside Australia), relevant archaeological employment history and publications. It remains to be seen whether AIPA will become widely accepted by Australian archaeologists. Attempts a few years ago by a group of archaeologists in Western Australia to set up their own 'professional association', born largely from dissatisfaction with AACAI, came to little.[65]

Rival organisations can be established by different groups because such organisations have no official status. There is no legal or other requirement for any archaeologist to join AAA, ASHA, AACAI, AIPA or any organisation to do archaeology or work in consulting. Many well-qualified, successful archaeologists don't join AACAI or AIPA because they see no benefit. Rightly or wrongly such organisations are dismissed by many archaeologists as irrelevant, or as existing to serve the interests of the people who set them up or to exclude competition for consulting work. An effective professional association needs to be accepted by the majority of Australian archaeologists as useful and as genuinely promoting high standards of professional practice. Australian archaeologists commonly work in isolation from colleagues in other states and territories. Even attending regular meetings and conferences can be prohibitively expensive, given the travel involved. This makes interaction and communication between archaeologists in different parts of Australia difficult; such interaction might otherwise facilitate the establishment of a national professional association with wide grassroots support.

Codes of ethics

An important function of archaeological associations in Australia, as elsewhere, is the development of codes of ethics.[66] A number of common themes run through such codes. Most promote the idea of minimum standards for archaeological work and professional training and qualifications. Archaeologists should abide by legislation and not accept bribes or condone looting or illegal trade in antiquities. Most codes support the conservation ethic.

Several codes set out the responsibilities of the archaeologist and the rights of various stakeholders (e.g. archaeologists, professional clients, students, special community groups such as traditional owners and Indigenous people, taxpayers and the public in general). Many of these rights and responsibilities conflict with each other, but only some codes acknowledge this. For example, it is commonly stated that archaeologists should publish their work and make their data available to other researchers and the public. This is in response both to the public's 'right to know' about archaeological work and to the idea that archaeological excavation is a means of conserving the material remains of the past by converting them into a data record for posterity. However, many

Indigenous people object to free and open publication of information about their cultural places. If archaeologists are also obliged by their codes of ethics to respect the wishes of Indigenous people they cannot also comply with the public's 'right to know'.

In Australia, the Code of Ethics of the Australian Association of Consulting Archaeologists conforms closely with codes of ethics developed by archaeological organisations in Britain and the United States. The AACAI code is a wide-ranging document which states in its introduction that 'members agree that as archaeologists we have certain responsibilities to the public, our employers and clients and our colleagues'. These responsibilities are then laid out in some detail. The AACAI code also provides guidance on professional standards, training, credit to colleagues, acceptance of favours, confidential information, consulting practice, legal requirements, preference of employment and duty to employees. AACAI has also adopted a separate policy on consultation with Indigenous communities which acknowledges that Indigenous people have legitimate interests in their own cultural places and should be consulted in an appropriate manner about archaeological work and paid for their involvement in consulting projects. AACAI's policy on Indigenous consultation has been less widely discussed in the academic literature than the Code of Ethics of the Australian Archaeological Association (Members' obligations to Australian Aboriginal and Torres Strait Islander people). The AAA introduced its code in the early 1990s, following lobbying by Indigenous people at AAA conferences. The AAA code of ethics derives from the World Archaeological Congress First Code of Ethics (Member's obligations to indigenous peoples). Indigenous delegates from Australia at World Archaeological Congress meetings brought home the idea of a similar code of ethics for Australian archaeology.[67]

There seems to be a certain amount of confusion about the status and role of the AAA code of ethics, particularly among some Indigenous people. Unlike the AACAI code of ethics, which covers a wide range of issues which may arise in the course of consulting archaeology, the AAA code is only about Indigenous ownership of cultural property and the way archaeologists should respond. Neither code is binding in any sense. AACAI and AAA can choose to expel members who are in breach of their respective codes of ethics. However, as discussed above, there is no requirement for anyone to be a member of either organisation to practise archaeology. The AAA code of ethics is more a statement of moral intent than anything else.

Archaeological knowledge and cultural heritage management

At the time much heritage legislation was introduced, Australian prehistory was dominated by a particular kind of modernist thinking in which cutting-edge research claimed to be about testing hypotheses through the application of scientific methods to archaeological data. Archaeological knowledge was regarded by many prehistorians as objective and isolated from social and political considerations. Archaeology was written into heritage legislation as a type of 'scientific' value, distinct and separate from other values of place (social, historic, aesthetic), and with a narrowly defined set of methods, techniques and approaches. This has had major consequences for the practice of Australian archaeology and its interaction with cultural heritage management. For example, Laurajane Smith argues that because the philosophy and principles of such modernist (processual) archaeology are embedded in much heritage bureaucracy, archaeologists have wielded major power in the decision-making processes of Australian cultural heritage management, often in direct opposition to the wishes of many Indigenous people, and that archaeology has been used as an instrument of government against Indigenous interests.[68]

The finer complexities of such an argument are explored in later chapters. Only some kinds of archaeological knowledge fall comfortably within the rubric of science and scientific value. In many cases archaeology contributes to, and is part of, the *social* value of places. Legislation which gives primacy to a set of values which does not even represent the whole of archaeology, let alone interests and understandings outside the discipline, does not help cultural heritage managers deal with a key question in their work: which versions of the past to take into account when making decisions about the conservation and management of cultural places?

3

Archaeologists and Indigenous people in Australia

When a woman called Truganini died and was buried in Hobart in May 1876, her body was exhumed soon after her death by scientists who wanted her remains for research. This was against her expressed wishes to be buried at sea. Her skeleton was acquired by the museum of the Royal Society of Tasmania in Hobart and was placed on general display from 1904 until 1947, when public pressure persuaded the museum to remove it to a storage vault. Tasmanian Aborigines fought a campaign for the return of Truganini's remains, and after a long legal struggle led by the Tasmanian Aboriginal Centre against the Hobart Museum they were eventually successful in 1975. Truganini's remains were returned to members of the Tasmanian Aboriginal community who cremated her skeleton and scattered her ashes at sea.[1]

The return of Truganini and the remains of other Tasmanian Aborigines collected in the nineteenth century is a well-known example of Indigenous Australians successfully campaigning for the repatriation of ancestral remains previously excavated for research purposes. Since then there have been several other well-documented cases of successful repatriation in Victoria and New South Wales. The Murray Black collection, for example, consisted of over 1600 skeletons removed from burials along the Murray River between 1929 and 1951 by amateur collector George Murray Black, and was variously housed in museums in Canberra and Melbourne. In the mid-1980s the collection was returned to Indigenous people in Victoria after a campaign involving the director of the Aboriginal Legal Service of Fitzroy, Jim Berg. In 1990 the Echuca Aboriginal Cooperative was given back human remains and grave goods dated between 9000 and 15 000 years old, which had been excavated from Kow

Swamp in the early 1970s by Alan Thorne of the Department of Pre-history, Australian National University. The fate of these bones is not on public record, but it is believed they were reburied. This repatriation followed unsuccessful campaigns in the 1970s by Koori people in Victoria, including David Anderson of the Wamba Wamba people on the Murray, to stop the Kow Swamp excavations and to then have the Kow Swamp remains returned to the local community. In 1984 Jim Berg successfully prevented the National Museum of Victoria from sending two skulls from Victoria overseas for an exhibition.[2]

In 1992, after protracted negotiations with the Indigenous communities in western New South Wales, a female burial at least 25 000 years old and known as Mungo Lady, which had been excavated by Thorne and other researchers from the Australian National University in the late 1960s, was returned to traditional owners to be held under joint community and archaeological control in a keeping place. The arrangement does not preclude either further research or future reburial of the remains. In 1995, as noted in the Preface, the Tasmanian Aboriginal Land Council (TALC) was successful in terminating the research work of La Trobe University archaeologists when a court ordered excavated materials—which did not include any human skeletal remains—be removed from Melbourne and returned to Tasmania on behalf of the TALC.[3]

All these cases are familiar to Australian archaeologists and to many Indigenous people. The story of Truganini's life and death is especially well known and significant, particularly in Tasmania. In each case the media have reported and provided comment on the politics of competing claims by Indigenous people and archaeologists, usually in terms of science versus religion and the loss of important scientific knowledge as a result of repatriation and reburial.

Following the widely publicised dispute between the TALC and the La Trobe archaeologists, an article by science reporter Cheryl Jones in the *Bulletin* of May 1997 described a perceived crisis in Australian archaeology in which some leading prehistorians felt no longer able to pursue their legitimate scientific research due to interference from Aborigines. The article also discussed other pertinent developments including the fact that some Australian archaeologists were now not just afraid of Aborigines but of 'anti-scientific theories borrowed from cultural and literary studies', which were described as 'politicising and weakening what was once a scientific discipline'. Proponents of postmodernism, which questioned the objectivity of archaeologists' interpretations of the past, were clearly seen by some prehistorians as the enemy.[4]

On another archaeological front, in an article in *Science* of May 1998 Elizabeth Finkel described the sorry state of government funding for Australian prehistory research projects in the 1990s, many of which had had to be abandoned due to lack of continuing financial support. She also reported the 1997 decision of the Australian National University to close its Department of Prehistory in the Institute of Advanced Studies. Finkel did deliver some better news for Australian prehistory in another story headlined 'Aboriginal Groups Warm to Studies of Early Australians', which described examples of successful collaboration between archaeologists and Indigenous communities following a process of community consultation about research work.[5]

These media reports highlight some important themes relevant to the practice of Australian archaeology since the 1970s. Since that time, Australian archaeology has become more fragmented and diverse in its theory and practice, and more overtly political and politicised. It has also been affected by wider socio-economic forces such as globalisation, economic rationalism and the rise of managerialism. These have influenced the kinds of work Australian archaeologists do and the kinds of archaeological research and teaching which gets supported. As the university system endured significant funding cuts over the last decade, archaeologists have increasingly looked for employment in cultural heritage management. Museums, too, have had to cope with reduced government funding which has impacted on their capacity to conduct archaeological research.[6] Changes in the direction of archaeological research are also linked to greater Indigenous involvement in and control of archaeology. Indigenous people are often more interested in their own oral and community history from the recent past than in what archaeology has to say about Australia tens of thousands of years ago, and have directed research accordingly.

Although there are still commonalities and overlaps in the kinds of research questions which occupy Australian archaeologists today, compared with the 1970s archaeologists in different camps are not necessarily interested in each other's work and may share little common intellectual ground. If the sentiments expressed in Cheryl Jones' article are accurate, some prehistorians have even felt threatened by diversification which seemingly challenges their own position.[7]

Despite these trends, Australian archaeologists have continued to work with Indigenous communities on a variety of projects. While conflicts and disagreements can and do happen, in fact these rarely make headline news, and most are resolved by a process of negotiation. This point is made well by Colin Pardoe, who described his own experiences studying human skeletal remains with communities in New South Wales and Victoria in the late 1980s and early 1990s. He does not deny the difficulties he faced as a scientist who wished to conduct research on human bones which many people do not want studied at all. But that is only part of the picture. While no Indigenous community would permit excavations of burials for research purposes, many communities invited Pardoe to excavate, record and study human bones which were exposed in eroding sand dunes or otherwise threatened, because they trusted him and felt there was some value in his research. Communities also invited him to play a major and active part in re-burial ceremonies. With the permission of the relevant people, he was able to collect measurements and other data which he then used for his research in biological anthropology.[8]

There are many examples of amicable cooperation between Indigenous communities and archaeologists. It was precisely to make this point that Iain Davidson, Christine Lovell-Jones and Robyne Bancroft organised a session at the 1991 Australian Archaeological Association on the theme of Archaeologists and Aborigines Working Together, which was then published as a book.[9] This is not to suggest that everything is easy and straightforward between Indigenous people and archaeologists. Nevertheless, through a process of negotiation and compromise, much archaeology continues to get done with the approval and involvement of Indigenous people. Many Indigenous people are interested in archaeology; some to the extent that they have gained formal qualifications and university degrees in the subject, and work as professionals in the discipline.

So what are the issues here? Why have some archaeologists been able to work successfully with Indigenous communities on research projects, while others have become embroiled in major conflicts which have seriously threatened or even terminated their work? Why do some Indigenous people seemingly reject archaeology, while others value it? What role have the government and wider public attitudes played in such developments?

In the following discussion of these questions I make no claim to be objective. My main aims are to clarify what I believe are some common misunderstandings and to present a range of views about questions to which there are no right or wrong answers. My experience as a university teacher and researcher is that many people who are not directly involved in Australian archaeology or cultural heritage management often don't appreciate the complexities and finer details of the relationship between Indigenous people, archaeologists, government and the public. Such comments apply to some Australian academics in other disciplines (such as history, anthropology and cultural studies) and to overseas archaeologists. They also apply to members of the public, including some Indigenous people themselves. My other observation is that many non-Indigenous people know very little about Indigenous people and their experiences. Such factors can cloud an informed and reasonably sophisticated under-standing of the relationship between archaeologists and Indigenous people.

Colonialism, Indigenous identity and black–white politics

The way Indigenous Australians feel about archaeology and the attitude of archaeologists towards Indigenous issues need to be understood in the context of British invasion and colonisation of Australia, and Indigenous people's struggle for survival and social justice in the face of this. This story has been increasingly well documented since the 1970s as part of an ever-growing literature on Indigenous history written by both Indigenous and non-Indigenous people.[10]

British invasion and subsequent colonial settlement of Australia from AD 1788 onwards have had devastating consequences for Indigenous Australians. This is a story of overwhelming dispossession, loss and human suffering, tempered by ultimate survival and the assertion of cultural and political rights against seemingly insurmountable odds. We don't know exactly how many people lived here when the British first arrived but it is likely that tens of thousands of them died during the early years of invasion from disease, violence and other forms of abuse. Many atrocities were committed against Indigenous people, who often fought back with acts of violence against settlers in what has been characterised by some historians as a colonial or guerrilla war.[11] A major long-term result of this invasion was that Indigenous peoples were forcibly driven or moved off most of their lands and many communities and families were broken up.

For a long time white society commonly believed that so called full-blood Aborigines were a dying race, which would eventually become extinct, thus resolving the 'Aboriginal problem'. Under government policies of segregation, many Indigenous people were moved onto missions and reserves away from white society. Here missionaries and government officials controlled their lives. Major elements of traditional culture and language were destroyed by attempts to 'civilise' and convert Indigenous people to Christianity. Others managed to avoid being institutionalised in this way and survived outside the reserve system. Eventually all state governments changed their policies from segregation to assimilation, and closed the missions and reserves and moved people back into mainstream 'white' Australian society. The way people survived in and around white society, and the extent to which they were able to maintain their cultural identity and links with their land, varied greatly across the country and with individual circumstances.

However, the overall outcome of the last 200 years or so of Australia's history is that Indigenous people have suffered gross economic and social disadvantage in white society compared with other Australians. Even at the start of the twenty-first century, Indigenous people are generally much poorer and less well educated than most other Australians. They are more likely to live in substandard housing, to be out of work, to be in jail, to have poor health and lower life expectancy. Many Indigenous communities are plagued with social problems associated with unemployment, alcohol and drug abuse, domestic and other forms of violence and crime. Such issues were highlighted by the 1987–1990 Royal Commission into Aboriginal Deaths in Custody, which made a number of recommendations for improving Indigenous health, wellbeing and rights. Sadly, but not surprisingly, such problems still remain. These are not just Indigenous problems—they affect all Australians. So does insidious racism against Aborigines which is rife in many segments of Australian society. Unsympathetic Australians blame Indigenous people for not dealing with their own problems, for not integrating into 'white' society, for demanding handouts, hindering economic developments and 'progress' and wasting government money. Yet many problems people face are the direct result of dispossession, racism and lack of understanding of Indigenous history and culture.

Over the last 200 years or so, white society has been responsible for denying many Indigenous people the skills and resources they need to deal with what has happened to them due to invasion and settlement. Despite this, Indigenous people have not been passive. Since early colonial times they have resisted and struggled for their rights, and from the mid-twentieth century they have made major political gains. From the early 1920s emerging Indigenous politicians formed organisations to promote their people's rights.[12] In 1938 activists declared Australia Day (commemorating the 150th anniversary of the establishment of the first British settlement at Sydney Cove on 26 January 1788) as a Day of Mourning for their people. This became an important symbol for Indigenous rights struggles. The changing social and political climate of the 1960s, which among other things made non-Indigenous Australians more sympathetic to Indigenous issues, culminated in a national referendum in 1967, supported by an overwhelming majority of Australians, which meant that for the first time Indigenous people were counted in the national census and that the Commonwealth government was given the power to override state powers in the area of Indigenous affairs.[13]

Indigenous people don't separate their interests in cultural heritage and history from other elements of their lives. In general, people want control and ownership of their own cultural places and the remains of their ancestors and their history as part of their struggle for social justice, self-determination and sovereignty. These things are closely linked to Indigenous people's relationship to land, and their desire for land rights. As Mudrooroo, writing from an Indigenous perspective, explains:

> The whole question of Land Rights and the correction of injustice must be preceded by a recognition of the enormous damage done through spiritual deprivation. The denial of cultural and spiritual heritage and lack of recognition of relationship to the land are the root cause of loss of identity, loss of health, and subsequent degradation.[14]

Land rights have been a central focus of Indigenous people's struggles for self-determination. Land rights legislation was enacted in several states from the 1970s onwards in response to a growing land rights lobby. This has had major political implications. The most significant recent political gain was the 1992 Mabo decision. Eddie Mabo and other Miriam people of the Torres Strait began action in the High Court of Australia seeking recognition of their traditional land rights. The Court eventually ruled in their favour and upheld their claim that Australia was not *terra nullius* (land belonging to no one) when British settlers arrived, but belonged to Indigenous people whose native title to land had in some cases survived Britain's annexation of Australia. The Commonwealth government then passed the 1993 *Native Title Act* codifying the High Court's decision in legislation. This provided a mechanism whereby Indigenous people could in principle claim Native Title rights in some types of Crown land. The status of pastoral and mining leases on Crown land remained uncertain. The issue was taken back to the High Court in the Wik case of 1993 which ruled by a narrow majority that pastoral and mining leases did not necessarily extinguish all Native Title rights. Both Mabo and Wik unleashed a torrent of anti-Indigenous political rhetoric, as many mining companies, pastoralists and the succeeding Liberal–National Coalition Commonwealth government under John Howard sought to constrain what they regard as a major threat to their economic and political interests. In 1998, after long and protracted negotiations and discussion, the Commonwealth government passed the *Native Title Amendment Act* in an attempt to deal with what some commentators have called the uncertainty for pastoral and mining interests created by the Mabo and Wik rulings of the High Court. Debate still rages and is unlikely to be settled for some time. Many issues have been raised by these developments which have thrust black–white relations to the centre of the political stage once more.

To some extent the Mabo and Wik decisions overshadowed the other major development of the 1990s: Reconciliation between Indigenous and non-Indigenous Australians. The Reconciliation process began in 1991 when a unanimous vote in both houses of the Federal Parliament established the National Council for Aboriginal Reconciliation with the aim of improving relations between Aboriginal and Torres Strait Islander people and the wider community. Following its establishment the Council became involved in a number of projects which aimed to define and explain the core elements of Reconciliation and raise awareness of and support for such a process across Australia. The Council believed it was especially important to promote Reconciliation between Indigenous and other Australians in the lead-up to the Sydney Olympic Games of

September 2000 and the Centenary of Federation on 1 January 2001, in order to create a better Australian society. At the time of writing, the Reconciliation process had gone awry in an atmosphere of growing antagonism between many Indigenous leaders and John Howard's Federal government over a number of issues.[15]

Views of the past and the politics of identity

Indigenous understandings of land, culture, society and identity have been noted in the studies of many archaeologists. Archaeologist Anne Ross and the members of the Quandamooka Aboriginal Land Council have described Indigenous values associated with the land and waters making up the islands and sea around Moreton Bay in south-east Queensland. While local people acknowledge the scientific value of shell middens and other archaeological sites in their area, such values are insignificant compared with other heritage values associated with living oyster beds, which continue to be used for people's livelihood.[16] In South Australia, in another example, James Knight has described Indigenous understandings of landscapes which incorporate places and things archaeologists call sites and artefacts in terms of messages which knowledgeable Indigenous people can read through a series of cultural rules:

> The travels of Dreaming ancestors create a pattern of friendships and enmities, as well as giving ceremony, law and social relationships to humans. Things discarded during this process leave traces which can be found and pieced together to tell stories. As each flaked stone artefact is made, retouched or resharpened, debitage, retouch chips and finally the retouched stone itself leave physical evidence which can be read as an archaeological text.[17]

Writing about the situation in New South Wales, Denis Byrne also comments on places which archaeologists call sites but which can have their own Indigenous significance. He argues that it is important for people involved in the heritage management process (which often divides heritage into separate natural and cultural components) to appreciate that the distinction some archaeologists have made between archaeological sites on the one hand and 'sacred' sites on the other may have little meaning for Indigenous people. Middens, rock shelter deposits, scarred trees, stone quarries, burials and cemeteries and a range of other places are as likely to have spiritual and cultural value as are ceremonial sites (e.g. bora rings) or Dreaming sites. In addition to religious or spiritual meanings, Indigenous people value sites for their historical associations or other significance as 'memory' places. Many places are also important for collecting traditional bush foods and other resources, which are themselves significant for people's lifestyle and physical wellbeing, as well as for maintaining elements of traditional culture.[18]

For historical reasons, as we have seen, archaeology and archaeologists have been instrumental in defining what Indigenous cultural places are (i.e. archaeological sites and 'relics') and the way they should be managed (i.e. through government-controlled heritage bureaucracies in which archaeologists play a central role). Defining and managing Indigenous cultural heritage in this way is a product of colonialism and has rarely suited the needs and aspirations of Indigenous people themselves.

Archaeology also produces knowledge which may be quite different from the way non-archaeologists understand the past. Views of the past, including those produced by archaeologists, are often important to people's identity, and questions surrounding identity are central to Indigenous rights in Australia. This is well demonstrated in Tasmania, where archaeology has been important to the way white Australians have defined Aboriginality. While Tom Haydon's documentary *The Last Tasmanian* made an impression on many people for its moving and deeply disturbing depiction of the genocide of Tasmania's Indigenous peoples, it was condemned by Aboriginal Tasmanians and their supporters for being racist. Tasmanian Aborigines were indeed present in the film, but were denied their own voice. In the film archaeological evidence from Rocky Cape and other Tasmanian sites was presented to support a version of history which seemingly justified the notion of genocide and denied Tasmanian Aboriginal survival and rights. Today many people still believe there are no Aborigines in Tasmania. People are either unaware that several thousand people living in Tasmania identify themselves as Aboriginal, or they dismiss such claims as fallacious.

Indigenous identity is currently defined by the Australian government in social terms. An Indigenous person is someone of Aboriginal or Torres Strait Islander descent, who identifies him or herself as being Aboriginal or Torres Strait Islander and is accepted as such by the Indigenous community where they live or used to live. In such terms Tasmanian Aborigines are no less Indigenous than many other people on the Australian mainland. Fundamental to the Tasmanian case is the widespread belief that Tasmanian Aborigines were completely wiped out by British invasion and colonial settlement. However, in Tasmania, as elsewhere in Australia, Indigenous identity is not simply about physical appearance and biological descent. It is about history and culture. Ironically many Tasmanian Aborigines have suffered racial discrimination, economic and other disadvantage precisely because other people have considered them to be Aboriginal while at the same time denying them their cultural identity.[19] Such ideas are part of the continuing legacy of colonial history in Tasmania. They are racist and they explain much about many Tasmanian Aboriginal people's attitudes towards archaeology and archaeologists.

The entanglement of archaeology, history and the politics of Indigenous identity go back to the time of first contact between Europeans and Tasmanian Aborigines. Following Abel Tasman's voyage to the islands in AD 1642, Europeans became fascinated by the people living there. Many colonial writers regarded the Indigenous Tasmanian Aborigines as so different from other Australian Aborigines that they must be a different race of people altogether. Nineteenth-century colonialist ideology classified Tasmanian Aborigines as 'living fossils' representing the lowest stage of human cultural and physical evolution. Their skeletons and body parts were highly valued for study by some scientists who were especially eager to acquire the bodies of the few remaining 'full-blooded' Tasmanian Aborigines who had been moved from Wybalenna to Oyster Cove by the colonial government. This interest resulted in grave robbing and the illegal dismemberment of people's bodies—a further insult and outrage against these people who had already suffered and lost so much from British invasion and colonial settlement.[20]

This early history and its legacy set the stage for the way archaeologists have chosen to interpret Tasmanian prehistory and archaeology, and it shaped the broader social context within which archaeologists have worked there. Key questions posed by prehistorians have concerned the origins and antiquity of human occupation of Tasmania and the wider implications of this for early human settlement of Australia as a whole. Archaeologists have also been interested in explaining the historical relationship between Tasmanian and other Indigenous groups, and in tracing the origins and causes of the supposedly distinct features of the Tasmanian Aborigines and their culture. Compared with their immediate neighbours across Bass Strait, for example, the Tasmanians were described by early colonial writers as being much shorter in height, and as having distinctive facial features and curlier hair. They made and used a much smaller range of tools, weapons and ornaments than Indigenous groups in Victoria and South Australia. As discussed elsewhere, they did not eat scale fish. The distinct features of the Tasmanian Aborigines are generally considered to have resulted from over 10 000 years of isolation; however, more recent research by Colin Pardoe has added to the puzzle. He suggests that while Tasmania does indeed appear to have been physically isolated by Bass Strait for a long time period, the Tasmanians themselves are no more physically different from other Indigenous groups than might be expected if the island were still attached to the mainland.[21]

Archaeological research has provided important information about ice age settlement of Australia and the relationship between the Tasmanian Aborigines and other Indigenous populations. It has also featured in theoretical debates about the validity of using eighteenth- and nineteenth-century accounts of Tasmanian Aborigines to interpret human behaviour in the south-west tens of thousands of years earlier (a subject discussed in Chapter 1). Some archaeologists have been particularly keen to distance their interpretations of ancient Tasmania from historical accounts and have instead used models drawn from ecology. They point out that there are no historical accounts of Aboriginal people living in the south-west forests of Tasmania at the time of early European contact in any case. Archaeological evidence from rock shelters in the area suggests that people stopped using many sites some time after 12 000 years ago. Southern Forests Archaeological Project archaeologists Richard Cosgrove, Jim Allen and Brendan Marshall argue that areas of the south-west were abandoned after this time for reasons associated with the development of the rainforests, when large-scale environmental change restricted people's ability to collect food.[22] Yet Ian Thomas interprets environmental and archaeological evidence to suggest that the south-west forests were not entirely abandoned at the end of the last ice age, and that people were living in and using the region during the last few thousand years.[23]

Arguments over this south-west Tasmania evidence are presented in a series of often acrimoniously worded papers in the journal *Australian*

Archaeology, in which the researchers hint at a 'subtext' to the scientific debate: the extent to which their interpretations seemingly support or contradict contemporary Aboriginal claims to sites in the area. No one, including contemporary Aboriginal people, was aware that anyone had ever lived in the south-west Tasmanian forests until the discovery of Kutikina Cave during the Franklin Dam dispute. Members of the Tasmanian Aboriginal community have since claimed archaeological sites in south-west Tasmania as part of their heritage.[24]

In such a context, archaeological interpretation which distances very old sites from historically documented Indigenous groups and demonstrates the area was abandoned until the arrival of Europeans could be seen as undermining contemporary Indigenous claims to control cultural places and materials from the south-west. Archaeological interpretation which demonstrates more recent and continuous use of the area by Indigenous people seemingly supports contemporary Aboriginal claims. The archaeological evidence of the south-west does not speak for itself. Archaeologists interpret such evidence to write (pre-)history. When such prehistory enters the public domain it can become embroiled in political debates about identity and cultural rights.

Do Indigenous Australians need archaeology?

At a very fundamental level, traditional Indigenous beliefs hold that Indigenous people have always lived in Australia and were created here during the Dreaming. Archaeologists argue that the ancestors of today's Aborigines are ultimately descended, albeit millions of years ago, from early hominids in Africa, in common with all other human populations, and that people first arrived in what is now Australia some time before 40 000 years ago. Here archaeology is in fundamental disagreement with the basic Indigenous spiritual beliefs and some Indigenous people reject archaeology outright on such grounds. Such disagreement is similar to clashes between archaeology and fundamentalist religious beliefs in other parts of the world.

Some Indigenous people prefer their own understanding of their past; they may not be particularly opposed to archaeology as such but simply see it as largely irrelevant, as succinctly expressed by Sammy Watson (from Kuku Djungu, Mt Mulligan, North Queensland): 'We were the first lot here in this country and I think we were placed here. That story about coming from somewhere, well no, no, no, that's a bit far fetched.'[25]

Likewise archaeologist Laila Haglund, working on environmental impact assessments in New South Wales, has commented how some Indigenous people are not especially opposed to archaeology—they are just not very interested in it because they can't see that it tells them anything that they'd like to know.[26]

Even when Indigenous people know about archaeology and the kinds of knowledge it can produce, they may choose to ignore it. Ian McNiven discusses a case from Fraser Island in Queensland, where Badtjala people, who are quite familiar with archaeological research about aspects of their culture, nevertheless deliberately exclude any mention of such work from their own writings about the history of their island. According to McNiven this stems from Badtjala people's rejection of the colonialist nature of key and highly significant nineteenth-century historic texts about the wreck of the European ship the *Stirling Castle* in 1836 and the 'kidnap' of Eliza Fraser by local Indigenous people on the island. Eliza Fraser was one of the few survivors of the wreck. She spent about 50 days living on the island with local people before being rescued by a government party. Eliza Fraser has become an almost mythological figure in Australian history and culture. Versions of her story attracted huge popular interest at the time and have continued to since. As generally related in the nineteenth century, her story depicts an innocent and vulnerable white woman who suffered a horrific ordeal when she was 'kidnapped' by cruel and wild savages and suffered many hardships in their hands. In the twentieth century the story shifted focus, to reflect contemporary attitudes to race, gender and class under conditions of colonialism and postcolonialism.

The nineteenth-century accounts, which are derogatory in their descriptions of Badtjala people, were also used by archaeologist Peter Lauer in the 1970s to reconstruct the lifestyle of Indigenous people at the time of European contact and to directly interpret the archaeological record of the island. He located numerous coastal shell middens and inland stone tool scatters. Scientific dating showed the middens were all less than 500 years old and some could be as recent as the eighteenth and nineteenth centuries. The stone tool scatters were not dated, but Lauer assumed they too were less than 500 years old, and that both types of sites represented the direct remains of Indigenous food collecting and subsistence activities described in the *Stirling Castle* archives and other documentary accounts. This is a classic example of the 'direct historical' use of ethnography for archaeological interpretation (see Chapter 1).

New archaeological research in the region by McNiven showed that the middens dated to the last 200 years, but the stone tool scatters were much older—between 1000 to 5000 years old. According to McNiven, the archaeological record of the Fraser Island region demonstrated two chronologically distinct phases of Indigenous use and Lauer's previous interpretation based on documentary accounts was flawed. Badtjala people, however, prefer to represent their own culture and their own history without reference to any of this archaeology even though archaeology does not necessarily involve using colonialist historical accounts.[27]

Harry Allen also discusses Indigenous people's rejection of archaeological interpretations of the past, and of any archaeological practice, in the Kakadu National Park in the Northern Territory. Kakadu National Park was declared and sections placed on the World Heritage List in a series of developments between 1979 and 1991. Land rights claims were successful in granting legal ownership of the park to Indigenous owners, but only on the condition that the land be leased back to the government for a national park. Currently the park is jointly managed by the Commonwealth Australian Nature Conservation Agency (ANCA) and representatives of traditional owners. The last twenty years have seen increasing Indigenous input into park management and there is now a majority of Indigenous people on the Kakadu Board of Management. The Indigenous Bininj Heritage Management Committee has also been established to deal with cultural heritage defined as including 'knowledge, beliefs, customs and practices, and tangible evidence of these such as artefacts, rock art and other archaeological sites, historic sites and sites of significance'.[28]

Allen explains how the Kakadu National Park has been the focus of a number of major research projects encompassing environmental history, archaeology and rock art studies over a number of decades. Such research has been central to many of the key questions addressed by Australian prehistorians and archaeologists, including the date of early human settlement of the continent, human–environment interactions, and models for cultural change in pre-European Australia. Yet the 1995 Draft Plan of Management only acknowledges archaeology in a very limited way. For example, it states that archaeological sites can provide information about people's daily activities—'what they did, what they ate, how they hunted, how they processed their food, what type of shelter they used'—and notes that some sites in the park date back to 50 000 years. At the same time the draft plan totally fails to acknowledge the wealth of knowledge about the Kakadu National Park area which has resulted from archaeological research—about long-term environmental change through time linked to changes in art styles and other aspects of people's culture and way of life.

When consulted about their views on research in the park, traditional owners thought that archaeological and rock art research had been over-emphasised. Traditional owners requested ANCA to support them in protecting their traditional intellectual property rights by giving them control over how their lands are managed, and particularly how their culture and history is interpreted. Allen notes the comments of the Bininj Heritage Management Committee that:

> . . . cultural heritage research should be directed away from archaeology and art site management towards the oral history of elders associated with the park . . . the Heritage Management Committee argued that any further archaeological research should be left until Bininj people themselves are suitably trained to undertake it.[29]

Peter Thorley comments that the forms in which people choose to represent themselves are highly culturally specific. Archaeology is one of many Western methods of collecting and transmitting information. 'Aboriginal people are unlikely to dump their own traditions to embrace archaeology as a form of self-representation any more than archaeologists are likely to throw out their research questions, although there may be some borrowing between respective cultures.'[30]

When archaeologists point out the value and benefits of their research to Indigenous people and to Australians more generally, many Indigenous Australians remain unimpressed. They ask why they need to feel grateful for being judged by white people in white terms. Why should they need to prove themselves to white society through archaeology? Furthermore, they point out, Indigenous people are perfectly capable of representing themselves, their culture, history, technological and artistic achievements, and many people would prefer to do so rather than being represented by archaeologists.[31] Linda Tuhiwai Smith, writing from an Indigenous perspective, discusses the many reasons why Indigenous people are generally suspicious of research which has so often been carried out against their interests under conditions of imperialism and colonialism. In particular, she stresses the power dynamics which exist between researcher and researched:

> Research in itself is a powerful intervention, even if carried out at a distance, which has traditionally benefited the researcher, and the knowledge base of the dominant group in society . . . Researchers are in receipt of privileged information. They may interpret it within an overt theoretical framework, but also in terms of a covert ideological framework. They have the power to distort, to make invisible, to overlook, to exaggerate and to draw conclusions, based not on factual data, but on assumptions, hidden value judgements, and often downright misunderstandings. They have the potential to extend knowledge or to perpetuate ignorance.[32]

Archaeology as physical and spiritual threat

Doing archaeology often involves direct action and physical impact. For example, archaeologists need to visit places which are significant to Indigenous people to conduct their research. While many archaeological techniques, such as photography, drawing, measuring and taking notes, do not cause any direct physical damage, the mere presence of archaeologists can be regarded as offensive and inappropriate by some Indigenous people. Indigenous Australian societies have their own strict protocols about who is and isn't allowed to visit certain places, and under what circumstances. For example, many places are classified as men's or women's places and it is inappropriate for the wrong gender to visit them. Other places are regarded as sacred, powerful or dangerous, and there are strict rules about who can and cannot go there. In the course of their work, merely by walking across the landscape to visit and record sites, archaeologists can transgress such rules and cause offence.[33]

Archaeological excavation is especially problematic as it involves digging into the ground, uncovering buried objects and sometimes human skeletal remains. Archaeologists aim to conserve the objects they dig up, and keep detailed records about their spatial associations. However, there is no question that archaeological excavations can cause great physical disturbance to places. Techniques such as radiocarbon dating and thin sectioning for microscopic analyses also involve the destruction of materials such as bone, charcoal and shell, albeit in small amounts. Excavated materials are frequently removed for study to remote locations and are often never returned, but kept stored in museums and university departments.

Many Indigenous people regard such activities as highly disrespectful, if not sacrilegious, especially when human burials and ancestral remains are involved. From an Indigenous perspective, these need to be treated correctly, both out of respect for the dead and so that the spirits of the dead can be laid to rest in the proper way that does not disturb the living. It is not just Indigenous Australians who feel like this about digging up human burials, especially when they are of known individuals. Many people don't want the remains of their relatives or ancestors interfered with.[34]

If some people object to archaeology on the grounds that archaeologists commit sacrilege in the practice of their profession, what can archaeologists say? Archaeologists could choose to disregard such beliefs and continue with their research. This is only possible if archaeologists have more power than other people. This was certainly the case in Australia until legislation gave Indigenous people more control over archaeological fieldwork, following political campaigns of the 1960s and 1970s. Currently, the balance of power between archaeologists and Indigenous Australians is far less clear. Because the government will not give archaeologists excavation permits without the permission of relevant communities, researchers are now unable to dig up sites in the face of expressed Indigenous objections, regardless of land ownership. One consequence of this has been to halt all research excavations of Indigenous burial sites.

Pragmatic concerns

In addition to the physical and spiritual threat to places which archaeology can pose, there are more mundane and practical reasons why some Indigenous people are wary of archaeologists. As we have seen, Indigenous people view archaeologists as yet another group of white people from outside the community with whom they have to deal. Unless there is some tangible benefit to the community, why should archaeologists expect people to help them with their research? What do Indigenous people get out of it? Some Indigenous people in Tasmania have been very blunt on this point. Writing in 1996 the TALC described archaeology primarily as an activity which earns archaeologists money and prestige and is of little real use to them. The title of Ros Langford's classic 1983 article about the politics of archaeologists studying Indigenous places—Our Heritage— Your Playground—is extremely telling.[35]

Many Indigenous Australian people are severely economically disadvantaged. Communities are struggling to deal with their own problems of health, housing, education, unemployment and other issues. Understandably these things are far more pressing to them than assisting some usually middle-class, relatively wealthy archaeologists, who live and work in a faraway city, with a research project which in the eyes of the community does little more than serve the career aspirations and employment prospects of the researchers, especially when many members of the community are themselves unemployed.

Indigenous people employed in land councils and other community organisations, whom archaeologists often deal with in the first instance, are usually coping with a large range of demands on their time and energy with very limited resources. Requests for help and support with research simply impose on these resources further. Dealings with archaeologists may place individuals in difficult or invidious positions regarding local community politics, especially if archaeologists pressure them to negotiate on their behalf with other members of the community.

On top of all this, and ignoring all the reservations Indigenous people may have, communicating what the archaeologist wants to do can be another hurdle. Some archaeologists seem unable to express what they are doing in clear terms to their colleagues, let alone to the wider public. How are those many Indigenous people who are poorly educated and have literacy problems expected to understand or be interested in what archaeologists want to do?

Despite such problems there are many circumstances where archaeology *is* seen to bring tangible benefits to members of Indigenous communities in the form of paid, if usually temporary, employment, opportunities to gain new knowledge and skills, educational materials for use in schools, opportunities to get involved in fieldwork in places which are interesting and important to community members, and social interaction with new people from outside the community.

Ownership and ethics

Both the codes of ethics of the Australian Archaeological Association (AAA) and the Australian Association of Consulting Archaeologists Incorporated (AACAI) among other things acknowledge that Indigenous cultural heritage belongs first and foremost to Indigenous people, whatever the current state of legal ownership of 'relics' and sites. But as we have seen, these codes are not binding, and indeed it is pertinent to ask to what extent they really reflect what archaeologists believe.

Many archaeologists are probably broadly sympathetic to Indigenous aspirations.[35] However, the AAA and AACAI codes of ethics are not universally accepted by all archaeologists working in Australia, nor is there any legal obligation for archaeologists to abide by them, although current government policies require archaeologists to comply with the basic tenets of the AAA and AACAI codes of ethics to obtain excavation permits. Some archaeologists clearly disagree that they should have to seek permission from communities for their work, or are only prepared to pay lip service to the idea of consultation. However, few have said so publicly for fear of expressing unpopular political opinions and being ostracised by their colleagues and Indigenous people on whom they might need to rely for permission to conduct future research work. An exception is Malcolm McKay, who openly criticised the AAA code of ethics in an article in the journal *Australian Archaeology* on the grounds that archaeology is an objective science, the practice of which should be kept separate from contemporary political concerns. McKay refers to the World Archaeological Congress (WAC) code of ethics, when he in fact means the AAA code. This has arisen because the AAA code derived from the WAC First Code of Ethics (Members' obligations to Indigenous peoples).[37]

McKay is critical of the wording of some of the AAA code of ethics and doubts its workability in many cases. He also disagrees with the view that Indigenous people necessarily own the past of the area where they now live, because of demonstrated changes to Indigenous culture in the precolonial and historic period. He puts forward an argument, which has been made by other archaeologists in the context of Indigenous claims to ancestral remains and cultural materials, that the remains of the human past cannot be owned by any one group but are the common heritage of all humankind and belong to the world. Tom Griffiths has discussed how notions of universal scientific value and the shared common ancestry of all mankind (epitomised by 'man the hunter') developed especially in the context of post-Second World War concerns about racism and ethnic nationalism associated with the Holocaust. The idea of a universal man was promoted by the United Nations to argue that all peoples were equal, and to combat racism. As he also notes, the 'problem was that man the hunter, although "a natural global citizen", was also "a natural neo-imperialist"'.[38]

The concept of world heritage and the universal scientific value of archaeological remains has been a central and recurrent theme in arguments between archaeologists and various ethnic, national and other groups worldwide. Some Australian prehistorians have argued that certain Australian sites, artefacts and human remains cannot be considered sole property of contemporary Indigenous communities. As regards very early Australian human skeletal remains and other items that are tens of thousands of years old, present-day people who just happen to live in places where these finds are unearthed should have no particular rights. Study of such material is important to scientific understanding of human evolution and cultural development as a whole, not just to Indigenous Australian history, and the material should therefore belong to all humankind. The return for reburial of such remains threatens scientific research of worldwide interest.[39]

Many Indigenous Australians disagree. To them it does not matter how old this material is. They argue that it still forms part of their cultural heritage and the remains are still those of their ancestors more than anyone else's, no matter how much Australia has changed over the past 40 000 years or so. In addition, Indigenous people have had huge changes imposed on them and their culture by British invasion and colonisation which, more than anything else, has served to disrupt links between people, their land and their past. Some Indigenous people explicitly reject the notion of world heritage and universal scientific value. For example, Langford, writing on behalf of the Tasmanian Aboriginal Centre in 1983, argues that such ideas are based on promoting a white, Western view of the world which is neither objective nor value-free. It is not 'humankind' or 'the world' who want this material, but individual white scientists.[40] In a recent discussion of postcolonial nationalism from a cultural studies perspective, Ken Gelder and Jane Jacobs also analyse claims to ownership of human skeletal remains and cultural materials by Indigenous people, and published counterclaims by archaeologists John Mulvaney and Tim Murray. Statements by Mulvaney and Murray stress the power of archaeology to speak for 'all of us' and for 'all Australians' and emphasise the 'loss to us all' in a democratic Australia if archaeologists are prevented from studying Indigenous skeletal remains and other cultural materials. Gelder and Jacobs query such a characterisation of archaeology in contemporary Australia in the following terms:

> A discipline that may itself appear utterly 'obscure' to many Australians thus represents itself as emblematic of a democratic, pluralist nation state. Aboriginal people are coded as *un*Australian, standing for closure, standing against 'freedom' and 'diversity'. This is an increasingly familiar form of postcolonial racism . . .[41]

This may be the case for the statements of these particular archaeologists in this particular context (the discussion was primarily about the return of the Kow Swamp material and the *TALC v. La Trobe* case). Claims by Tim Murray in a slightly different context about the ownership of Indigenous and non-Indigenous material remains from the historic period raise another set of issues, as discussed below. Gelder and Jacobs also concede that Mulvaney and Murray do not speak for all Australian archaeologists, and quote work by Colin Pardoe, who presents a different set of perspectives, including negotiation with Indigenous communities about research. Indeed, as discussed elsewhere in this book, archaeologists in Australia have a range of different perspectives on the nature of their work.

Nevertheless, statements like that of Gelder and Jacobs stem from a current postmodern loss of faith among many Western intellectuals in the validity of their own knowledge and a rejection of universal principles. Indigenous critiques of archaeological knowledge are aimed at reclaiming cultural and other human rights denied by colonialism. The motivation of Indigenous people in making such statements is different from those of white academics. Yet in Australia, as the introduction to this chapter suggested, postmodern and Indigenous critiques of archaeological knowledge are closely linked to each other. A counterargument to the postmodern view is that there are some universal principles and some of these are worth aspiring to, including some Western intellectual traditions. True pluralism, which accommodates a range of understandings, should also be able to accommodate scientific and other forms of Western knowledge.

Ownership and contact archaeology

Historical and contact archaeology raise their own particular problems about ownership of the material remains of the past and their interpretation. Who owns places and remains which are the product of interactions between Indigenous Australians and settlers during the colonial period? For example, Murray has argued that many places from the last 200 years or so of Australia's colonial history are part of a heritage shared by all Australians, black and white.[42] Yet many of these places, as well as places associated with Indigenous life following British colonisation, are as important to Indigenous Australians as the more 'traditional' and older places. Most states require that Indigenous people be consulted about archaeological research on Indigenous historic places just as they are for prehistoric sites. Yet it is not always clear exactly what constitutes an 'Aboriginal site' in the colonial period.

Some post-AD1788 places are more clearly Indigenous than others; these include the remains of missions and reserves established by governments to segregate Aborigines from the rest of Australian society until the 1940s, and cemeteries associated with such places.[43] Other kinds of historic places also have strong Indigenous significance, including prisons where Indigenous people were incarcerated and massacre sites where Aborigines died in inter-racial conflict. Places where Indigenous people lived outside white society, such as fringe camps and shanty towns, and sites associated with mining, pastoralism and other industries which relied heavily on Indigenous labour are frequently nominated to heritage registers by Indigenous people, as are places associated with political struggles for self-determination, including community resource centres, museums and 'keeping places', Indigenous business ventures and land successfully reclaimed by Indigenous people under land rights legislation.[44] In most cases, no one would dispute that Indigenous people are legitimate stakeholders in such places and should be consulted about any proposed research on them. Yet some of these places also have a strong non-Indigenous history. So far governments have not usually insisted that archaeologists also seek consent for research from non-Indigenous communities or individuals with interests in such places, except for historic burials where, in New South Wales at least, it is now government policy to consult with descendants.[45]

Many historic places are primarily about white history and their fabric is non-Indigenous, yet they may contain small quantities of Indigenous materials such as flaked glass or stone, or isolated Indigenous burials. In such cases, because much state legislation protects Indigenous 'relics' regardless of where they are found, governments require that Indigenous communities be consulted about the treatment of these items. Yet the mere presence of items of Indigenous material on an otherwise European site does not necessarily indicate that the whole site is Indigenous. Early colonial settlers may have built on a pre-existing Indigenous site, and stone tools and other items may have been disturbed and incorporated into the European structures by accident. In other cases, items of Indigenous material in an otherwise European site do indicate that Indigenous people were present and living at that place during the colonial period. The exact nature of such places and the degree to which they represent Indigenous, European or contact archaeology depends on very careful study of the archaeological deposits and supporting documentary research. The question then becomes: who 'owns' such sites? And should Indigenous communities be able to veto archaeological research into such places on the basis of some demonstrated historical association with the place (either physical or documentary) when such places also have an equally strongly documented non-Indigenous history and significance?

A well-known example of such a place is the site of Sydney's First Government House, the remains of which were first excavated by Anne Bickford in the 1980s.[46] First Government House, which was built in AD 1788 and demolished in 1845, was the earliest colonial building in Australia and the seat of government in New South Wales. Most of the structures and finds from the site relate to British colonial occupation, yet documentary records attest to the presence of Indigenous people there during the course of its history. Small quantities of Indigenous artefacts were recovered during the excavations, which have been interpreted as material evidence for Indigenous presence at the site during the colonial period. In the early 1990s, the Museum of Sydney was built over the remains of First Government House in a way which preserves some of the foundations and other structures recovered by the excavations, stores finds from the dig and interprets the place to the public. There is currently a strong Indigenous emphasis in the interpretation of the First Government House site at the Museum of Sydney (MoS), which is presented as a place of significance to both Aborigines and Europeans—albeit for different reasons. The MoS has adopted a deliberately postmodern approach to historical and archaeological interpretation by presenting several sometimes contradictory and conflicting views on the significance and history of the place. However, as explained by Bickford, one active and vocal interest group, the Friends of First Government House, feels that its views of the significance of the place have been sidelined by the MoS in favour of Indigenous people.[47]

In a pluralist and democratic society there should be room for people to express differences of opinion and to tolerate each other's beliefs. Postmodern approaches in museums and on-site interpretation displays encourage multi-vocality, in which different versions of history and views of the past are acknowledged, even if these are in opposition to each other. No attempt is made to reconcile these views. They are presented as equal but different. Such an approach neatly sidesteps a range of key questions about power and representation. Given that there may be a very wide range of differing opinions about a place, it is rarely practical to give every voice space in a museum display or on-site interpretation. This then raises questions about who controls the content of the display, who the audience is and who has been silenced. In an attempt to avoid being didactic, many postmodern museum exhibitions try not to make any direct statements about the meaning that visitors should read from what they see. The idea is that visitors should make up their own minds. Yet by the very action of producing an exhibition and selecting items for display, a curator cannot avoid making some statement. Indeed the display itself is a statement. In addition, if there is no clear message and no information the end result can just be confusing. There are no neat and easy answers to these problems.[48]

Censorship, academic freedom and intellectual property rights

Legal and spiritual ownership of Indigenous places, objects and ancestral remains are closely linked to questions of the ownership of ideas and information associated with these things. To what degree does consultation with Indigenous people about archaeology mean that a community can or should be able to dictate and control the kinds of research archaeologists pursue or the ideas they express in their work? Who owns information and ideas produced from archaeological research?[49]

To some archaeologists the need to negotiate with Indigenous communities about archaeology projects smacks of unacceptable censorship and a denial of academic freedom. For example, in discussing his objections to the AAA code of ethics, Malcolm McKay takes particular issue with Principle 7 of the code, which requires archaeologists to enter into contractual arrangements with Indigenous people about their research:

> But what does it mean? Is it a suggestion that archaeologists seek paid work from indigenous communities, or is it a rather unclear expression of the laudable idea that archaeologists should share their findings with the locals? Or does it express rather obscurely the dangerous idea that indigenous people should have the power of veto over research? If so this is enshrining the evil of political censorship which is totally untenable in any scientific community.[50]

For reasons discussed below, such issues have been particularly pertinent in Tasmania. In the mid-1990s, following the *TALC v. La Trobe* case, a series of letters and editorials was published in national newspapers about censorship and the control of archaeological research agendas by Indigenous people. For example, Pamela Gait, then a postgraduate research student at La Trobe University's Department of Archaeology, complained that following a lengthy process of consultation, the TALC had rejected a research proposal she presented to them because they objected to its focus. She cited correspondence to her from the TALC as follows:

> Pamela Gait's proposal as it stands is not acceptable, but she should be given the opportunity to revise her proposal but along the lines that the proposal should be about the resistance of Aboriginal women instead of the blending of Aboriginal and European cultures.[51]

Gait's letter prompted a response in her support from archaeologist and biological anthropologist Richard Wright, who also complained that current government policies placed some archaeologists in the invidious position of having to move overseas to work, or else conduct their research as 'a member of the propaganda wing of a political organisation'. He regarded such a situation as being unacceptable.[52] This prompted letters in response from archaeologist Jeanette Hope and prominent Tasmanian Indigenous rights campaigner, and Legal Manager of the Tasmanian Aboriginal Centre, Michael Mansell. Both essentially made the point that, given the history of archaeology in Tasmania, it was hardly surprising that such a research proposal would be rejected by the TALC, and that archaeology is not and never has been politically neutral. Both letters also acknowledged that most Australian archaeologists do now accept that Indigenous people are entitled to veto any field research which they deem to be unacceptable and, despite this, numerous archaeological projects go ahead. The whole notion of consultation implies that the people being consulted have the right to say no.[53]

In her letter Hope also picked up an interesting and significant point when she suggested Gait could continue dialogue with the TALC by asking how it would expect to recognise 'resistance' in the archaeological record. If an archaeologist goes looking for evidence of resistance, cultural blending or anything else, will they inevitably find it? Apart from the question of whether archaeology can be used to make meaningful statements about such aspects of history,[54] Hope's point raises key issues about the nature of archaeological knowledge. Are archaeological data value-free, even if archaeologists aren't? Can archaeologists dig up evidence which proves one particular view of the past is more valid, reliable or correct than another? Such questions have vexed archaeologists themselves for some time and are at the core of postmodern and feminist critiques of archaeology.

The TALC itself has countered accusations of censorship by arguing that academics already censor research when they reject, through the process of peer review, applications for research funding or articles for publication in scholarly journals, on the grounds of insufficient 'academic merit': 'Why is it that when an archaeologist says no to an archaeologist it is peer review, but when we say no to an archaeologist it is censorship? Why are you afraid of censorship by non-archaeologists?'[55]

Very few archaeologists now attempt to argue for absolute academic freedom. Most are fully aware that archaeological research agendas have always been subject to controls of various kinds, including peer review and funding constraints, and always will be. However, there are different degrees of academic freedom and different kinds of constraint. For example, the peer review process which the TALC commented upon is a long-standing tradition in which research archaeologists, as academics, impose their own standards to decide which projects get funding and which work gets published in professional archaeology journals and books. For publication, the peer review process is more like a public endorsement of what different sectors of the profession regard as good research scholarship, methodology and argument rather than direct and open censorship of politically unacceptable work. If an archaeologist fails to get their paper published in one journal, they often succeed in getting it published elsewhere. Members of the profession who are asked to review work for publication do so anonymously and in isolation from each other. They don't even necessarily agree with each other.

Applications for research grants are also subject to a peer review process. Here personal and other biases about acceptable research agendas and methods have more serious consequences for the applicant—if they don't get the money there is usually no appeal process and alternative sources of funding may be impossible to find. Peer review panels do constrain the kind of archaeological research which gets funded. With greatly increased competition for research money in recent years, many archaeologists have failed to get their work funded, often after negative comments from anonymous peers. In such circumstances complaints of unfairness and bias are common. Yet peer review panels of government research funding bodies are not drawn from a single organisation, such as the TALC, which has its own openly political aims. Bias is not quite the same as censorship.

Some kinds of archaeological research funding are also subject to ethical approval. For example, the Australian Institute of Aboriginal and Torres Strait Islander Studies (AIATSIS) will only fund research work, including archaeology, which meets the approval of its ethics committee. Research will only be supported by AIATSIS if the researcher provides written evidence of approval from the relevant Indigenous community. Researchers are also asked to provide references stating that they are people who are likely to be acceptable to Indigenous communities. Universities have also created their own ethics committees to control certain types of research involving people or animals. In some universities such internal ethics approval is required for archaeological research. In many cases this involves duplication, as archaeologists must already consult with communities for excavation permits. However, universities could, if they wished, impose much tighter controls on the types of research projects they permit their staff to undertake. What is new about the current situation is that the Australian government has to some degree empowered Indigenous people to veto archaeological research they don't agree with by restricting the issue of excavation permits.

Through the *Aboriginal and Torres Strait Islander Heritage Protection Act 1984* and by insisting on Indigenous community consultation, the government has also placed pressure on archaeologists to return human skeletal remains and other cultural items to Indigenous communities. But what about placing restrictions on the ownership and use of research results and data collected by archaeologists?

As part of agreements for excavation, Indigenous communities often request that archaeologists seek their approval before publishing results of the work. Some archaeologists would no doubt regard this as unacceptable censorship. However, it is worth considering that commercial organisations who sponsor archaeology often require similar agreements and no one describes this as censorship. In practice such arrangements are usually a matter of commonsense and politeness. Doing archaeology in the public domain does raise a number of unresolved issues about intellectual property rights in general, and there have long been unresolved ethical issues about the rights of individual archaeologists to own particular data sets.[56]

Australian Indigenous cultural and intellectual property rights in general are both important and topical, given the recently commissioned report into the subject by the Australian Institute of Aboriginal and Torres Strait Islander Studies and the Aboriginal and Torres Strait Islander Commission. *Our Culture: Our Future. Report on Australian Indigenous Cultural and Intellectual Property Rights* picks up a wide range of Indigenous concerns about commodification and commercial exploitation of Indigenous cultural and intellectual property which have for some time been voiced by Indigenous people in the media, at conferences and elsewhere.[57] With a growth of public interest in many elements of Indigenous culture, in Australia and overseas, non-Indigenous people and commercial organisations have increasingly started to exploit elements of Indigenous culture, often in highly culturally inappropriate ways, to make a commercial profit. In most cases Indigenous people have received no compensation for such exploitation.

The report was commissioned to canvas a wide range of Indigenous opinion on the topic and to suggest possible strategies. While most discussion focuses on areas of major commercial activity (e.g. arts and crafts, cultural tourism, biotechnology and music) several areas of the report are relevant to archaeology. These include the commercial and cultural exploitation of what the report describes as 'Indigenous cultural and intellectual property' by museums and the 'academic/research industry'. Here a major concern is that universities sell course materials in Aboriginal studies for a profit and that Indigenous people should be compensated for this. The extent to which universities and other educational institutions can and should be described as an industry in this sense, and the degree to which they are profitable, is itself a contentious statement and seriously misrepresents the current status of Australian universities and their funding. Unless these courses are run by private profit-making organisations this is hardly 'commercial' exploitation—although it could obviously be regarded as cultural exploitation. And exactly what part of course materials and other teaching resources produced by academics and others for educational purposes is Indigenous 'intellectual property'? The author or creator of the materials and the university or other organisation which funded their production also have some intellectual property rights—at least in a Western legal sense.

Significantly, in its submission to the report the TALC proposed that 'scientific knowledge' produced from the observation of Indigenous people and their culture is Indigenous intellectual property. This most certainly applies to archaeology. The Queensland Museum countered this suggestion by noting that while Indigenous people might claim such documentation of their heritage as intellectual property, the person or organisation that researched and produced the documentation would also have a valid claim. However, the author of the report (Terri Janke, Principal Consultant, Michael Frankel and Company, Solicitors) notes that the rights of such parties are already protected, at least in theory, under current intellectual property laws, while Indigenous people enjoy no such legal protection. Problems also arise because Indigenous people do not traditionally 'own' their knowledge and culture in a Western sense. Notions of 'intellectual property', 'copyright' and 'cultural products' with monetary value are completely alien to people's relationship with traditional knowledge.

Whether this report will have any real impact on the practice of Australian archaeology remains to be seen. Essentially most of the issues it raises in connection with archaeology have already been discussed, argued, debated and negotiated at length by archaeologists and Indigenous people. Interestingly, one recommendation of the report is that various professions and sectors of industry should develop codes of ethics for their dealings with Indigenous peoples. The 'Australian Association of Archaeologists [sic] Code of Ethics' is cited as a good example of such a code.[58]

What is the value of archaeological research?

Since Tindale and McCarthy conducted their pioneering excavations in the late 1920s and 1930s, Australian archaeologists have gone on to produce an extensive body of knowledge about Australia's Indigenous and colonial past which has the potential to enrich people's understanding of their own history and heritage. Archaeology demonstrates that for tens of thousands of years before British invasion and colonisation, people were living in all parts of the continent and had developed their own separate identities and beliefs—reflected in differences in rock art styles, grave goods, burials and ceremonial sites. Archaeology shows how over time people developed and adopted new technologies and lifestyles to make the most of available natural resources, allowing them and their descendants to live for thousands of years in places where climate and environment defeated later attempts at settlement by Europeans. Archaeology can tell us where people camped, what they ate, how they hunted and collected their food, what kinds of tools, weapons and ornaments they used. Research on human skeletal remains also reveals much about the origins, physical appearance, health, lifestyle and diet of the ancestors of today's Indigenous people. Archaeology and related disciplines provide unique insight into what life may have been like in the distant past. In conjunction with historical evidence it also provides information about the impact of invasion and British colonisation on Indigenous people and their culture, and on changes to both Indigenous and settler cultures over the last 200 years or so.

While not denying the importance of local amateur interest in historic places and artefacts, or the production of local histories and Indigenous people's own knowledge of their own places, it has usually been archaeologists who have drawn wider public attention to the historic and archaeological research values of a range of cultural places. Archaeologists have produced prehistory and history, much of which has not only local but also regional, national and in some cases international significance. They have also been responsible for helping conserve and manage important places from Australia's past through their direct role in the cultural heritage management process.

Archaeologists have explained their work and ideas to the public through the media, and by their direct involvement in secondary, tertiary and public education programmes, and in processes of community consultation. They have also engaged in academic discourse in Australia and internationally through their specialist publications and active participation in professional conferences, workshops and seminars. This ensures that Australian voices and Australian archaeological evidence are represented and taken into account in debates of worldwide interest.

It is not just some Indigenous people who have questioned the value of archaeological research over the last twenty years. In tightened economic circumstances Australian governments of all political persuasions have increasingly chosen to fund research which seemingly produces short-term economic gains at the expense of research deemed less worthy because it produces no obvious short-term monetary outcome. Consequently, funding for research in archaeology, in common with other humanities and social sciences, has been greatly reduced.

Parallel changes have occurred in government attitudes to cultural heritage management. When heritage legislation was first introduced by the Commonwealth and state governments in the 1960s and 1970s, archaeological values of places were given precedence over Indigenous values. Over the years, government departments have changed their policies in favour of Indigenous people, and have consequently placed less emphasis on the purely scientific or archaeological values of Indigenous places. In particular the Commonwealth government's *Aboriginal and Torres Strait Islander Heritage Protection Act* was introduced in the mid-1980s quite specifically to protect Indigenous values of places and objects, regardless of what archaeologists might think. Whatever the ethical questions raised by Indigenous demands for the return of their cultural heritage from the grasp of archaeologists, the reality is that such demands also conveniently suit government policies of withdrawing research funding from universities and other research institutions. One could cynically argue that it is very convenient, and very cheap, for governments to give Indigenous people back their cultural heritage at the expense of a few academics, whom nobody cares very much about anyway. Politicians can make good political mileage from such moves, as they can be seen to be doing the right thing by Indigenous people while neatly sidestepping much more costly and difficult issues like health, housing, unemployment and land rights.

4

Negotiating archaeological research

Despite the issues explored in the previous chapter, many Indigenous people do value archaeology and the knowledge it produces. Research still gets done, not only because Indigenous places continue to be threatened by development work, but also because archaeologists negotiate with Indigenous communities about their work.

When an archaeologist approaches an Indigenous community and seeks its permission to conduct an excavation or field survey for research purposes there are several possible outcomes. The community can say no to fieldwork it feels is inappropriate. It can suggest modifications to the archaeological research aims and methods to make the work more relevant to the community. Or, more commonly, the community will tell the archaeologists to go ahead with their dig or field survey under certain conditions. This chapter examines some of the complexities of the community consultation process associated with archaeological research projects, drawing mainly on examples from New South Wales and other parts of south-east Australia. (For reasons already discussed, the situation in other parts of Australia is different. The practice of consulting archaeology is discussed in Chapter 5.)[1]

Community consultation

Archaeologists must consult with Indigenous communities before government agencies will issue requisite excavation and fieldwork permits. Consultation is also necessary when archaeologists seek access to places on land legally owned by Indigenous people. It is also required by archaeologists' codes of ethics. Even before consultation became normal practice, archaeologists often employed local Indigenous people on their fieldwork projects as guides and informants. This was especially common in those areas of Australia where Indigenous people had managed to retain more continuing links with their land and lost less of their traditional knowledge.[2] However, such engagement was different from the situation now which requires archaeologists to seek permission from the community as a whole, not just individual members, and to negotiate with the community over the terms and conditions under which their project may proceed.

Not all Indigenous places are sacred and restricted to outsiders. If the correct protocols are observed, there are many circumstances in which Indigenous people are willing to allow archaeologists to conduct field survey and excavation, even for research purposes. It is also common for community members to disagree amongst themselves about giving permission for archaeological work. This is true even for the study of human skeletal remains. Many Indigenous people oppose such studies, yet others are interested and support them.[3]

So how do archaeologists react to such differences in opinion among Indigenous people about what is offensive and what is acceptable? In continuing to seek permission to go ahead with archaeological work which some people support and others find offensive, is an archaeologist disregarding genuine beliefs? There are three obvious responses to such a situation. One is to seek support from those in the community who favour archaeological work, and to disregard the beliefs and opinions of those who don't. Another response is to let the community members sort the problem out for themselves and abide by their collective decision. Another option is for the archaeologist to ask supportive community members to negotiate on their behalf with other community members.

A collective decision does not mean that the whole community is supportive of the work.[4] Peter Thorley has discussed this point in connection with relations between archaeologists and Indigenous people in the Northern Territory and poses the very valid question of who or what is represented by 'community'—is it the local community, a community organisation or specific individuals?[5] He comments that archaeologists frequently offer direct and indirect economic incentives to community members in exchange for their support and assistance. Archaeological research proceeds through relationships with individuals who do not necessarily represent the views of everyone who happens to reside in the locality.[6]

Ceding to Indigenous demands for control over Indigenous places and archaeological research has cost many archaeologists a great deal, though there have also been many gains. It seems unlikely that most archaeologists would have changed the way they interact with Indigenous communities, or have introduced codes of ethics acknowledging the legitimacy of Indigenous interests in cultural heritage matters and archaeology, if Indigenous people had not campaigned for their rights, influenced government departments to back them up, and put moral pressure on the archaeological community. Research by Christine Lovell-Jones[7] in the early 1990s into differences between the involvement of Indigenous people in archaeological research in Queensland, where the then state government did not enforce consultation, and in New South Wales, where the government did, supports this impression. Proportionately far more Indigenous people were consulted about, and were actively employed in, archaeological projects in New South Wales than in Queensland during the same period. This may suggest that, given a choice, archaeologists would prefer not to have to consult. This does not necessarily imply that most archaeologists are 'anti-Aboriginal'. However, consultation can cause complications and cost time and money, while resulting in outcomes which are beyond the control of the archaeologist and not always in their best interests.

Nevertheless, consult they must do. The first and often major stumbling block to negotiations is the basic question of why the project needs to be done at all, and whether its aims and methods are considered appropriate by the people concerned. Sometimes, such as in Tasmania in the mid-1990s, Indigenous demands for tighter control over research aims have had the effect of stopping most archaeological research projects altogether, at least for the time being. However, as indicated, most communities do not set conditions so tight that projects cannot proceed. Their conditions are more commonly that archaeologists may not publish anything about their work without prior approval from the community, or that excavation must stop immediately if any human bones are recovered. Indigenous communities frequently request copies of any publications arising from the work and ask archaeologists to return the results of their research to the community in the form of reports or posters written in 'plain English'. From a community perspective such conditions are a reasonable way for people to gain more control over their own cultural places and to get some benefit from the work. Indeed, requests by Indigenous people that archaeologists explain their work in terms understandable to non-specialists have been highly beneficial to the discipline as a whole, in forcing archaeologists to polish their writing skills and to present their work more clearly to students and colleagues as well as to Indigenous groups and other members of the public. This is no bad thing.[8]

Another common request is that Indigenous people be offered the opportunity to become actively involved in the fieldwork, and that they be paid for their time. Communities often want to be kept informed about the progress of the work. Consultation is viewed as an ongoing process, a working relationship between community members and archaeologists, and not just something that happens at the very start of a project, after which the archaeologist need have no further involvement with the community.

Such conditions are perfectly reasonable from the perspective of Indigenous communities. The problem is that for many archaeologists, even if they would like to comply with such requests, this is only rarely viable. For many projects the costs involved are too high for the individual researcher to pay. This is especially so for research work carried out through universities. In general, Indigenous people are exposed more to consulting archaeology than research projects, given the situation under much cultural heritage legislation and the fact that it is often in their own interests to permit such archaeology. If they refuse their places may get destroyed anyway. Archaeology, which at least results in the salvage of artefacts and information about Indigenous places, may be seen as the lesser of two evils. But the terms and conditions that apply under consulting archaeology do not apply to research projects. For example, research projects occur within a different time frame and are funded differently from consulting projects. For consulting projects Indigenous people commonly request employment of community members at standard consulting rates, and the costs are borne by developers or mining companies. Significant sums of money can be involved for large development projects.

However, many research projects work on tighter budgets than consulting work. Rightly or wrongly, research granting bodies may be unwilling to acknowledge payment to Indigenous assistants as a legitimate expense, or there may simply not be enough money to pay what the community wants. This especially applies to projects initiated by students for postgraduate research, where there may be barely enough funds to cover basic fieldwork expenses. Students are often subsidising their research from their own pockets. Some Indigenous people argue that students and researchers gain direct economic and other benefits from research work which essentially exploits Indigenous culture, and that Indigenous people are owed compensation for this.[9] In such cases, if the community insists on paid employment on the project at standard hourly consulting rates the project may be financially unviable. Such matters have to be negotiated between the individual researcher and the community in question.

Despite this, many communities do acknowledge the differences between research projects and consulting work and will reach some compromise if they feel the research project has some value to them, and if they develop a relationship of trust with the individual archaeologist. However, again there can be problems for the researcher. If such negotiation takes up too much time the project can again become unviable. Students are required to complete their research within strict time frames laid down by universities. The student may have no choice but to switch to a topic which does not involve lengthy and costly negotiation.

Similar constraints apply to archaeologists employed on short-term contracts by universities and museums, whose future employment depends on their completion of clearly specified research aims within strict timetables. Even those archaeologists lucky enough to have more secure employment can face problems.[10] In contrast to the situation even ten years ago, university-based archaeologists have fewer resources for research and are required by their employers to demonstrate tangible outcomes from their work in the form of high-quality peer-reviewed academic publications. Research funding favours quick results. This situation downgrades the value of time and effort spent in negotiation with Indigenous communities, writing 'plain English' reports and posters, making museum displays, talking at public meetings and to school groups, or producing educational materials.[11]

So even if Indigenous communities are not particularly opposed to individual archaeologists and their research, the reality for many research archaeologists is that extensive community consultation and negotiation takes time and resources which they cannot afford. At the present time, much university-based archaeological research on Indigenous places is caught between government funding policies and Indigenous community politics. Given a choice, most archaeologists would prefer to work in areas and with people who are generally sympathetic towards them, and where they know they will get a warm welcome, rather than entering into lengthy and protracted negotiations with people who may even be antagonistic towards them. That is human nature and explains why, in the late 1990s, some Australian prehistorians publicly announced they were so fed up with wrangling with Indigenous people about research that they preferred to work in historical archaeology or overseas where things were simpler.[12]

The cost in time and resources negotiating permissions and accommodating local issues and interests for historical or overseas projects is not always lower, however. Archaeologists must often negotiate with development companies, local councils and non-Indigenous community members in relation to historical archaeology research projects, and when they work overseas, permissions need to be sought, feelings may and do run high, and time and effort may be involved to resolve problems. Yet there are differences. The circumstances of black–white race relations in Australia raise particular political issues which are confrontingly 'close to home' and uncomfortable for many people to have to face.

Trust is a very important component of any working relationship and, as discussed elsewhere, some Indigenous people have good reasons not to trust archaeologists. However, when archaeologists are willing and able to spend the time and effort building up genuine working relationships with members of Indigenous communities, then many things are both possible and likely. Some archaeologists are better at developing these kinds of working relationships than others. They can be very personally demanding and require skills and personal qualities that not all archaeologists possess. But working with Indigenous communities in this way can also be very rewarding.

A case study: Cuddie Springs

Since the early 1990s, Judy Field has directed a long-term major archaeological research project at Cuddie Springs in western New South Wales, some 80 kilometres or so from Brewarrina. The aim of the project is to investigate the role of humans in the extinction of Australia's ancient megafauna, such as *Diprotodon*, *Megalania* and *Genyornis*, which once lived in Australia but became extinct some time during the last ice age.[13] Excavations have been conducted through over 3 metres of deposits in a shallow ephemeral lake where the bones of now extinct animals occur in close association with stone tools and charcoal dated back to at least 30 000 years. Cuddie Springs is one of very few places in Australia where the remains of megafauna have been found in direct association with stone tools, and provides strong archaeological evidence for the coexistence of humans and megafauna over a long period of time. There is no question that Cuddie Springs is a very important site, and the research being conducted by Field and her team has aroused wide scientific interest in Australia and overseas.[14]

In an environment of declining research funding and shrinking resources, Field has successfully obtained government research money to support her project over a number of years.[15] A major element of the project's continuing success has been support for the research from members of local Indigenous communities. Before it would issue her with an excavation permit, the NSW National Parks and Wildlife Service (NPWS) required Field to demonstrate that local Indigenous communities had been properly consulted and had given their fully informed consent to the work. Field was able to convince members of local Indigenous communities of the value of her research and she has obtained continuing Indigenous support for the project over a number of years without having to modify her research aims. Why has Field succeeded where several other projects have come unstuck, or the archaeologists have had to modify their research aims, even if they have not regarded this as a major problem?

Teasing out the finer complexities of negotiations between archaeologists and Indigenous communities over a particular piece of research requires at least some inside knowledge about the project, the views of the parties and individuals involved and the process of negotiation. I have been able to discuss Cuddie Springs here because Field was willing to talk to me about aspects of the community consultation involved in her project. Also, in early 1997, I accompanied Field and project photographer Georgia Britton on a visit to Cuddie Springs while they made arrangements for the forthcoming 1997 field season. During this trip, Field interviewed several Indigenous people about their experiences with archaeologists, the consultation process and community involvement in the Cuddie Springs project. I was present at several of these interviews and I met many local people connected with the Cuddie Springs dig, so I have at least some direct personal experience of the project.[16]

The most important element in Indigenous consultation at Cuddie Springs was Field's ability to persuade enough people in the community to trust her. People had to get to know her and feel that she was okay, and that she had the right attitude towards Indigenous people, before they were comfortable working with her. Several Indigenous people explained to Field how they distrusted many white people, especially when they didn't know them. Previous negative experiences with individual consulting archaeologists and NPWS staff had left many people mistrustful of archaeologists in general. Several Indigenous people complained that consultants and NPWS personnel did not spend enough time getting to know people in the community, and that the community was not kept adequately informed about the outcomes and results of archaeological survey work. The long-term nature of the Cuddie Springs project has allowed Field to travel to Brewarrina and Walgett on many occasions over several years and build real and lasting working relations, and in some cases personal friendships, with people in the area. This includes many non-Indigenous people as well. Field has been able to solicit support for the Cuddie Springs project from a wide section of the local community including landowners, local businesses and the Walgett Shire Council. In one sense Field has become a member of the local community herself, even though she lives and works many hundreds of kilometres away in Sydney.

Another important element of community consultation at Cuddie Springs has been the direct and continuing involvement of Indigenous people in the fieldwork and post-excavation analysis, including in paid employment and training. In this Field showed some flexibility and competent use of resources, at one stage obtaining funding from the former Commonwealth Department of Employment, Education and Training (DEET) to employ Indigenous people as part of the Training Aboriginal People Programme.

Finally, Field has made sure that she has kept people informed about all stages of her project by welcoming visitors and organising site tours during the fieldwork season. She has also written and produced easy-to-read and well-illustrated community reports on each season's work, as well as poster displays and other materials which have been freely distributed to the local community.

Engendering community support for her project so that she can get on with her research has been expensive for Field. She estimates that at least one-third of her work time is spent maintaining relationships with the local Indigenous community.[17] She also has to find money for travel and related expenses every time she goes to Brewarrina and Walgett to see people. If she chose to work on a project which did not require such intense consultation, for example in historical archaeology, the time and money saved could be spent directly on archaeological research.

Like all researchers, Field has to constantly re-apply for funding to support her work. Each year she must renegotiate the terms of her field-work with local Indigenous community organisations in order to get her excavation permit. In common with politics everywhere, internal factions and infighting can blow up and threaten support for Field's project at any time. At least one local Indigenous authority in the past has openly opposed her work, forcing Field into a whole new round of negotiation and lobbying. As a white outsider Field can have no say or direct role in local Indigenous community politics. The only option for an archaeologist in these circumstances is to persuade members of the Indigenous community who are supportive to negotiate with other Indigenous people on their behalf. In a setback in 1998, two government agencies which had previously provided funding to employ Indigenous people on the Cuddie Springs project decided not to support archaeology any more. This has ended programmes that Field had set up to train and employ Aborigines, and removed a source of income for community members, weakening her links with the community.[18]

Field has been unwilling to compromise on the major aims of her research. The project involves studying the environmental prehistory of Cuddie Springs and the role of humans in megafaunal extinction. As such it contributes to a wider series of research questions about the history of human impacts on the Australian environment. Had the Indigenous community insisted that she change her project from megafauna to oral history, or had it refused her permission to excavate, then there would have been little point in her continuing. Nor is she as likely to have been as successful in obtaining government research funding for a substantially different project. Cuddie Springs has in part been able to attract Australian Research Council and similar funding over other projects precisely because of the perceived scientific importance of the work.

The nature of the site itself has perhaps made it easier than might otherwise have been the case to persuade local people to support her work.

Cuddie Springs is important in a traditional sense to local Indigenous people, and there are Dreaming stories which explain the formation of the site and the presence of fossil bones. However, Field is not digging up human burials or trying to study rock art or ceremonial sites, which are often particularly sensitive for Indigenous people. Many people in the area, both black and white, are fascinated by the bones of giant extinct animals, which have been recovered from the site since at least the nineteenth century. Field's particular contribution has been to recognise that humanly produced stone tools are associated with these fossil animals. To many Indigenous people, this provides scientific proof that their ancestors lived in the area when these giant animals came to drink at what would have been a lake many thousands of years ago. This also links in with Dreamtime stories. On a more pragmatic level, many members of the community believe that Cuddie Springs has the potential to draw tourists to the region because the wider public is also interested in fossils and giant animals.

Because Field's scientific research objectives have been broadly in line with Indigenous interests in the site, she has been able to pursue her own research agenda. While she has involved Indigenous people by providing basic training in archaeological techniques, in the same way that students and other inexperienced people have been able to join in the work, the research aims, methods and directions have remained under Field's control.

'Indigenous-controlled' archaeology

Cuddie Springs was chosen here as an example of amicable and fruitful cooperation between archaeologists and Indigenous communities, but which also demonstrates some of the complexities of negotiating archaeological research in the late 1990s. There are many other examples where archaeologists and Indigenous people work together under similar circumstances. Numerous Australian archaeologists report the results of their research in Australian and overseas journals each year. None of this work could have been done without the support and direct involvement of the members of relevant Indigenous communities. The driving force behind most of these projects has been the desire of professional archaeologists—individually or in small research teams—to conduct their own research to address questions which other archaeologists also think are important and valuable.

Many Australian archaeologists enjoy working with local Indigenous people and welcome community support and involvement in their research work. Some archaeologists seek the active involvement of community members in defining their research questions and approaches. Examples of this 'community-based' archaeology are the projects of Anne Clarke on Groote Eylandt (Northern Territory) and Shelley Greer in Cape York (Queensland). Both of these archaeologists first went to work in these places to address fairly standard archaeological research questions about prehistory. When members of local Indigenous communities indicated they were much more interested in different questions—about more recent sites, local history and cultural matters—the archaeologists in each case changed the focus of their research accordingly.[19] Whatever such projects are called, this and similar work was initiated by outside archaeologists for research purposes rather than being something that arose internally from community interests or needs. It is still uncommon for Indigenous communities to initiate and seek funding for their own archaeology projects—if archaeology is defined as being aimed at answering academic research questions and commonly involving excavation. However, there are an increasing number of examples where Indigenous communities do initiate projects and invite archaeologists to study their places. The introduction of Native Title legislation, for example, has resulted in archaeologists being invited to conduct archaeological research by communities in support of Native Title claims.[20]

More often Indigenous communities seek the input of archaeologists for projects aimed at recording and conserving their own places. Such studies are sometimes described as being 'archaeology', which raises several questions about the nature of archaeology practised in the context of cultural heritage management. In their book *Archaeologists and Aborigines Working Together*, Iain Davidson, Christine Lovell-Jones and Robyne Bancroft document six projects described as having been specifically requested by Indigenous people and compared them with twelve or so projects where outside archaeologists or government departments initiated the work and the community agreed to cooperate and get involved.[21] Not surprisingly there are interesting differences in the aims and scope of these different projects. For example, most of the work initiated by professional archaeologists was conducted to answer specific research questions about Indigenous prehistory and most, but not all, involved excavation. In contrast, none of the projects initiated by Indigenous communities them-selves involved any excavation. Most of these projects involved site survey and recording using standard archaeological methods in conjunction with interviews with traditional owners about the meaning and history of the places recorded. In all cases the work was conducted because sites were under threat by proposed development or related activities, or because recording information about Indigenous places was thought to be useful or necessary for management and conservation purposes, rather than being initiated to address academic research questions.

This state of affairs is not surprising. It is obvious that members of local Indigenous communities will usually have different interests in their own cultural heritage, and ideas about why and how it should be studied and recorded, from outside professional archaeologists. Indigenous control over archaeology often replaces excavation aimed at answering academic research questions with non-intrusive site survey methods aimed at site management and conservation. It combines field-recording methods drawn from archaeology with interviews and oral history methods to record traditional knowledge not just about 'archaeological' sites but about other places significant to Indigenous people, many of which are not amenable to archaeological study at all.

A recent initiative between archaeologists at La Trobe University in Melbourne, Aboriginal Affairs Victoria (AAV—the state government agency currently responsible for Indigenous places) and local Indigenous communities in Victoria aims to combine academic archaeological research objectives and community interests in site management and interpretation. The project involves undertaking new analysis of collec-tions of archaeological materials which resulted from numerous excava-tions conducted in the 1970s and 1980s by the Victoria Archaeological Survey (VAS). During this period VAS (which has since been disbanded) was responsible for managing Indigenous heritage in Victoria. Most of the archaeological material has never been properly studied or published.

The link between AAV and the university has been a key to commu-nity consultation and involvement in this case. The project took advan-tage of a collaborative grants scheme through the Australian Research Council designed to link university research with industry. To date the project has resulted in publication of two research papers on the archae-ology of the area in peer-reviewed journals, and education materials (posters, a computer-based presentation and 48-slide kit with text) for community use only at Brambuk Aboriginal Cultural Centre in Gariwerd (the local name for Grampians National Park). Community represent-atives made it clear they wanted to have access to the information and teaching materials but would handle its dissemination to the wider com-munity and other Indigenous groups themselves. The archaeologists are currently near completing their major formal report on all the sites under study. Continuing relations with the community have provided the context for several honours degree projects on other old VAS collections and on new survey work.[22]

5
Indigenous places and consulting archaeology

As we have noted, most archaeology in Australia today gets done because places are threatened by development work. Planning legislation requires that archaeology be considered as part of environmental impact assessment (EIA) work ahead of development proposals. Legislation does not necessarily stop development work; it merely makes provision for the cultural value of places to be taken into account during the planning process. If places are deemed to be particularly significant then the government can step in and preserve them. Depending on the circumstances, if a development cannot be easily modified to minimise its impact on heritage sites, the government might eventually give permission for such places to be destroyed, with or without salvage excavation by archaeologists.[1]

In New South Wales the *National Parks and Wildlife Act 1974* empowers the director of the National Parks and Wildlife Service (NPWS) to issue 'Consent to Destroy' Aboriginal 'relics' as defined under the Act (e.g. artefacts, sites, human skeletal remains), even on private land. In considering applications for Consent to Destroy, NPWS policy takes into account the views of Indigenous communities. For example, the NPWS currently proposes what it calls 'Partnership with Aboriginal Communities'. This is based on principles laid out in its *Aboriginal Cultural Heritage Standards and Guidelines Kit*, which includes the policy that NPWS recognises Indigenous culture as living and unique, that Indigenous people are the rightful owners of Indigenous cultural heritage information and Indigenous sites and objects, and that they have a right to protect, preserve and promote their culture. Elsewhere in Australia heritage legislation has been changed or is currently subject to review with the aim of providing Indigenous people greater legal control of their own places. Native Title rights and legislation, introduced after the Mabo and Wik court decisions, is also relevant in some cases to greater Indigenous control of cultural places.[2]

All well and good. But as many writers have commented, government response to Indigenous concerns has been slow and sporadic.[3] Indeed, in the current political climate the tide seems to have turned against many Indigenous interests. In essence, Indigenous people still have very limited legal right to be involved in protecting and managing their own heritage. Community consultation is a government policy decision, which could always be reversed. Despite all the rhetoric about consultation, Indigenous people, in common with many other members of the Australian community, are effectively powerless to prevent the wholesale destruction of many of their cultural places in the face of relentless development pressures and overriding economic interests. In New South Wales, as elsewhere, government agencies have no absolute legal obligation to abide by the views of Indigenous people. Conservation organisations such as NPWS and comparable heritage agencies in other states will try to protect important Indigenous places if they can. But economic and other realities dictate that many places will eventually be destroyed.

Not all Indigenous people are against all development. Many land councils and other Indigenous organisations take a pragmatic view. They acknowledge the economic benefits development can bring and accept that this will inevitably mean the destruction of some cultural places. The main issue is that Indigenous people want to be in control of, and actively involved in, making decisions about what happens to their cultural places. They want to decide which places are too important to be touched and which are less important and can be sacrificed. Indigenous people also want employment opportunities in the cultural heritage management and environmental impact assessment business, and some Indigenous people want financial compensation from private companies which make profits through activities which often result in the destruction of their culture.[4]

However, it is the government which regulates the development process, and governments are subject to a wide range of political pressures. Politicians can easily pay lip service to Indigenous demands for greater input into the conservation and management of Indigenous sites. But when such sites are on land which is not legally owned by Indigenous people, and large amounts of money are at stake, most development work eventually goes ahead, whether Indigenous people like it or not.

Heritage assessment work forces Indigenous people to have dealings with archaeology and archaeologists in ways which are somewhat different from research projects. As already discussed, archaeological excavation is not usually a priority for most Indigenous people. Government policy has empowered Indigenous people to say no to research excavation they don't want by refusing to issue permits. Consultant archaeologists are also required to obtain Indigenous permission to undertake test or salvage excavations as part of the EIA process, even if the place will otherwise be destroyed by development. In contrast with many research projects, for which permission to excavate is often only granted under tightly controlled circumstances or is refused altogether, test and salvage excavations are a common part of the EIA process.

Building the M2 motorway

The construction of the M2 motorway in the north of Sydney in the mid-1990s highlighted issues which can arise when Indigenous places are threatened by large and controversial development proposals. The finer details of this case, and the exact outcomes, were dictated by the provisions of the relevant legislation and planning regulations, the nature of the local environment, the kinds of Indigenous places commonly found in the Sydney region, and particular historical and political factors relevant to this part of New South Wales. However, the general issues raised are widely applicable to other parts of south-east Australia (especially in Victoria and Tasmania) where Indigenous places located on private land and governed by 'relics' legislation come under threat from development pressures.[5]

In the late 1980s the NSW state government entered into a joint venture with two private companies, Australian road builder Abigroup and Japan's Obayashi Corporation, to construct the M2 motorway, a tollway which runs 21 kilometres through Sydney's northern suburbs and bushland. As required by law, the developer undertook EIA work, which included contracting archaeologists to survey and make recommendations about any Indigenous 'relics' (e.g. stone artefacts) likely to be affected by the proposed road. A number of rock shelters, stone artefact scatters and other formally recognised archaeological sites were duly located and investigated by Sydney-based consulting archaeologists Laila Haglund and Tessa Corkill, to the satisfaction of the NPWS. Local Indigenous groups were consulted about, and involved in, this archaeology work.

According to Corkill, several route options were examined by the archaeologists at different times, because the detailed plan for the motorway kept changing.[6] On the finally determined route only a few known archaeological sites were physically endangered by the road and subject to salvage recording and excavation. These included a rock shelter site (CF6), three open artefact scatter sites, a possible scarred tree (bearing marks which possibly demonstrated that bark had been previously removed in a traditional manner by Indigenous people), and two sites with 'potential archaeological deposit' which proved to contain artefacts. A number of other rock shelters were located during survey work, but the road construction was modified to avoid any physical damage to the 'relics' contained in them. Apart from this, no other identified potential archaeological sites were physically threatened. Road building did eventually destroy one or two small rock overhangs. These were initially identified as having 'potential archaeological deposit' but when examined turned out not to contain any artefacts.

The M2 case was extreme. This very large, expensive road development in an urban area was already unpopular with many people when archaeologists were brought in under the requirements of EIA legislation. By its very nature a road like this cuts a corridor through communities and affects many people. There was much organised opposition to road construction and this was widely reported by local media. The exact route of the road was sometimes uncertain until very late in the construction process and the relevant NSW heritage legislation is not always well suited to dealing with impacts on a broad area of landscape like this. These and other factors created pressures for the archaeologists involved and for local Indigenous people when sites came under threat.

The M2 was and is a huge development in which some 153 hectares of land were cleared and six million tonnes of soil excavated. Large tracts of urban bushland and many previously desirable residential areas were ripped apart. A range of protest and lobby groups mounted campaigns against the state government and the developers. Many people were angry at the failure of the planning system to protect adequately the environment from a road which they argued would not only fail to solve Sydney's traffic problems, but was constructed primarily to return a profit to private companies subsidised by the state government. Over 100 local residents also threatened to sue the government over its backflip on moneys they had been promised in compensation for the loss of value to their property caused by the proximity of a noisy new road. A community action group called Freeway Busters, angered by the large-scale environmental destruction wrought by the road and by what they regarded as the futility of the whole project, staged sit-down protests ahead of development work, which resulted in the arrest of several of its members and attracted a flurry of media interest.[7]

At the height of the dispute, Indigenous activist and local resident Ian Bundeluk (Rosella) Watson, angered by the destruction of bushland which had spiritual and other cultural values to local Darug people, staged his own protest. In October 1994 he started proceedings to claim part of the area affected by the road under the *Native Title Act*. In May 1995 he also mounted a case in the NSW Land and Environment Court to obtain an urgent interim injunction to stop road construction. He claimed that the building work threatened to destroy Indigenous 'relics', burials and sacred sites, which the developer had completely failed to take into account in previous EIA work.[8] This story was reported in the media, with little mention of the survey and excavation work already undertaken as required by law by Haglund and Corkill in full consultation with other local Indigenous people. University- and museum-based anthropologists and archaeologists, myself included, were approached by legal representatives of local Indigenous people and asked to visit the area to provide professional comment about sacred sites which were supposedly under threat. One of those who chose to get involved was Australian Museum archaeologist and anthropologist Paul Taçon. Taçon was cited in some media reports as supporting Watson's claim, even though he was cautious about the situation and concurred that, whatever the broader rights and wrongs of the situation, the relevant NSW legislation had been complied with.[9]

Environmentalists and others opposed to the development also claimed that sacred sites and other Indigenous places were indeed under threat, as this provided further ammunition for their case against the road construction. One of the people arrested at an environmental protest happened to be studying for an undergraduate Arts degree at Sydney University which included some units of archaeology. When members of the media discovered this, the student was interviewed and cited as yet another 'archaeologist' who supported Indigenous claims that 'relics' were under threat. Although this may have not been the intent, Haglund and Corkill's professional reputations were quite unjustifiably called into question in media reports.

Writing in her regular 'Breccia' column in the *Australian Association of Consulting Archaeologists Incorporated Newsletter*, Corkill described developments thus: 'The impression was given, and in some cases this was actually stated, that there had been no surveys as part of the EIS or that the archaeologists had missed or "overlooked" sites. Such was not the case . . .'[10]

Corkill also commented that the instigators of the protests about sacred sites did not represent the majority of local Aborigines, 'who have naturally been very worried about the damage this kind of thing does to their credibility', but that local community politics made it difficult for Indigenous people to speak openly on the issue to the media and to non-Aborigines. Watson eventually withdrew his legal action because, according to reports in the *Sydney Morning Herald*, he did not have evidence that sites were actually under threat.

The *Herald* also reported that Watson wished to 'erect a fence to protect several piles of rocks of Indigenous significance'.[11] However, as Corkill commented:

> The majority of reported sites were found, after much time, public money and two court cases, either to have been fully investigated and documented or not to be Aboriginal sites at all. In the latter case, stone piles that were reported as burial mounds (and later as initiation circles) were found to be part of a jungle warfare training 'ambuscade', constructed during World War II.[12]

Corkill reported further developments in the M2 protest saga in the September 1995 issue of the *AACAI Newsletter*. Soon after the developer had agreed to re-route a section of the road alignment to avoid 'the most archaeologically and environmentally sensitive area along the route', Corkill found a previously unrecorded rock shelter site (CF6) in the direct line of the newly proposed road construction while on a visit to the area with representatives of the road builder, the NPWS and two Aboriginal land councils. No archaeological material was immediately obvious. Test excavation proved the rock shelter to contain 'relics' (and therefore to be legally protected by the *National Parks and Wildlife Act*), although the deposit was very shallow and heavily disturbed. Corkill commented:

> Moving the road one way would endanger a very significant site nearby, moving it the other would require destruction of extra houses and further enrage local residents (not to mention costing several million dollars more). A Consent to Destroy was applied for and there was frantic lobbying in the political halls of power . . . In the meantime various Indigenous groups (the Land Council, the Native Title claimant and an association of Daruk descendants) decided to join forces and oppose destruction.[13]

The road did get built. The CF6 rock shelter was eventually fully excavated by the archaeologists and the site destroyed. It was only threatened at a very late stage in the process because the developer re-routed this section of the road to avoid other problems, including destroying another rock shelter with demonstrated high archaeological significance. According to Corkill, salvage excavation of the CF6 rock shelter was not approved by local Indigenous people but the NPWS issued the permit for this work anyway, due to political pressure to complete the road building.[14] The M2 finally opened on 18 May 1997, amid continuing protests from Freeway Busters and the Coalition of Transport Action Groups.

Legislative limits and practical constraints

The M2 case highlights several key issues about archaeology, the 'protection' of Indigenous cultural heritage and the EIA process. In the first place it demonstrates how 'relics' legislation, like the NSW *National Parks and Wildlife Act*, which defines the Indigenous archaeological record primarily in terms of individual artefacts, groups of artefacts and spatially bounded archaeological sites, often promotes a disjointed and piecemeal approach to understanding and 'conserving' the archaeological record. Such legislation forces the archaeologist to break the archaeological record of a region into its smallest constituent parts, each of which has to be considered individually as and when each 'relic' or site is threatened by development. As many archaeologists who advocate landscape-based approaches have discussed, individual 'relics' or sites considered in isolation from other sites in a region, and from the broader landscape in which they are located, can only answer very limited questions about the behaviour of the people who created them.

Hence, the potential research results from archaeological survey and excavation conducted as a by-product of a development such as the M2 are limited.[15] In the M2 case, the developer paid only for the archaeological study of sites immediately in line with its roadway, producing data about sites which happened to lie along a 21-kilometre transect to the north of Sydney. Such data may have no necessary relevance to the way people used the landscape in the past. The archaeological sampling strategy was dictated by the shape and size of the development rather than by the requirements of any particular archaeological research agenda. In addition, the fact that the route kept changing made it very difficult for the archaeologists to anticipate where it might go next and how far away from the route as designated they should survey. It was for this reason that the CF6 rock shelter was only discovered at such a late stage in the development process.[16]

Despite all this, results from the M2 work have made a useful contribution to regional archaeology, primarily because they are relevant to a longer term and larger scale archaeological research project being conducted by Val Attenbrow of Sydney's Australian Museum. Attenbrow's Port Jackson Archaeological Project aims to document spatial and temporal variations in the subsistence patterns and material culture of coastal Indigenous people living in the area which is now Sydney Harbour (Port Jackson) prior to AD 1788. As part of this work, Attenbrow had previously excavated a rock shelter in the area of the proposed M2 motorway development, which she found to contain thousands of Indigenous stone tools, and radiocarbon dated to 10 000 years old. This very significant site became threatened by the proposed M2. When Haglund and Corkill notified the developers of this, that part of the route was re-designed (resulting in subsequent threats to the CF6 rock shelter). Results from archaeological work conducted by Haglund and Corkill as part of the EIA for the M2 could be usefully compared with research results from Attenbrow's own excavations, and this information has been incorporated into Attenbrow's book about the archaeology of the region.[17]

The M2 case also demonstrates very clearly the inadequacy of the NSW planning process and legislation to readily take into account anything other than a very narrowly defined set of archaeological values when cultural places come under threat from development work. The EIA work ensured that most archaeological sites along the line of the M2 were saved from immediate physical threat, and data about those that were destroyed were recorded through 'salvage' excavation.[18] Yet the area and places within it clearly had a range of cultural and social values which were not protected by the existing legislation and planning framework. Technically speaking, the developers 'did the right thing' in terms of the archaeology. The consultant archaeologists acted professionally, did what was expected of them and complied with the law. Local people, including Indigenous community members, were consulted in the process. Yet many people were very unhappy with the outcome.

There are provisions within the *National Parks and Wildlife Act* for the minister to declare an 'Aboriginal place', which allows for legal recognition and protection of places of spiritual and anthropological significance to Indigenous people, regardless of whether 'relics' are present. In addition the NSW *Heritage Act* (which primarily protects non-Indigenous heritage in the state) can also be used to stop development of places which have spiritual value to Indigenous people to allow time for the place to be declared an 'Aboriginal place' under the *National Parks and Wildlife Act*. In the early 1970s, when Mumbulla Mountain on the NSW south coast was threatened by logging, local Indigenous people mounted a successful claim to have parts of the area declared an 'Aboriginal place' in this way to halt further destruction of an important cultural landscape.[19] Since then, however, for a range of political and financial reasons, state provisions have rarely been used to stop a development impacting on the cultural values of Indigenous places in the context of EIA work in New South Wales. In general, it has required the intervention of the Commonwealth government in collaboration with state agencies to protect Indigenous values of place, especially when such places are not already part of existing national parks and protected areas. The situation is complex and varies from state to state.

Heritage agencies are well aware of the problems with legislation. Many of the problems can be avoided if cultural heritage management issues are taken into account early in the planning process. Indeed this is happening. For example, as part of planning for large-scale rezoning, urban development and mining in New South Wales, the NPWS has been involved in negotiating agreements with developers and Indigenous communities to develop conservation areas to preserve landscapes rather than just isolated 'archaeological sites'. The conservation values of such areas have been agreed on by members of local Indigenous communities and archaeologists. The trade-off is that outside such conservation areas the NPWS will facilitate the development process by reducing the need for test excavation or salvage, and expediting Consents to Destroy. Such action is regarded as acceptable to NPWS, Indigenous communities and archaeologists as it produces a much better conservation outcome overall than might otherwise be the case.[20]

On a practical level, archaeologists on projects like the M2 must work to a strictly defined brief. Prior to commencing the job they must outline exactly how they will approach the work and estimate what the likely costs will be. If they then find something unexpected which requires extra time and money, they must re-negotiate with the developer. As discussed above, given the size of the area to be surveyed, the generally low visibility of many Indigenous archaeological sites, and the absence of detailed prior knowledge about exactly what sites might be found where, it is almost inevitable that some sites and 'relics' will be missed by initial survey work. This does not mean that the consultants are either corrupt or incompetent, as was implied in some media reports in the M2 case. It simply means that the EIA process rarely if ever allows consultants adequate resources to find every single site present in a development area, even if this were physically possible.

Community consultation

Whose opinions are really represented when a 'community' reaches a decision over an issue? We discussed this issue in Chapter 4 regarding research-based archaeology. The situation in consulting archaeology is no less vexed. Not surprisingly, in the M2 case people had different views about the value of places threatened by the motorway, what should be done, and whether they wanted to get involved with the archaeology work. One individual took matters into his own hands by making claims on land and sites in the area and taking part in the protest against the road. Other Indigenous people from the area worked *with* the consultant archaeologists on the EIA project. There was no one 'community opinion'— rather a range of views.

Reaching consensus may take time and effort and require special skills in negotiation. Indeed, there may be no general agreement reached at all. Formal consultation with Indigenous groups in some areas has become more complex following the introduction of Native Title legislation. Among other things, this has led to the formation of new kinds of Indigenous organisations such as councils of elders and descendants groups, some of whom are in direct and open opposition to Aboriginal land councils (created under previous land rights legislation) and other Indigenous community organisations.

The situation for consulting archaeologists is further complicated by the fact that in the past it has been common practice for heritage agencies and developers to require archaeologists to negotiate with communities not only about archaeology but about other Indigenous values of place which have nothing to do with archaeology at all. This is not appropriate. Indigenous organisations want to negotiate with developers and government agencies directly and in their own right—and archaeologists want to do the job they were hired for and assess and record the archaeological significance of sites. If a development proposal is controversial, or if places of particular significance are threatened, it is best (and increasingly common) practice for the developer to hire a professional negotiator to deal with all matters to do with community consultation at an early stage of the project. If archaeology is required under the relevant legislation, archaeologists can be invited to take part in the consultation and negotiation process. But this is quite different from heritage agencies or developers expecting archaeologists to automatically take responsibility for extensive and protracted negotiations with community members about whether salvage excavation and other archaeological intervention are appropriate in the first place. Archaeologists are only there because of the development proposal and legislation which requires archaeological values to be taken into account. The developer and the heritage agency must take responsibility for negotiating with people impacted on by the development.

War of words

Consulting archaeologists and Indigenous people often get caught up in battles between environmentalists and developers which are played out in the print media and in radio and television broadcasts (rather than the academic literature).[21] The M2 protest contained many elements of a good media story. 'Expert' anthropologists and archaeologists were called in to 'confirm' that Indigenous 'sacred sites' and 'burials' were threatened by 'corrupt and greedy' developers. An Indigenous 'activist' was making a Native Title claim. 'Angry residents' threatened to sue the government over 'property prices'. Such stereotypical language and imagery frequently occur in media reportage of Australian archaeology and Indigenous issues. Key facts, which may have changed the tone of the story, failed to be mentioned. These included the full extent of Corkill and Haglund's EIA work; the existence of a range of Indigenous opinions on the matter; and the actual provisions of the NSW planning and heritage legislation in relation to 'relics' and 'sacred sites'.

Making a Native Title claim and instigating various court actions to stall the development by claiming breaches of environmental planning and other regulations did not stop the eventual completion of the M2 motorway. Yet in this and similar cases such tactics can be effective political weapons in the war against environmental destruction caused by development. They create delay and cost the developer money. In some cases, development projects have gone broke in the face of lengthy and protracted court battles. Such actions also attract media attention which, if properly handled, can generate negative and damaging publicity for the developer. In such cases archaeology and archaeologists are often used by the protagonists to support their own positions. Further examples of such 'regional agreements' are discussed below. The way they can be set up, and their effectiveness in conserving cultural places, varies across Australia.

Authenticity

Another interesting issue raised by the M2 case was the role played by archaeologists and archaeological evidence in determining the 'authenticity' of Indigenous claims to place. This operated in several different ways. In the first instance, because the NSW legislation defined Indigenous heritage primarily in terms of archaeology, the EIA work only needed to take account of 'relics'. The *National Parks and Wildlife Act* defines a 'relic' as any deposit, object or material evidence (not being a handicraft made for sale) relating to Indigenous and non-European habitation of the areas that comprise New South Wales. The term also includes Indigenous human remains. It was the job of the consulting archaeologist to make a professional judgement about whether anything found in the line of the M2 met this definition and was therefore protected as an archaeological site. Because of current NPWS policy, Indigenous groups were also consulted for their views about the recorded sites, which they also helped to find during survey.

While many 'relics' are easy to recognise, not all archaeological sites are immediately obvious even to professionals. For example, a common feature of the archaeology of the Sydney area are places known as potential archaeological deposits (or PADs). The sandstone terrain which characterises much of the region includes numerous rock overhangs and shelters, many of which could have been used by Indigenous people. We know that people used some of these places because many contain physical evidence which demonstrates human presence (e.g. rock paintings, stone tools, hearths). Historical accounts and paintings and drawings by early European settlers also describe and depict Indigenous people camping in and making use of rock shelters. Shelters identified within a project area may contain archaeological material which is buried within the floor deposits and is not discernible without excavation. The investigating archaeologist must first decide whether the rock shelter is likely to contain archaeological remains or not (i.e. what its potential to contain archaeological material is) and whether it merits further investigation. Such a decision is usually based on the presence of floor deposits which could harbour stone tools and other 'relics', and also on the size and physical layout of the shelter itself. The assumption here is that people are more likely to have used an overhang which is large enough to provide shelter, has a fairly level and soft floor which offers them somewhere to sit and make a fire, is near water or food resources, and so on.[22]

A few places with potential archaeological deposits were found as part of the M2 survey work. Some of these were not physically threatened by the road buildings (e.g. they were located under bridges and left physically intact). Any shelter which proved on subsequent examination to contain artefacts (or 'relics') was protected by the *National Parks and Wildlife Act*. But what of any other shelters which may have been used by Indigenous people in the past but which did not contain any actual physical evidence of use? It is perfectly possible that people used some of these places but did not leave anything behind, or what they did leave behind has long since rotted away. Archaeologists cannot determine with absolute certainty if every rock shelter was used by people. They might feel that some shelters are likely to have been used, but only those that actually contain visible 'relics' are protected by the Act.

This also applies to landscape features which contain no archaeological evidence of human use but which are nevertheless likely to have been used by Indigenous people in the past and to have formed part of their belief system. The media, members of the public, and many Indigenous people themselves often call important Indigenous places of this kind 'sacred sites'. Yet the term 'sacred site' distorts and oversimplifies Indigenous people's traditional relations with and understanding of land. Before Indigenous people's links with and spiritual knowledge of their land were disrupted and, in many cases, shattered and destroyed by British colonisation, all elements of the landscape were known as important in some way. Some of these places had particular and special religious significance. In many parts of Australia, especially in the more remote north, west and centre, Indigenous people have been able to maintain much of their traditional knowledge despite the history of invasion and colonialism. Elsewhere, colonial history has effectively destroyed such detailed knowledge. This particularly applies in the south-eastern states, including New South Wales. When white people require Indigenous people to demonstrate the 'authenticity' of their claims to 'traditional' places by reference to continuity of traditional knowledge, the likelihood of successful claims to place by many Indigenous people in south-eastern Australia is seriously undermined. As already discussed, Tasmania presents the most extreme example of this situation.

In the M2 case the media reported that 'sacred sites' were threatened by the road. Researchers were invited to inspect the area to 'verify' that these places were indeed 'sacred sites'. For example, journalists asked Paul Taçon to comment on whether particular rock formations were likely to have Indigenous significance. In some media reports he was quoted as saying that they were similar to places significant to Indigenous people in the Northern Territory, and with which he was personally familiar through his own fieldwork. According to Taçon himself, he visited the M2 area with, and at the request of, local Indigenous people, and was shown scarred trees and unusual rock formations. What people were saying about these places was very similar to the kinds of things Taçon had heard Indigenous people in the Northern Territory saying about their own places. In his opinion the rock formations near the M2 also looked like the kinds of places which would traditionally have had important spiritual significance to Indigenous people.[23]

Such statements 'prove' nothing about the M2 rock formations. Indeed, no archaeologist could 'prove' whether a particular place was or wasn't 'sacred' to Indigenous people simply by inspecting it. This applies whether there are 'relics' present or not. Recognising archaeological evidence (or identifying the archaeological value of 'relics') is a very different process from assessing the social and cultural values of places.[24] Yet there is often confusion in the public mind about this matter. Social anthropologists (who are qualified in the study of living people's culture and belief systems) have often been called upon to give evidence about the 'authenticity' of Indigenous claims. For example, the Commonwealth *Aboriginal and Torres Strait Islander Heritage Protection Act 1984* provides for the protection of Indigenous cultural values of places irrespective of whether there are 'relics' or other archaeological evidence present. There have been several well-publicised cases in which Indigenous people have used such legislation in an attempt to block mining and other developments. When social anthropologists have been asked to present evidence about the 'authenticity' of Indigenous claims to such places,[25] this has had nothing to do with archaeology in the strict sense, although archaeologists may have been involved in a minor way.

In the M2 case, the piles of rocks which some people claimed were Indigenous 'burial mounds' or 'initiation sites' raised a slightly different set of issues. Here Corkill was able to provide proof (by documentary research and talking to several informants with direct experience and knowledge) that these structures were built during the Second World War for military purposes and had no 'authentic' Indigenous value.[26] Yet, at least on a temporary basis, these piles of rocks had acquired some contemporary Indigenous or political value to at least some people as a site of contention in the fight to save the area from the development. As discussed in other chapters, members of the public frequently make claims about places and about the past which are patently 'inauthentic' or 'false' when tested against archaeological, historical and scientific evidence. When such claims are made by non-Indigenous people, most archaeologists feel free to publicly dismiss them as 'pseudo-science' or 'New Age nonsense'. Yet when some Indigenous people make claims about their own places which are incompatible with archaeological or scientific evidence, there can be significant political implications if white 'experts' publicly dismiss such claims as 'false' or 'inauthentic'.

The importance of title

Land ownership is crucial in determining the process and outcomes of heritage assessment when places are threatened by development. Where Indigenous peoples have been granted legal ownership of their lands through land rights or Native Title claims, or have substantial input into the management of government-controlled national parks and reserves, for example through joint management agreements, they are in a much stronger position to negotiate with developers, mining companies and others about the treatment of cultural places located on this land. This is much more common in remoter parts of northern, central and western Australia than in the south-east. This, and the fact that heritage and other relevant legislation varies between states and territories, means the process and outcomes of heritage assessment work differently in different parts of Australia.[27]

The Mabo and Wik High Court rulings and subsequent Native Title legislation have been very important in supporting Indigenous aspirations for control of cultural places and country. A significant outcome of Native Title legislation has been the establishment of various kinds of 'regional agreements' between Indigenous owners and local government, mining companies and other major stakeholders on issues such as service delivery, joint management arrangements for protected areas, resource sharing and Native Title claims.[28] In parts of Australia where Indigenous people's Native Title has been legally recognised, such agreements have included arrangements for 'looking after country'. Mining companies such as RTZ-CRA Ltd (in the Northern Territory) and Hamersley Iron Pty Ltd (in Western Australia) have entered into their own arrangements with traditional owners and Native Title holders over cultural heritage matters. This has included these companies funding Indigenous cultural heritage protection programmes, employing Indigenous people, and paying compensation in return for access to mining rights.[29]

To have their Native Title rights recognised, the Commonwealth government requires that Indigenous people demonstrate traditional or long-term links with any land or rights being claimed. As many writers have commented, this has made it much easier for Indigenous groups in remoter areas of northern, western and central Australia to claim Native Title rights than people in other regions, especially those in urban areas and in most parts of the south-east, who were forcibly removed from their traditional lands.[30] However, this has not stopped Indigenous people across Australia from aspiring to similar types of arrangements. Such aspirations have been given support by sympathetic government departments and policies which favour Indigenous control of cultural heritage matters, even in the absence of extensive Native Title and Indigenous land ownership. For example, NSW NPWS policy currently advocates the goal of Indigenous *coordination* of heritage assessment work, including archaeology, as a natural extension of its current policy of Indigenous consultation and participation. Denis Byrne, writing from the position of a non-Indigenous person and NSW NPWS cultural heritage manager, regards such a step as an important and necessary part of any process of Reconciliation between Indigenous and non-Indigenous Australians.[31] The extent to which this is achievable, given the political and other constraints within which cultural heritage agencies in New South Wales must operate, is debatable. While Indigenous people in New South Wales certainly have more direct involvement in heritage assessment work and archaeology than they did in the past, they are certainly not in control of all elements of their own heritage at the present time.

Professionalism, archaeology and Indigenous control of heritage management

The prospect of Indigenous coordination and control of heritage assessment work in New South Wales and elsewhere raises issues about professionalism as well as fears from some consulting archaeologists that they will be squeezed out of business unless they conform to acceptable Indigenous political agendas. Their concern is that if Indigenous communities reject archaeology completely, or insist that only community members carry out assessment work instead of outside consultants, professionally qualified archaeologists may have to switch to historical archaeology or other areas of the discipline to find work. Many archaeologists also fear that the quality of archaeological assessment work conducted by community members who have no formal archaeology qualifications and only limited experience will be substandard from the perspective of research archaeology.

There are several issues here. First, it is reasonable to assume, given the sentiments expressed in documents such as the Australian Archaeological Association (AAA) Code of Ethics and the Australian Association of Consulting Archaeologists Incorporated (AACAI) policy on Indigenous consultation, that most (if not all) Australian consulting archaeologists agree that Indigenous people have the right to own and control their own cultural heritage. Therefore, archaeologists should have no problem with the notion of Indigenous people assessing the cultural values of their own places in their own terms—even if this means 'substandard' archaeology or no archaeology at all.

Denis Byrne notes that Indigenous people's concept of land and heritage does not conform to Western 'scientific' analysis:

> What an archaeologist may perceive as a lack of scientific detail or rigour in an assessment carried out by Aboriginal people may, from the Aboriginal point of view be elements of an alternative and culturally appropriate assessment strategy. Aboriginal people, for their part, may perceive there to be too much emphasis on measurement and quantification in the archaeological approach, too much science and not enough culture.[32]

Taking an extreme view, Indigenous people could reject professional archaeology altogether and take only Indigenous values into account in making decisions about place. This is a distinct possibility. We have already noted Badtjala people's rejection of and lack of interest in archaeological understandings of the prehistory of Fraser Island in Queensland (see Chapter 3).[33] If archaeology is excluded altogether from the heritage assessment process, in the event of destruction we will lose both the archaeological record and the information it holds. From the perspective of archaeologists this is definitely an undesirable outcome.

In many parts of Australia a more likely outcome is that archaeology of some kind will continue to get done.[34] As discussed in other parts of this book, archaeological and Indigenous values are not completely distinct. Frequently Indigenous people cite the scientific or archaeological values of places, such as radiocarbon dates demonstrating great antiquity or archaeological evidence demonstrating continuity of traditional practices into the historical period, as reasons why places are important to them. For example, members of the local Indigenous community have described Indigenous sites around the Jervis Bay area on the NSW south coast as important because of what archaeologists had excavated there in the 1970s. This 'validation' is probably more common in south-eastern Australia where Indigenous people have retained fewer ties with their land. However, Indigenous people across Australia incorporate knowledge gained from archaeology into public statements about the significance of their culture and history (e.g. 60 000 years for first human settlement in the Northern Territory). In some cases Aborigines rely on archaeology to fill gaps in knowledge lost as a consequence of invasion and colonialism, such as at Lake Condah in Victoria (discussed in Chapter 8). Indigenous communities request the services of and employ consultant archaeologists when archaeological information is useful to them. Archaeological evidence has sometimes been tendered in land rights and, more recently, in Native Title claims where Indigenous people need to demonstrate long-term links with land.[35]

The questions—for professional archaeologists—are who will actually do this archaeology work? Will it be members of the community—even if they have no formal professional qualifications or training in archaeology? Will community members themselves seek further training in professional archaeology? Will they still want to employ professional archaeologists from outside the community? In this context, professional qualifications mean that a person has a university degree or equivalent academic qualification in archaeology, that they can demonstrate a thorough knowledge and understanding of archaeological theory and method through the production of an acceptable research design, and that they are sufficiently experienced to carry out the work (see Chapter 2).

No one can predict the answers to these questions. It seems likely there will be a range of outcomes depending on the circumstances. As already discussed, many Indigenous people are already qualified and involved in archaeology and heritage management in a very wide and varied range of ways. Indigenous people already control a lot of Australian archaeology. In New South Wales Byrne predicts the development of what he calls 'genuinely cross-cultural heritage management'—under Indigenous control and blending those elements of professional archaeological practice which community members find useful and excluding those which they don't. He sees archaeologists' acceptance of such developments—even if this may lead in some instances to a reduction in professional standards—as part of the process of Reconciliation between non-Indigenous and Indigenous Australians.

In some parts of Australia compromises are already being made when Indigenous places are threatened by development work and archaeologists called in. For example, in north-west Queensland in 1999 archaeologists Ian McNiven and Luke Godwin undertook salvage excavations and surface collection of materials from a road construction project. As far as representatives of the local Kalkadoon community were concerned, redeposition of any materials found was an integral part of the archaeological work. To conserve the archaeological significance of the finds, certain details of excavated hearths and collected artefacts were recorded by the archaeologists. Charcoal samples were collected for radiocarbon dating. However, to conserve the overall significance of the place, all materials except charcoal for dates were immediately redeposited off the side of the road easement, under trees. McNiven comments that this was a negotiated compromise between the heritage consultants and local community representatives.[36]

If archaeologists really respect Indigenous people's rights to their own cultural heritage they will not oppose Indigenous control of the heritage assessment process, whatever the consequences for them and their profession. Like much else to do with Indigenous cultural heritage, this all comes back to a basic point about control which was clearly stated in the now much-quoted article by Tasmanian Aboriginal Ros Langford in 1983: 'We say that it is our past, our culture and heritage, and forms part of our present life. As such it is ours to control and it is ours to share on our terms. That is the Central Issue in this debate.'[37]

The question of who is 'qualified' to assess the heritage values of places, the inclusion or exclusion of archaeological values in this process, and whether government heritage agencies should allow people without formal professional qualifications to excavate archaeological sites is not just about Indigenous heritage. It is enlightening to think about similar issues for historical archaeology on non-Indigenous sites. Many of the concerns raised by archaeologists for historic sites are very similar—but people's reactions are often different. Historical archaeologists frequently complain that heritage assessment work for many non-Indigenous places and the 'built environment' in urban areas is carried out by people whose major professional qualifications are in architecture, history or urban planning. This can and does result in archaeology being ignored or mis-understood in such studies—by other professionals.

It is uncommon in historical archaeology for non-professionals to want to conduct their own formal heritage assessment work and conduct their own archaeological excavations. But there are conflicts between his-torical archaeologists and amateur bottle collectors digging into sites, or hobby divers who want to remove items from historic shipwrecks. Digging into protected historic sites to collect bottles is illegal in many states. This causes resentment from some bottle collectors and it is hard if not impos-sible for heritage managers to fully control the activities of such collectors under current policy. Heritage Victoria (the agency responsible in that state) has recently introduced an amnesty on some bottle-collecting activ-ities and is working to educate people about the damage their activities can do to important historic sites—while devising ways archaeologists and collectors could work together for mutual benefit.[38] When this subject was discussed at a recent conference of the Australasian Society for Historical Archaeology (ASHA), some archaeologists expressed anger that the government should make such concessions to bottle collectors—but this was a minority view.

Community-based archaeology—getting local school groups and members of the public more actively involved in the archaeology of their own places—on non-Indigenous historic sites also featured strongly at the ASHA conference. Most archaeologists recognise that if they want to continue doing archaeology, they have a responsibility to educate people about the value of their work, explain what it is about, get people involved, and demonstrate that archaeology can have some real benefits to the public. This issue is much broader than just the relationship between archaeologists and some Indigenous communities. It is about Australian archaeology more generally—in all its forms.[39]

6
Archaeology and the public

Many Australian archaeologists don't work in Australia at all. They travel overseas to investigate ancient civilisations and cultures in Asia, the Pacific, Europe, the Middle East and elsewhere. Their work and the places and sites they study are of interest to Australians—often more so than 'home-grown' archaeology. Even when people are interested in archaeology conducted in Australia, they can misunderstand what it is and the kind of knowledge it produces. Public attitudes towards archaeology form an essential backdrop to relationships between Indigenous peoples, archaeologists and government. Such attitudes colour the way archaeological knowledge about Australia's Indigenous past is received, produced, reproduced and acted upon by Australians inside and outside the archaeology profession.

Public perceptions of archaeology

In the early 1990s Hilary du Cros asked several Australian archaeologists to describe how people other than professional colleagues reacted to their occupation. When archaeologists were conducting excavations, passers-by most frequently asked, usually half-jokingly: 'Have you found any treasure yet?' In social settings archaeologists were most commonly asked if they worked overseas, if there were actually anything old enough in Australia to count as archaeology, and if it were really possible to make a living as an archaeologist. Du Cros also documented inquiries about archaeology from 24 members of the public who telephoned her Victoria-based archaeological consulting business. Eight callers confused archaeology with palaeontology (the study of fossils and dinosaurs). Others sought information about Egypt, New Age aspects of Aboriginal places, how they could go on a dig, and the likely market value of illegally obtained antiquities.

On the basis of this research and an analysis of the way archaeology was portrayed in a sample of Australian newspapers, du Cros identified several common misconceptions and stereotypes about Australian archaeology. People thought of a typical archaeologist as male, bearded, academic, harmless and eccentric. Archaeology was considered to be about digging for fossils, treasure or dinosaurs. Archaeologists mainly excavated very slowly using brushes and trowels (making archaeology expensive and time-consuming), and the activity was fun (and therefore self-indulgent). Most people thought of archaeological sites as ruins or garbage, which should belong to everyone equally, and were not usually worth conserving. People believed archaeology was an objective science and involved digging up facts. Apart from providing dates for Aboriginal occupation possibly relevant to land rights claims, people regarded archaeology as politically neutral and largely irrelevant to society.

Du Cros' study of public attitudes is limited, yet her results concur with other work and anecdotal evidence about wider public attitudes towards archaeology in Australia. As discussed by du Cros herself and others, changing school curricula, public education programmes and well-informed media reports about major Australian archaeology projects do seem to be having some impact in making a wider cross-section of the public aware that there is archaeology in Australia, and that archaeology is not primarily about finding treasure or digging up fossils.[1] Nevertheless, the broad popular appeal of archaeology still seems to be based more on myth and fantasy than the reality of what Australian archaeologists do.

Digging up fossils

The common confusion in Australia between archaeology (the study of Australia's human past and history from material evidence) and palaeontology (a branch of geology which studies now extinct plants and animals and their environments) relates partly to the way Australian Aboriginal archaeology developed as something called 'prehistory', by which it is still often referred to (see Chapter 1). In Australia the term 'archaeology' has most often been used when describing studies of things and places from overseas, especially the classical and ancient Mediterranean and Near East. In contrast, the term 'prehistory' has been applied both to the study of

fossils and dinosaurs, and to the study of human or Aboriginal history in
Australia before the arrival of Europeans.

Palaeontology usually involves studying fossils. The term 'fossil'
implies something which is now extinct, and many Aboriginal people
object to ancestral remains and elements of their culture being described
as such. A dictionary definition of a fossil is 'organic traces buried by
natural processes and subsequently permanently preserved'. Fossils include
skeletal material, impressions of organisms, excremental material, tracks,
trails and borings. Human artefacts are not regarded as fossils by geologists or palaeontologists, but human remains are.[2] Some Australian archaeology does involve the study of 'fossils' in this sense, including some early
human remains which have become fossilised and the remains of now
extinct megafauna, some of which lived during the early period of human
occupation of Australia. Archaeology and palaeontology also share similar
methods such as careful excavation of bones and stones, the observation of
stratigraphic associations and the use of scientific dating methods.

Romance and adventure
An important element of archaeological mythology is romance and adventure. These are epitomised by the Indiana Jones films about a fictional
archaeologist played by actor Harrison Ford: *Raiders of the Lost Ark* (1981),
Indiana Jones and the Temple of Doom (1984) and *Indiana Jones and the last Crusade*
(1989). Jones is a handsome hero who travels the world, with attractive
women in tow, seeking treasure and lost civilisations while fighting evil
forces. The Indiana Jones films have been criticised by some for promoting American imperialism and offensive racial and gender politics.[3] Jones'
attitude towards the archaeological record and the conservation and ownership of antiquities also contravenes all archaeological codes of ethics.
According to research by R. Weissensteiner at the Australian National
University, Indiana Jones' behaviour in removing artefacts from sites categorises him as a simple looter and so angered the Society for American
Archaeology that it complained to the filmmakers and was then given the
script of the third Indiana Jones film to review.[4]

Indiana Jones still retains his popular appeal. For example, Internet
searches in early 2000 produced tens of thousands of web pages which contained the text 'Indiana Jones'. This compared to fewer than 200 each for
real-life archaeologists Colin Renfrew, Mortimer Wheeler and Heinrich

Schliemann. Obviously the nature and purpose of the websites varied. Real-life archaeologists featured mainly in sites produced by academic institutions and book publishers, while Indiana Jones was mainly found at sites produced by fan clubs and marketing operations for Indiana Jones computer games and related products. Such numbers nevertheless say something about the broad public appeal of the Indiana Jones character. A more recently created character comparable in many ways to Indiana Jones is computer game 'Tomb Raider' heroine Lara Croft, whom the *Sydney Morning Herald* ICON section described as 'an upper-class English archaeologist-adventurer—the straight man's Indiana Jones' and as 'Woman of the Decade'.[5] Information from the Internet[6] describes Croft as a British aristocrat-turned-traveller-and-adventurer who, over the years, has acquired 'an intimate knowledge of ancient civilizations across the globe' and is famed for 'discovering several ancient sites of profound archaeological interest'. Needless to say, all such sites are fictitious.

Despite the fact that sustained public interest in figures such as Indiana Jones and Lara Croft has been largely created by the marketing strategies of media corporations, these characters must embody values and ideas which appeal to the public in the first place in order for them to be so successful.

Most real-life archaeology projects don't offer the glamour and adventure of Indiana Jones movies, yet the media often refer to Indiana Jones in their reportage of archaeology. Some archaeologists welcome this, in part because Indiana Jones has great public appeal. From an Australian perspective, the Indiana Jones image perpetuates the notion that archaeology happens overseas and is primarily about treasure hunting. It also celebrates certain masculinist values and ideals.[7]

Archaeology, science and technology
The 'archaeologist as scientist' is another image often promoted in the media and by many archaeologists themselves. Archaeology stories often feature in science programmes on television and radio, and images of scientists in white coats standing near laboratory equipment, staring down microscopes or through lenses at archaeological finds are recurrent in newspaper and magazine coverage of Australian archaeology. Such representation is more complex than the Indiana Jones 'archaeologist as hero' image, because much archaeology really does involve science, or the

application of scientific methods to the study of archaeological materials. Forensic archaeology and closely related disciplines such as biological anthropology actually contribute to forensic science, police work and the investigation of war crimes.[8]

Julian Thomas has discussed the ambivalent theoretical position occupied by archaeological science in the United Kingdom. In Australia very few natural scientists work primarily or exclusively in archaeology, compared with the United Kingdom, but Thomas' general comments are valid here. The term 'science' is used loosely and in different ways by different archaeologists. 'Archaeological science' or 'archaeometry' is used to denote the application of scientific methods and technology to measuring and describing archaeological data. Obvious examples include dating methods such as radiocarbon and thermoluminescence, DNA analysis, residue analysis, pollen analysis, and the use of information technology. Used in this way, Thomas argues 'archaeological science' is not science at all (in the sense of the natural sciences), but is rather an assemblage of techniques with no coherent theoretical underpinnings or common objectives in understanding or explaining the past.[9] Yet during a period when successive UK governments have slashed funding for humanities research, including archaeology because they deem it to have insufficient practical application, 'archaeological science' has retained a central role in government-funded research programmes. In such circumstances it suits archaeologists to classify themselves as scientists and what they do as science. Archaeology is a practical discipline. Most archaeologists need access to laboratories, vehicles and other equipment and facilities, regardless of their particular theoretical stand. Such infrastructure costs money, which is increasingly beyond the means of most university humanities faculties. If in order to secure funding archaeologists need to present their work as science, who can blame them?

However, identifying with science is not always beneficial for archaeologists. Not all public perceptions of science are positive. For example, in Australia many archaeologists have chosen to distance themselves and their work from science, choosing instead to emphasise the historical and cultural studies aspects of their research. Science is unpopular with many Indigenous people. 'Western science' is viewed as a colonial practice which has exploited Aboriginal people.[10] In particular, many Indigenous people castigate scientific study of human skeletal remains—in which bones are stored in what they regard as a disrespectful way in boxes in laboratories, skulls are measured with callipers, and 'specimens' are seemingly ground up in test tubes and destroyed in machines. 'Mad scientists', like Frankenstein and his monster, pursuing their own obscure research agendas with complete disrespect for Indigenous sensibilities, are viewed as undesirable and unacceptable.[11]

Alternative archaeologies

Ethereal elements of mystery and the unknown are important to many people's interest in ancient places. Numerous popular 'archaeology' books and other publications blend descriptions of real archaeological sites with the mythical and the mysterious. A fairly conservative and scholarly example of this genre is a book called *The Atlas of Mysterious Places*, edited by Jennifer Westwood.[12] This presents a detailed overview and description of a very wide range of places from across the world categorised into sacred sites, symbolic landscapes, ancient cities and lost lands. Many of these are well known places which have been put on the World Heritage List for their archaeological values. Included are prehistoric stone circles at Stonehenge and Avebury in England, carved stone temples in Malta, the site of the Oracle at Delphi in Greece, the Great Pyramid of King Cheops at Giza in Egypt, the Inca settlement of Machu Picchu in Peru, and many other well known archaeological sites. The book also documents mythical places such as the lost city of Atlantis, the elusive continent of Lemuria, and the secret utopia of Shangri-La. It discusses geomancy and ley lines (see below) and also includes a description of Uluru (Ayers Rock) in Australia, described as 'The Dreamtime Sanctuary'.

In her introduction, Westwood justifies the inclusion of this disparate collection of places and topics in the book, describing them in terms of enigmas, secrets, riddles and mysteries which are of interest to 'scholars and adventurers, curiosity seekers and tourists'. Such places fire the imagination and generate awe, as well as raise questions about how people lived in the past. In particular, 'They challenge modern thinking and its ideas about the supremacy of twentieth century technology and the "foolproof" dogma of the scientific method'.[13]

The mythical and mysterious cases in Westwood's book are examples of what are often described as 'alternative archaeologies'. In fact, this term is a misnomer. Such ideas are not archaeology at all, but something else. Perhaps the most famous alternative archaeologist is American Erich von Daniken, whose books such as *Chariots of the Gods* (1971) and *Return to the Stars* (1972), which espouse the theory that prehistoric technological achievements are largely the result of visits to the earth by aliens from outer space, have sold over 40 million copies.[14] Aliens and spacemen are a common theme in alternative archaeologies, as are lost civilisations such as Atlantis. Historically known Ancient Egyptians and their pyramids are especially popular, together with Phoenicians, Celts and Mayans. Anti-scientific sentiments are also common in these 'archaeologies'.

Peter Hiscock, who is particularly interested in the currency of such ideas in an Australian context, divides alternative archaeologies into two main types. The first is what he terms 'pseudo-science', which uses scientific terminology comparable with conventional archaeology and refers to material evidence to 'prove' various theories about what happened in the past. Such views may also rely on the acceptance of some elements of conventional archaeology such as geological chronologies and radiocarbon dates.[15] Claims by Australian writer and collector Rex Gilroy to have found evidence for visits by ancient Phoenicians and Egyptians to New South Wales and Queensland fall into this category. Hiscock also regards creation science and some types of Biblical archaeology as 'pseudo-science'.

Hiscock's second alternative archaeology category is what he terms 'New Age' archaeology. This rejects conventional archaeology and science altogether as a legitimate means of understanding the past. Instead, knowledge of the past comes to chosen individuals via mystic forces, time travel, channelling of psychic energy and similar phenomena. There may be some reference to archaeological remains, but New Age archaeologies rely more on revelation than on any systematic examination of physical evidence. Hiscock describes several examples of such interpretations of the past, some of which have an international following, including some ecofeminists who associate particular archaeological sites with the Goddess who embodies feminine forces. These forces are believed to have been overturned by masculine forces some time in prehistory as part of a continuing spiritual cycle of feminine and masculine energies, which will in time see the Goddess rise to power again.[16] The long-standing interest by Goddess worshippers in the prehistoric site of Çatalhöyük in Turkey, which is currently being excavated by a team of archaeologists led by Ian Hodder (see Chapter 8), is an example of both pseudo-science and New Age archaeology.

Another of Hiscock's examples is that of New Age archaeologies originating in northern Europe which propose that the earth is circled by a grid or lines of psychic or biomagnetic power (sometimes called leys) on which important places, such as the ancient Egyptian pyramids at Giza, are located.[17] Hiscock describes examples where similar ideas have been applied to the interpretation of Australian Aboriginal rock art sites. In an Australian context there is often a conflation of New Age ideologies and Indigenous understandings of place which, as discussed elsewhere (see below and Chapter 8), can have political and other implications for archaeologists and heritage managers.

In true 'X-Files' fashion, conspiracy theories abound in alternative archaeologies. Proponents of both pseudo-science and New Age archaeologies commonly accuse scientists, archaeologists and the government of ignoring them and perpetuating a cover-up about the True meaning of archaeological sites and what Really happened in the past. As Hiscock notes, the main aim of much alternative archaeology, in all its forms, is to discover or reveal 'hidden histories' (i.e. 'the Truth') which the government, scientists and archaeologists don't want the public to know.[18]

Alternative archaeologies have existed in Australia for some time and are alive and well.[19] Hiscock documents a thriving audience for information on the subject. He quotes the readily available *Nexus* magazine, which is produced in Queensland, has offices in the United Kingdom, United States, New Zealand and Italy and claims to sell 75 000 copies every two months. Local academic archaeology journals such as *Australian Archaeology* and *Archaeology in Oceania* can only dream of such circulation figures. According to Hiscock, desktop publishing and the Internet become very effective media for the widespread dissemination of ideas about alternative archaeologies, which might otherwise be restricted in their distribution by the peer-review process and the constraints of conventional publication.[20]

One organisation using this media is a Queensland-based organisation called Awareness Quest, which states on its website that it aims to 'preserve Ancient sites including Pyramids, Stone Circles, and Petroglyphs from destruction and denial'. Its Australian Archaeological Anomalies web page lists example after example from every state in Australia of objects people have supposedly found, many of them illustrated with black and white photographs, which support alternative interpretations of Australian history.[21]

Several common themes run through the views about the past put forward by Awareness Quest. While 'alternative archaeology' finds come from most Australian states (excluding Tasmania) most claims come from parts of New South Wales (the Blue Mountains, central and north coast, and the Hawkesbury area) and south-east Queensland. The region around Gympie on Queensland's Sunshine Coast gets special mention as an area with a high concentration of pyramids and other relevant finds. Kingaroy, well known in Australia as the home of ex-Queensland premier Joh Bjelke-Petersen, also gets a mention as the find spot of an onyx scarab, which is described as having been unearthed many years ago.

The kinds of things found by contributors to Awareness Quest fall into a limited range of categories. Most of them are isolated finds from a general area or region rather than a very specific location. Most common are stones (both large and small), which are usually carved in the shape of gods, animals and humans, or decorated with motifs and inscriptions. Other common finds are coins (in gold, silver, bronze, copper), Egyptian scarabs, and tools, knives and axe blades made from copper, iron and bronze. Other finds mentioned include clay pipes, broken pottery, giant stone tools, human skeletons, metal armour, helmets and jewellery. Sites and settlements are less common than individual artefacts. Of these, pyramids, obelisks, stone alignments, stone circles, 'megaliths' and shipwrecks are most frequent. Also mentioned are a 'stone fort' and a 'lost city' in northern Australia, marked by stone walls and other features. Plants and plant remains from outside Australia (e.g. 'Egyptian' papyrus and 'southern European' cork and fig trees) are also described.

The 'artefacts' are ascribed to particular ethnic groups, all of them from outside Australia. Ancient Egyptians, Phoenicians and people from 'the ancient middle east' are by far the most common. For example, carvings are said to represent Egyptian gods (Ra, Thoth, Horus), Phoenician writing, Egyptian hieroglyphs, and symbols such as the sun and winged griffins. Other groups mentioned include Greeks and Romans, Celts, 'pre-Mayans', Chinese, Hindus and people from Easter Island in the Pacific. Very specific dates are often given ('2000 BC', '28 BC', '700 years ago'). Such people are presumed to have visited Australia long before recorded history and to have interacted with the Aborigines whose burial customs, art styles, belief systems, languages and 'genetic makeup' have been influenced by them.

In a slightly different category are claims for 'pre-Aboriginal' occupation of Australia by mythical fossil hominids such as 'Meganthropus', who is said to have originated in South East Asia, stood 12 feet (about 3–4 metres) tall, and left behind fossilised skulls' and giant stone tools including a '25 lb [about 12 kilograms] hand axe'.[22] Extensive 'megalithic' stone alignments and other astronomical structures dating back 10 000 to 15 000 years are said to demonstrate the former presence in Australia of a highly advanced civilisation of unknown origin. Aliens from outer space are actually rarely implicated, but they are thought to be responsible for building a ruined city in northern Australia, the location of which is now lost and known only to local Aborigines whose traditions record 'white men' living there thousands of years ago.

In a slightly different category again are claims to 'pre-Cook' exploration and settlement of Australia in the fifteenth, sixteenth and seventeenth centuries by Spanish, 'Castillians' and Portuguese. Shipwrecks, skeletons, armoury and 'European' plants testify to this 'hidden history'. There is also mention of Dutch clay pipes being found in shell middens in south-east Queensland.[23]

Public and private archaeology

Archaeology is a leisure activity to many people. Its major public benefit, perhaps *the* major benefit, is as entertainment—or at least infotainment—and education. Archaeology stimulates the imagination. It can offer escape into other worlds, as do science fiction and fantasy. People want to know about the activities and findings of archaeologists by reading magazines and books, watching television programmes and films, and attending lectures given by real archaeologists. People want to visit sites and exhibitions to see, touch and experience real things from the past found by archaeologists. Even if people don't want to be archaeologists or get actively involved themselves, they want archaeology and archaeologists to exist.

Professional, or academic, archaeology developed in northern Europe from amateur collecting and antiquarian traditions pursued and supported by wealthy and educated people. Bruce Trigger has argued that the historical development of Western archaeology corresponded with the rise to power of the middle classes, and that public interest in archaeology continues to be primarily among the educated middle classes, including some political leaders.[24] This seems to be true in Australia, although there have been no systematic studies of links between interest in archaeology and factors such as income, class, ethnicity and gender. Other than Gough Whitlam, few if any of Australia's political leaders have expressed any interest in archaeology, other than making occasional passing reference to a 40 000 year date for Aboriginal occupation of the continent (derived from archaeological research at sites such as Lake Mungo, NSW, and Swan River, WA, in the 1970s). Maritime archaeology was the only type of Australian archaeology mentioned at all in ex-Labor Prime Minister Paul Keating's 1994 cultural policy statement *Creative Nation*.[25]

The title of David Lowenthal's influential book about history and heritage—*The Past is a Foreign Country*—portrays elements of public interest in archaeology as exotic escapism, entertainment and travel.[26] Many people, including archaeologists themselves, associate archaeology with adventure and visits to interesting and exotic destinations. Here archaeology is part of a cultural tourism experience. It can also be about pilgrimage and journeying to places significant to people's beliefs or cultural identity. This is certainly true for those Australians whose interest in Biblical archaeology and visits to ancient places in the Bible Lands derive from their religion. Many Australians also want to visit places in the Mediterranean and Near East which they regard as nurturing the cultural roots of European civilisation, from which modern Australian society ultimately derives. The multiculturalism of Australian society also impacts on people's interest in archaeology. Many people have a continuing and special interest in the history and archaeology of their country of origin. For example, members of Melbourne's Cypriot community have been interested in and supportive of archaeological research conducted in Cyprus by Australian archaeologist David Frankel.[27]

People seeking active engagement with archaeology can pay to attend study tours with professional archaeologists, and participate in fieldwork and excavation. Australian archaeology, especially overseas, relies in part on such private donations and volunteer assistance. Several organisations facilitate public involvement in archaeology through fundraising, public education and building links between professionals and amateurs. The international Earthwatch Institute aims to promote the conservation of natural resources and cultural heritage by creating partnerships between scientists, educators and the public, and by organising for paying volunteers to participate in projects, including archaeology projects. Examples of Australian projects sponsored by Earthwatch include archaeological fieldwork and excavations at Ngarrabullgan Cave, North Queensland (Bruno David), and the Lightning Brothers rock art project in the Northern Territory (Josephine Flood).[28]

Another organisation is the University of Sydney's Near Eastern Archaeology Foundation, which promotes research and public understanding of archaeology in the Mediterranean and Near East. This is achieved by raising private funds for student research and organising public lectures, adult education courses and professionally guided overseas tours. The Near Eastern Archaeology Foundation's volunteer system enables fee-paying members of the public to participate in overseas excavations with professional archaeologists.[29]

Going on a dig

Excavation frequently involves heavy and dirty manual work, shifting soil, rubble and other materials. Other jobs, like brushing soil from stone structures and cleaning and labelling finds, are routine, repetitive and time-consuming. Archaeology first developed as a pastime for wealthy, upper-class people who did not move the dirt themselves, but employed others for such work.[30] This tradition has continued, and manual and routine work on excavations often provides employment opportunities for local people, although most archaeologists now get actively involved in the digging themselves. Machinery is used to move earth, circumstances permitting, but most work still needs to be done by hand. Excavations also involve specialists like photographers, illustrators and surveyors. Large field projects require a cook and someone to manage domestic tasks, transport, equipment and personnel. Few archaeologists can afford to pay for all this—most rely on volunteers.

The Australian public is very eager to donate its time and labour to help with a dig. In Australia most volunteer participation occurs on large-scale historical archaeology projects in urban centres. Government departments and consulting archaeology companies are often keen to encourage volunteers as part of public education about Australian archaeology. For example, excavations in Sydney's historic Rocks area in the mid-1990s, conducted by consulting company Godden Mackay Logan for the Sydney Harbour Foreshore Authority, involved an extensive public education programme, including a volunteer scheme which attracted over 2000 people.[31] In the 1970s the then Victoria Archaeological Survey organised extensive volunteer participation in Aboriginal archaeology in the state, and Earthwatch has sponsored several successful volunteer programmes on Indigenous sites elsewhere in Australia. On the whole, however, volunteers are less common on projects involving Indigenous places, in part because there are fewer opportunities to get involved. Most archaeology on Indigenous sites involves small teams, and archaeologists don't want or need many volunteers. Indigenous people themselves also want to be involved, and political sensibilities can preclude outsider volunteer participation by people who are essentially there for a cultural tourism experience.

Using volunteers and charging people to go on a dig raises practical and professional issues. Volunteers are a mixed blessing. Not everyone has a natural aptitude for field archaeology. Many people mistakenly imagine excavation as an easy and exciting activity where you flick dirt off interesting and significant finds with a paintbrush and trowel. But apart from the routine and boring, digging can involve considerable hard physical labour and discomfort—you can't always stop for bad weather—and living conditions can be very basic. Great care and patience are required, and many of the more interesting jobs are too technical and important to be left to untrained and inexperienced volunteers. Many people who go on a dig find themselves disappointed by the reality. Disgruntled volunteers, especially when they are paying for their experience, feel justified in complaining about the work and conditions. They can fail to complete tasks to an adequate standard or simply walk off the job. An archaeologist who relies on volunteer labour needs to spend time and effort in providing people with a positive experience. Good people management skills are essential.

Volunteers and consulting archaeology don't always mix well. Given the time and money constraints of many consulting projects, supervising too many inexperienced volunteers can be a luxury which archaeologists can't afford. It is often better (and cheaper) to employ a small team of experienced professionals paid at proper rates to ensure work gets done on time to the required standard. Only some consulting projects (usually the larger and longer-term projects) are volunteer friendly. On a professional level, if a consulting company's bid for a job includes use of volunteer and (unpaid) student labour, this can undercut competition from other teams comprising fully paid professionals. This raises questions about quality control and contravenes the Australian Association of Consulting Archaeologists Incorporated Code of Ethics about undercutting.

Private funding and sponsorship

As public funds for archaeology and heritage conservation have declined, private support and sponsorship have become more important. Archaeologists in the United Kingdom, for example, have commented how governments have sometimes actively promoted this trend.[32] All money for archaeology, whether public or private, comes with some strings attached. However, the saying 'He who pays the piper calls the tune' is much more obvious where private money is concerned.

Ian McNiven has described an interesting and unusual example of private money being donated to Australian Indigenous archaeology for overtly political reasons. In the mid-1970s, in the middle of a campaign by environmentalists to prevent sand mining on Fraser Island in Queensland, the Australian novelist Patrick White paid $1000 of his own money to employ archaeologist Peter Lauer to conduct an archaeological field survey to locate Aboriginal sites on the island as part of the anti-mining struggle.[33]

If Australian archaeology relied totally on private funding, little archaeology would be done at all. Archaeology projects based overseas in exotic holiday locations or places linked to the roots of European civilisation are more attractive to the paying public and to sponsors than other digs. Understandably, when private companies sponsor archaeology they want to be associated with something highly attractive to the public which buys their products and services. The Australian Associated Press Group would seem to have done this with their sponsorship of historical archaeology and conservation work being conducted at huts associated with early Antarctic exploration by Sir Douglas Mawson at Cape Denison, Australian Antarctic Territory. The project is sponsored by the media organisation through the AAP Mawson's Huts Foundation, with the full and active support of the present Commonwealth government.[34] AAP and other private-company support for the Mawson's Huts project relies on enormous positive public interest in Australia generated by anything to do with the Antarctic. And significantly, while Sir Douglas Mawson was a prominent Australian who currently features on $100 banknotes and the site is Australian, it is also located off the Australian mainland in an overseas territory.

Concerns about private funding go beyond a simple consideration of whether a project can attract funds. In the Mawson's Huts case, for example, John Mulvaney expressed his concern that good conservation practice and government control of this important Australian place might be too compromised by commercial interests.[35] In a slightly different context, Yannis Hamilakis has discussed issues raised by major international company sponsorship of Ian Hodder's excavation of the prehistoric site of Çatalhöyük in Turkey. The team has adopted what it describes as reflexive practices aimed at maintaining self-awareness of its role in producing archaeological knowledge, including considering the New Age interests in Çatalhöyük of Goddess worshippers. This is a post-modern approach to archaeology, pioneered by Hodder, in which the subjectivity of archaeological practice is fully and openly acknowledged. The team also claims such an approach challenges racist Orientalist stereotyping. Yet Hamilakis argues the project cannot avoid promoting other messages because of the high-profile involvement of the sponsors. For example, the Visa credit card company has influenced the way some of the results of the archaeology have been interpreted and presented, while the Shell oil company has been condemned by environmental organisation Greenpeace for its unethical practices. At the same time, such a long-term and large-scale project could not proceed without the money provided by such companies. While an extreme example, the Çatalhöyük case clearly highlights the costs and benefits which can come with private sponsorship.[36]

Amateur archaeology

Archaeologists actively encourage some amateur involvement in their work, but they can be ambivalent about or opposed to private organisations and individuals who operate beyond and outside the profession. As explained in Chapter 2, government heritage agencies control some aspects of archaeology through the issue of excavation and fieldwork permits. Legislation makes it illegal for anyone other than an archaeologist to deliberately dig into an archaeological site and remove anything. This limits, for example, the activities of bottle collectors and other groups classified as 'looters'. A permit is also unlikely to be issued for research which is thought to be too unorthodox. For example, it seems unlikely that a government heritage agency would issue anyone (including a fully qualified professional archaeologist) with an excavation or survey permit to seek evidence of Ancient Egyptians in Queensland or alien cities in northern Australia. Yet some types of archaeological research and fieldwork which lie on or beyond the fringes of orthodoxy proceed and even flourish, despite such constraints.

Interpretations of rock art feature frequently in amateur study of Australia's past. Academics such as art historians, art theorists and anthropologists are interested in rock art as well as archaeologists, and there seems to be room for a variety of approaches and more professional tolerance of the unorthodox and the amateur. Studying rock art primarily involves methods which do not physically damage the art or the site (e.g. observation, photography and drawing). Researchers sometimes wish to obtain samples of pigments and other materials for scientific dating, but such samples are small and any damage is minimal. Physically destructive archaeological excavation is a minor component of rock art research. This means that studying rock art is less restricted by the government permit system than other kinds of archaeological fieldwork. Many rock art sites are located in places such as national parks, which are freely accessible to the public. While some Indigenous people may take offence at inappropriate visits to some rock art sites, they can only control these in places where they officially own the land or are involved in visitor management.[37]

Permit restrictions apply to archaeologists who wish to conduct research work which requires access to rock art sites located on government-controlled land. As private individuals, archaeologists like anyone else may enter national parks to observe, contemplate, photograph or draw rock art, so long as they don't physically damage anything. But formal permission is usually needed before government land managers and heritage agencies will allow anyone access to sites for specific research purposes. Professional archaeologists are also bound by their own codes of ethics to consult with Indigenous owners before recording rock art, regardless of land ownership, access or permits.

An interesting case study of an amateur in rock art studies is Robert Bednarik, who has no formal qualifications in archaeology but who has pursued his own privately funded research into Indigenous archaeology and rock art for many years. In an interview with Nicholas Rothwell in the *Weekend Australian*, Bednarik described how he developed a long-standing amateur interest in Australian Aboriginal archaeology and rock art. He conducted extensive study of Aboriginal art sites in the Pilbarra and other regions of northern and western Australia while travelling in his job as an engineer. Over the years he established a reputation as a dedicated worker outside the institutional research system. In 1980 an article he wrote on his work was rejected for publication by a professional Australian archaeology journal, yet three years later the same journal published a paper by someone else based on Bednarik's ideas.

Incensed by what he saw as blatant plagiarism and widespread professional disregard for the large amount of rock art research being conducted by dedicated amateurs in many countries, Bednarik took matters into his own hands and started his own rock art research organisations—the International Federation of Rock Art Organisations (IFRAO) and the Australian Rock Art Research Association (AURA)—and his own journal *Rock Art Research*.[38] Whatever they may think about Bednarik's work, many professional archaeologists and rock art specialists have become actively involved in the activities of AURA and the journal. *Rock Art Research* is now the leading international rock art journal, AURA has run several major large-scale international conferences, and Bednarik himself has published widely in leading international archaeology and anthropology journals. His publication record is better than many professional archaeologists.

Despite an apparent *rapprochement* between Bednarik and many professional archaeologists, Rothwell noted in his interview that Bednarik is not a 'natural friend of the academy'. Bednarik's views about aspects of rock art and archaeology are rejected by many academics. In reply, Bednarik pushes the theme that free thinking is best pursued independently of establishment structures. Rothwell described him as having a pure and idealistic commitment to seeking out the Truth and an outsider's scepticism towards institutions. On this he quoted Bednarik as saying:

> I accept you can't do science without big funding, but then you become part of the establishment and don't challenge it. I would suggest that I live for my science more than someone who is paid for it. I don't depend

on an institution, a system. I am eroding power systems, I am engaged in
a major battle and the only reason I can do it is that I'm independent—
if this is the only way I am able to challenge the existing paradigm, then
surely it's right![39]

Several other researchers have also funded and pursued significant
research in rock art outside the formal academic system. Most notable are
Percy Trezise, an artist, writer and bush pilot for the Royal Flying Doctor
Service, who in the 1960s began making extensive study of Indigenous
rock art in Quinkan Country in the area around Laura in North Queensland, and Graham Walsh, whose important work on the Bradshaw art of
the Kimberley area is discussed in detail in Chapter 8.[40]

Robert Bednarik also edits *The Artefact*, the journal of the Archaeological and Anthropological Society of Victoria Incorporated (AASV). The
AASV was set up by and for members of the public interested in archaeology, ethno-archaeology, ethno-history and anthropology. As explained by
Gary Presland, the present organisation developed from the Archaeological Society of Victoria (ASV) which was formed in 1965 and bridged the
'public' and 'professional' archaeology divide. The ASV/AASV provides an
interesting example of fruitful cooperation between amateur and professional archaeologists in Victoria. A number of professional archaeologists
have always been involved in the AASV and *The Artefact* regularly publishes
high-quality papers by professional archaeologists, several of whom also sit
on the journal's editorial board.[41]

The archaeological fieldwork and writing of the late Dr Alexander
Gallus was crucial in the development of the society. Gallus was a very well
known Australian archaeologist who, because of his overseas archaeological
training in Hungary and somewhat unorthodox ideas about Aboriginal
pre-history, was never quite accepted by other members of the Australian
archaeological establishment. He unsuccessfully applied for at least two
university positions in prehistory, although he made an important and
lasting contribution to the discipline. Writing about Gallus after his death
in 1996, John Mulvaney commented:

> With hindsight the title of Australia's first post-modern archaeologist and
> philosopher of the human mind may be assigned to Sandor Gallus . . .
> Some of his conjectures and interest in cognition forty years ago possess
> current relevance, even though most of his evidence must be rejected.[42]

Gary Presland discusses the relationship between 'amateur' and 'professional' in relation to excavations at Keilor in Victoria, which were directed by Gallus in the 1960s and 1970s. River terraces in this area had previously been identified by Edmund Gill as late glacial or earlier in age (i.e. more than 10 000 years old). Gallus began collecting artefacts and excavating in the area on his own in the 1950s, looking for evidence of early human occupation. In 1966 he approached the ASV and asked about carrying out excavations under its auspices. It was at first agreed that the ASV foundation president, Dr A. Cymons, would be appointed as co-director of the dig. After a falling out between the two, ASV appointed Gallus sole director in 1967. Most of the people working on the excavations were amateurs, some of whom went on to study archaeology at university and establish themselves in the profession. Presland notes that the ASV achieved a measure of credibility within professional archaeology circles through the Keilor excavations, which were conducted diligently and systematically, and many professionals visited the site, including Mulvaney.[43]

Gallus also made an important contribution to Australian archaeology through his amateur excavations at Koonalda Cave in South Australia. The site was later excavated by Richard Wright who then edited a publication based on his own and Gallus's work at the site, through the Australian Institute of Aboriginal Studies Press in 1971. Gallus's interpretations of Australian prehistory at Koonalda (as at Keilor and elsewhere) were based primarily on his personal intuition and strong opinion, without necessary recourse to evidence. Notably, he developed a complex classification system to determine the function and age of stone tools excavated at Koonalda. His system was based on long-established European stone tool terminology, which bore no relation to patterns observed by other Australian prehistorians. Many of the stone tool types which Gallus labelled and interpreted so meticulously were not stone tools at all but naturally flaked specimens, or examples of quarry and tool production waste, well known from other sites. Richard Wright rejected Gallus' interpretation of the Koonalda stone tools, commenting 'I do not find his conclusions accord with the realities of the Koonalda flints'.[44] Wright did not attempt to integrate his own interpretation of the site (based on accepted archaeological methods and theory) with Gallus' less orthodox view of the site's prehistory, but presented dual interpretations.[45]

Biblical archaeology

Biblical archaeology is another area which attracts a high degree of amateur interest and participation, and is regarded with varying degrees of ambivalence by many professionals. As Colin Renfrew and Paul Bahn explain, biblical archaeologists search the Near East for archaeological evidence of places, people and events described in the Old and New Testaments. Treated as a historical document, the Bible can provide valuable information for archaeologists in the same way as other documentary sources. In this sense, biblical archaeology is a type of text-aided or historical archaeology. However, fundamentalist Christian beliefs in the absolute religious truth of the texts often result in spurious pseudo-scientific claims about 'archaeological' evidence, which are as patently absurd, in a scientific sense, as claims made by alternative archaeologists for space men, aliens and Phoenicians visiting Australia.[46]

A number of Australians are involved in biblical archaeology. Diggings Tours, an organisation established and run by Australian David Down with other staff in the United Kingdom, Israel, Turkey and Jordan, lies at the archaeologically respectable end of the scale. It organises visits to archaeological sites in what it describes as the 'Bible Lands' of the Middle East, and publishes a popular bi-monthly magazine, *Archaeological Diggings*, which describes itself as 'Australia's top magazine of ancient history and archaeology'.[47] Many articles in the magazine are accounts of places visited on previous Diggings Tours. There is emphasis on the Bible, but other archaeological sites are discussed. The content is fairly descriptive and factual, and the authors actively distance themselves from the more outlandish claims of other Biblical archaeologists. For example, a recent copy of the magazine published an article by Down openly critical of American adventurer Ron Wyatt who, among other things, excavated in the grounds of the Garden Tomb in Jerusalem where Christ was supposed to have been buried and claimed he had found the Ark of the Covenant.[48] Yet Down and his organisation still view the archaeology of the Near East from a specifically fundamentalist Christian perspective. Archaeology is used primarily to support and promote their own religious beliefs—for example, in lectures delivered to the public at the Sydney Opera House. In this sense, their work is pseudo-science and outside the boundaries of orthodox, professional Near Eastern archaeology.

When another Australian-based Biblical archaeologist, Allen Roberts, claimed to have found the remains of Noah's Ark in Turkey in the early 1990s, he was publicly opposed by scientists amid public furore and high media interest. The Allen Roberts case is by no means unique—people from other countries say they have found the remains of the Ark in different geographical locations. This case is important to Australian archaeology because Roberts is Australian and his statements and actions provoked a chain of subsequent developments in Australia which were widely reported by the Australian media. Details of this particular Noah's Ark find hit the headlines in mid-1992 following a series of unruly public fund-raising lectures delivered by Roberts on behalf of organisations called The Noah's Ark Research Foundation and Ark Search Incorporated. According to Roberts and his associates, their scientific research proved that a boat-shaped geological formation on the side of a mountain at Ararat in Turkey was the fossilised remains of Noah's Ark as described in the Bible.[49]

This interpretation was challenged by several eminent Australian geologists (including Ian Plimer, Colin Murray-Wallace and Alex Ritchie), who pointed out that the formation was in fact an example of a well-known geological feature—a plunging syncline. When scientists raised other objections to Roberts' misuse of scientific evidence at a public meeting in Sydney, they were physically ejected from the room by security guards, and the case attracted much media attention. Plimer is a member of a society called the Australian Skeptics, whose aims include investigating and exposing fraudulent claims about pseudo-scientific and paranormal phenomena from what they describe as a responsible scientific viewpoint, and encouraging Australians and the Australian news media to adopt a critical attitude towards such matters.[50] Plimer's fight with Roberts became an important element of his ongoing campaign to discredit 'creation science' which he views as an abuse and misuse of science. Interviewed in the *Good Weekend* magazine, he stated his motivation as follows:

> I am not out to destroy their beliefs, and I am not anti-religious, as they would make out . . . [b]ut I am out to stop them teaching creationism as science. If you want to accept what they say, that the earth was formed 10,000 years ago, that Noah's ark physically existed and so on, then you have to throw not only all geology, but all astronomy, all physics, all biology into the garbage can. It is anti-science, and as one of the share-holders of knowledge I am employed by the community to rigorously attack it wherever I come across it.[51]

The case re-entered the news in 1997 when Plimer joined forces with another biblical archaeologist, David Fasold, and took Allen Roberts to court. Fasold claimed that Roberts and Ark Search Incorporated had breached copyright legislation by reproducing his drawings of the so called archaeological site without permission. Fasold and Plimer also alleged that Roberts was in breach of trades practices and fair trading legislation in making false or misleading claims during lectures to paying members of the public. Not surprisingly, the case was widely reported in the media. The judge ruled that Roberts had engaged in misleading and deceptive conduct, but that Roberts could not, and should not, be prosecuted under the *Fair Trading Act*, commenting that he did not think the court system should be used to provide a remedy for every false or misleading statement made in the course of public debate on matters of general interest.[52] Plimer had made his point, but the case cost him a lot of money.

Collectors of curios and antiquities
Collecting exotic and unusual items from archaeological sites and ancient places is another important area of amateur interest in archaeology and ancient history. Tom Griffiths has described how, before the introduction of heritage legislation in the 1960s made it illegal, there was thriving and active interest in Australia's Indigenous artefacts by many amateur collectors.[53] Most collectors were interested in ancient Indigenous objects for scientific and cultural reasons, rather than for making money. Ground and flaked stone tools were the primary focus, and items were either picked up where they were found lying on the ground or excavated from known sites. Many Australians, especially those who live and work in rural areas, still commonly find Aboriginal grindstones, axes and other items on their land, which they collect and keep. Such activity is illegal in those states where legislation classifies such items as 'relics' and prohibits people from removing, damaging or destroying them without a permit, even on private land. For both practical and political reasons, the government turns a blind eye to such minor contraventions of the legislation. Collections which were acquired before legislation was introduced are legal and items from these are commonly displayed in small private museums in many rural areas and small country towns.

Today worldwide more collectors than ever before are interested in exotic ancient objects and artworks (antiquities) from overseas countries.

Such items are valued for their perceived aesthetic, artistic and monetary value. In recent years many governments have become concerned about the loss and destruction of their history and cultural heritage caused by large-scale trade in such items, and have introduced legislation and signed international conventions to regulate and limit such trade. Antiquities can fetch large sums of money, and there is a thriving illegal trade in them.[54]

Within Australia, the attention of amateur collectors has shifted from Indigenous stone tools to historic items of European origin from ships wrecked around our coast, and old bottles from historic sites on land. The damaging and destructive activities of such amateur collectors pose considerable problems for cultural heritage managers. As noted earlier, Heritage Victoria is currently experimenting with a scheme to educate and work with bottle collectors whose illegal diggings physically threaten historic sites in that state, and legislation protecting historic shipwrecks from the illegal and damaging removal of significant items has been introduced across Australia.[55]

Australian archaeology and public education

Informal education about archaeology occurs in many contexts, as already discussed. However, public education also involves more formal teaching and learning in institutional settings, such as universities, colleges, schools, museums and visitor centres.[56]

School and university education
At least eleven Australian universities currently offer degrees and courses in archaeology. Several others teach cultural heritage management and related subjects with some archaeology content. Adult education courses in archaeology are also available through some universities and educational organisations such as community colleges and the Workers' Educational Association. According to Sue Feary, as much non-Australian archaeology is taught in Australian universities as is Australian Indigenous, historical and maritime archaeology.[57] Since 1990 successive funding cuts, staff retirements and restructuring in Australian universities have had a major impact on course content and teaching methods. Only some departments now have enough staff and resources to offer both a broad range and in-depth coverage of Australian (or other) archaeology to all students. Such changes have had most

impact on historical and maritime archaeology, which are less well represented in university courses than Australian Indigenous archaeology.[58]

Some archaeology is taught in Australian schools. Exactly what depends on the nature of the school curriculum in different states and territories, the knowledge and interests of individual teachers and the availability of teaching resources. Little if any Indigenous archaeology is included in Aboriginal studies curricula, the contents of which are generally based on consultation with Indigenous people and focus mainly on traditional culture, recent history and contemporary social and political issues. In New South Wales the only part of the curriculum in which any archaeology is compulsory is the present Years 11 and 12 ancient history syllabus taken by students aged sixteen to eighteen and who are finishing high school. This requires students to examine methods used by historians and archaeologists to investigate the past, and covers archaeological ethics and the role of science. According to archaeologist and high school educator Helen Nicholson, case studies can include Australian Indigenous or European historic sites (in part for pragmatic reasons of access to local materials and sites), but most teachers opt for overseas examples, such as Pompeii, Thera and Chinese warriors.[59]

Few ancient history teachers have any training in archaeology and if they don't really understand it, they can't teach it to their students. Indeed, it seems odd that Australian archaeology, comprising Indigenous prehistory and colonial history and historical archaeology, should feature in an ancient history syllabus at all. Helen Nicholson comments that even when teachers say they are using archaeology to teach ancient history, they are often using it in a very limited way. Many teachers, in common with other members of the Australian public, still think archaeology is something that happens overseas and is about coins and wall paintings at places like Pompeii and Thera. There are also few Australian text books suitable for teaching archaeology. Most are now dated, or they are about history rather than archaeology. An exception is the more recent publication by Louise Zarmati and Aedeen Cremin, *Experience Archaeology*, which is closely based on the NSW ancient history syllabus and includes case studies using archaeological ethics and methods from all over the world, including Australia.[60] Most teachers otherwise tend to pick cases from what is easily available in their school library, or in magazines like *National Geographic*. This limits the types of archaeology that get taught.

Archaeology and Australian museums

Australian museums play a relatively minor role in educating the public about archaeology, especially Australian archaeology. Small private museums with collections of Indigenous artefacts often emphasise traditional aspects of pre-contact Indigenous life and culture and present a colonialist view of Australia's past, which is not often based on archaeology. In state-sponsored museums archaeology of any kind is simply not a major part of their exhibitions and educational programmes. In New South Wales a major exception is Sydney University's Nicholson Museum. This was founded in 1860 to house a large private collection of Etruscan, Greek, Roman and Egyptian antiquities belonging to the then provost, Sir Charles Nicholson. As well as being the research and teaching collection of Sydney University's Department of Classical and Near Eastern archaeology, the museum organises fundraising and public education programmes through its Society of Friends of the Nicholson Museum, and a highly popular schools education programme which attracts hundreds of students each year from over 100 schools in the Sydney region. In Victoria, Melbourne's Australian Institute of Archaeology also plays an important role in educating the wider public about archaeology.[61]

In contrast, Sydney's Australian Museum is primarily devoted to Australian and Pacific natural history and anthropology collections. The museum is the legal repository for Aboriginal 'relics' (as defined by the *National Parks and Wildlife Act*) excavated by archaeologists in New South Wales, and houses extensive Aboriginal archaeological collections. The museum also employs archaeological research staff, several of whom work in Australia. Despite this, Australian Indigenous archaeology has formed at most a very minor component of the Australian Museum's exhibition and education programmes since the mid-1990s. This stems partly from the museum's policy of employing Indigenous staff to educate the public about Indigenous aspects of its activities and collections. Museum policy is also to consult Indigenous people about the content of exhibitions with Indigenous themes. For reasons explained elsewhere, archaeology is largely irrelevant to the way most Indigenous people want to represent their culture and history to the public.

In addition, the content of the schools education programmes offered by the Australian Museum's education section depends on what teachers want, and this rarely includes Australian Indigenous archaeology.[62] At the same time, the Australian Museum has hosted several travelling exhibitions about overseas archaeological projects, including Pompeii, Egyptian mummies and Tuscan antiquities, which have attracted many visitors. In common with many other Australian public institutions, the Australian Museum is under increasing pressure to justify its budget, and high visitor numbers are viewed as a good thing. Australian Indigenous archaeology is simply not competitive in this respect with Egyptian mummies or Mediterranean pottery.

The Museum of Sydney (MoS), on the site of First Government House, is unusual in an Australian context for being specially created to house and interpret finds from a major historical archaeological excavation which also recovered small numbers of Indigenous stone tools. Current museum displays include much about Indigenous history and culture, but almost nothing about the way archaeology can contribute to understanding such subjects. The way the MoS has represented Indigenous issues is part of its postmodern approach to presenting material from the archaeological dig overall and, as noted, this has been unpopular with some archaeologists.[63] A museum which has taken a very different postmodern approach from the MoS to presenting archaeology and a range of other topics is the Strahan Wharf Centre in south-west Tasmania, designed by Tasmanian writer and historian Richard Flanagan. In designing the content for the centre's exhibition, Flanagan aimed to provoke visitors into confronting issues of historical and current relevance to the region, such as conflicts over logging and 'wilderness', and notions of Aboriginality in Tasmania. The role of archaeology in such issues is woven into the displays. Flanagan describes the centre as an 'anti-Museum'.[64]

Education, consultation and consulting archaeology

Most public education about Australian archaeology occurs outside universities, schools and museums. Government authorities responsible for the management of Aboriginal and European cultural places often include at least some reference to archaeology in their visitor interpretation programmes in cases where research has produced interesting and significant results. Cultural heritage managers and consulting archaeologists are frequently involved in educating the public about archaeology as part of their day-to-day work. Education is an intrinsic part of community consultation, which is now mandatory for all archaeology on Indigenous sites and increasingly common for non-Indigenous sites. Some consulting archaeology projects have involved extensive public education and visitor programmes. The programme instigated by the Sydney Harbour Foreshore Authority (SHFA) and archaeological consulting company Godden Mackay Logan at the Cumberland/Gloucestershire Streets excavations at the Rocks was highly successful in informing and educating people about the meaning and significance of local archaeology, as noted by SHFA historical archaeologist and heritage manager Wayne Johnson. According to Johnson, whereas fifteen years ago passers-by at urban excavations in Sydney would probably have asked 'Have you found any treasure?', now people are more likely to ask if the archaeologists have uncovered anything significant, implying a slightly more sophisticated understanding of the archaeological process.[65]

For reasons of practicality and ethics, only some consulting projects can accommodate site visits and extensive public education programmes. While not all states require community consultation for removal of non-Indigenous remains, in New South Wales present government policies require extensive consultation with descendants and relatives when human skeletons are threatened by development work.[66] In recent cases in which historic cemeteries have been excavated by archaeologists, at the Prince of Wales Hospital site in Sydney and the Cadia Cemetery near Orange in New South Wales, relatives and descendants approved the excavation and research work being carried out, but they insisted on minimal publicity, no public visits and strictly controlled media access. In both cases, after the work was completed the human skeletal remains were reburied else-where with a religious ceremony.[67] Here non-Indigenous concerns about the study and treatment of human skeletal remains in Australia have seemingly been strongly influenced by the way Indigenous Australians view this issue.

An unstated assumption behind much discussion of public education and archaeology in Australia is that the public *should* be more interested in the archaeology of Australia than in what happens overseas, and that if people were better informed about what Australian archaeology is, they would be more interested in it and there would be more support and funds for Australian archaeologists.[68] For a variety of reasons, many of which have been discussed already, this seems somewhat naive. While education about archaeology is a very important part of the process of community consultation over archaeological projects, the whole notion of consultation is based on the community's right to reject the archaeology if they so wish. As discussed in earlier chapters of this book, many Indigenous people are knowledgeable about archaeology and reject it nevertheless. Education in such contexts is about enabling people to make better informed decisions about archaeology, not necessarily convincing them that they should support a particular piece of research.

Archaeology and the media

The media is central to shaping and reflecting public understanding of archaeology in Australia. Much of this book has already referred to archaeology and the media. Information about and from press reports, letters to newspapers, films, radio and television reports and Internet sites is woven through the previous chapters. Yet media representations of archaeology cannot always be taken at face value. In common with other archaeological texts (including this book), media reports reflect the motives and viewpoints of the writers, journalists and organisations who produce them. Postmodern approaches regard the production of archaeological knowledge to be primarily about writing and otherwise representing the past and the archaeological enterprise.[1]

Jinmium and early dates

In 1996 the Jinmium rock shelter in the Northern Territory became infamous for its role in the debate over the date of early human settlement in Australia. Jinmium was excavated by Richard Fullagar and Lesley Head as part of a long-term government-funded research project into the archaeology, environmental history and changing land-use patterns of the Keep River area of the Northern Territory. In 1996 Fullagar and Head, with dating specialist David Price, submitted an article for publication in the Cambridge-based international peer-reviewed archaeology journal *Antiquity*. They claimed thermoluminescence evidence for flaked stone artefacts from Jinmium demonstrated human presence in Australia at least 116 000 years ago. Claims were also made, in conjunction with Paul Taçon, for very early dates for Indigenous rock art at the site.[2]

While the detailed justification for such claims was awaiting publication in *Antiquity*, the team discussed their work with selected members of the Australian media for a news release to be published after the *Antiquity* issue. The claims were so startling that they attracted a wave of media attention in Australia and overseas. If correct, the Jinmium finds almost doubled the previously oldest date mooted for human settlement of Australia of between 50 000 to 60 000 years, claimed by Rhys Jones and Bert Roberts and based on thermoluminescence (TL) and optically stimulated luminescence (OSL) dates from the Malakunanja II and Nauwalabila rock shelters, also in the Northern Territory.[3]

Such dates are important to worldwide theories of human evolution. As explained by John Mulvaney and Johan Kamminga in their 1999 book, there are currently two general scientific views on this topic. The 'multiregional,' or 'regional continuity', view suggests that today's modern humans (*Homo sapiens*) evolved from more archaic *Homo erectus* populations across Africa, Asia and Europe. In contrast, the 'out-of-Africa' hypothesis suggests that modern humans evolved to *Homo erectus* in Africa, and spread from there to the rest of the world where they displaced more archaic forms. Under this theory, it is generally thought that modern humans started to move out of Africa some 150 000 to 100 000 years ago and only reached South East Asia well within the last 100 000 years, from where they then made a water crossing to Australia. Although this question has been the subject of much recent debate, proponents of the out-of-Africa model argue that Australia was settled by fully modern humans. Dates of less than 100 000 years for the earliest human settlement of Australia concur with such a theory.[4] If people were living in northern Australia as early as 116 000 years ago, as was being claimed by the Jinmium researchers, this could upset the more widely accepted out-of-Africa hypothesis.

Some media reports about Jinmium said, totally erroneously, that the site proved people were in Australia as long as 170 000 years ago. The researchers never made this claim. Confusion arose because Fullagar, Price and Head had reported a thermoluminescence date of 170 000 years for archaeologically sterile deposits beneath the earliest evidence of human occupation. Australian archaeologists commonly produce a series of dates throughout the depth of their excavations, including for the underlying soil. The 170 000-years-old date had nothing to do with human occupation at Jinmium, yet it was quite wrongly reported as such by some of the media, and even by some archaeologists.[5]

Several researchers questioned the reliability of the Jinmium evidence. Research published in scientific journals since strongly suggests that Jinmium is probably no more than 20 000 years old because the original samples were contaminated and the dating method used was less reliable than others which have since been applied.[6]

Making the findings public

Reflecting on Jinmium media coverage in the Australian cultural studies journal *Meanjin*, Lesley Head claimed that from the Jinmium team's perspective there was 'no way to whisper to Australia in 1996 that people might have been here more than 100 000 years ago'. Because of the perceived public significance of very old dates for Indigenous settlement of Australia, Jinmium was as important to Indigenous people and other Australians as it was to researchers. Head discussed the team's obligations to local Indigenous communities and traditional owners who had consented to the work. The researchers wished to inform the wider Indigenous community of their findings in a culturally appropriate way while minimising possible media misrepresentation. According to Head, they pondered how to release their news to the public in a way least likely to produce 'the sort of treasure hunt view of archaeology that we and dozens of our colleagues spend much time trying to dispel'.[7] They planned to inform the public at the same time as the research findings were published in the scientific literature, and agreed to give their story to journalist James Woodford for publication in the *Sydney Morning Herald*, and to provide materials for a half-hour documentary for regional Indigenous radio station Waringarri 6WR, based in Kununurra, Western Australia, which broadcasts to more than 30 remote outback communities.

For reasons which Head claims were neither the fault of the archaeologists nor the journalists, news of the find was made public several weeks before the *Antiquity* article was published. The *Sydney Morning Herald* and Waringarri Radio reported the story almost immediately, to avoid losing it to rival media organisations. James Woodford's exclusive report was the leading front-page story in the *Sydney Morning Herald* on Saturday 21 September 1996, under the headline 'Unveiled: outback Stonehenge that will rewrite our history'.[8] Inside the paper, the News Review Special section carried extensive coverage of Jinmium over several pages with many coloured illustrations, under headlines such as 'Unearthed. Australia's Lost Civilization', 'The arrival of man and nature of art', 'We believe it is better to present the evidence' and 'The people behind the discoveries'. The story then hit the rest of the Australian media, including as main item on the ABC television national evening news, which may be a first for Australian archaeology. It also went worldwide, on the front page of the *New York Times* and in the main BBC television evening news in the United Kingdom, and prompted comment in major international scientific journals *Nature* and *Science*.[9]

Fallout

Leading national newspaper the *Australian* then published a series of articles highly critical of the Jinmium claims and the supposed motives of the archaeologists involved. The paper was openly critical of the research team for releasing the story to the media before it was published in a peer-reviewed journal. The fact that rival newspaper the *Sydney Morning Herald* got the story first presumably had more than a little to do with the often vitriolic and highly personal tone of much subsequent coverage in the *Australian*. Science correspondent Graeme Leech's article entitled 'Challenge to the origin of man. Scientists split over rock find's implications for evolution' was the lead story in the *Australian* on Monday 23 September 1996. The article reported the facts of the find and their implications. It also quoted Rhys Jones and Australian National University (ANU) dating specialist Rainer Grun's doubts about the accuracy of the dating methods used. The following day the front page of the *Australian* carried an article further attacking the Jinmium dating methods, citing University of New England archaeologist and rock art specialist Mike Morwood. Morwood stated that he had been asked by the journal *Antiquity* to referee Fullagar, Head and Price's paper as part of the normal peer review procedure, and had recommended against publication on the grounds that the dating evidence was extremely tenuous and that once published it would be widely and wrongly quoted. In its Opinion section, the same issue of the *Australian* also published articles by Morwood and archaeologist Claire Smith, both expressing doubt about the Jinmium claim.[10]

Despite Morwood's reported reservations, the then editor of *Antiquity*, Christopher Chippindale, decided he would go ahead and publish

Fullagar, Head and Price's article anyway. In his accompanying editorial, Chippindale noted that the question 'How long have people lived in Australia?' was not proven one way or the other, and that resolution of such questions was built on 'debate, argument and disagreement as well as on agreement'. He commented that his decision to publish this article was no more contentious than many others, and was based on normal procedures and considerations.[11] There is no requirement that all referees must agree with each other before an article can be published in an archaeological journal. Such matters of policy are left to the discretion of the editor or the editorial board of the journal. Articles are commonly rejected by one journal and subsequently accepted by another. (This touches on broader issues, by no means confined to the Jinmium case, about the extent to which the peer review process guarantees the scientific or other academic credibility of all published work.)

The *Australian* (23 September 1996) also published a front-page article by Nicholas Rothwell about the politics of the Jinmium find. Rothwell criticised the way public release of the story, to the *Sydney Morning Herald* alone, had been 'tightly managed' and 'splashily presented'. He also attacked the archaeologists and the *Sydney Morning Herald* for their pro-Indigenous political stand, indicated for example by the rival newspaper's large and prominently displayed coloured photograph of an Indigenous person's hand lying across the Jinmium rock art. According to Rothwell, readers were here looking at 'the last triumphant stage in a more alarming process: the politicisation of Australian archaeology', and commented that it would be hard to imagine an archaeological research project that tended to work against Indigenous interests. The article prompted public response in the form of letters to the editor, some of them expressing pro-Indigenous sentiments. The *Sydney Morning Herald* subsequently published an article by Paul Taçon and Richard Fullagar pointing out the highly political nature of all archaeology, and some of the key issues in the relationship between Australian archaeologists and Indigenous people.[12]

An editorial in the *Australian* on 24 September 1996 was somewhat more conciliatory. Noting criticism (albeit mostly by the *Australian* itself) of the way the Jinmium find was initially publicised as a 'managed' media event, the editor commented that from the scientific community's viewpoint:

... the key issue here is whether interaction with mainstream journalism before *Antiquity's* publication of the Jinmium material interferes with the process of peer review and presentation. It does seem naive to believe that once the journal article had been published there would not anyway have been an international news media flurry. How much difference does a few months and an amount of 'background noise' from public discussion make to the scientific process?[13]

The next day the *Australian* carried a front-page article by Maria Ceresa reporting her visit to Jinmium, which mainly commented on local Indigenous connections with the site. An article on page two of the same paper by John Ellicott reported further doubts about the scientific dates.[14]

Other angles

Other Australian newspapers placed their own angle on the story. For example, Sunday newspaper the *Sun Herald* (which is aimed at a broader audience than the *Sydney Morning Herald* or the *Australian*) announced, next to a close-up picture of Lesley Head clutching a large stone tool, that 'The first man was an Aussie'.[15] The dubious logic of such a claim was not explained. The article reported the Jinmium evidence as fact, with no discussion of any of the doubts surrounding it. Regional newspaper the *Canberra Times* explained the issues in some detail, at the same time emphasising local connections. One article by science reporter Cheryl Jones featured a prominent photograph of Canberra-based ANU biological anthropologist Colin Groves with comments from him on the case. A second report under the headline 'ACT settlement could predate NT site' noted that during the 1980s bio-geographer Gurdip Singh had claimed a 125 000-year-old date for human occupation at Lake George near Canberra, which matched the Jinmium claim.[16]

Several months later, long after the story had been dropped by other media outlets, the *Australian* published a mainly human interest article by Graeme Leech about the possible motives of the Jinmium team, and of Richard Fullagar in particular, in first publicising and then standing by their dates for Jinmium in the face of so much opposition.[17] The article came in the wake of further assessment and rejection of the Jinmium dates by other scientists, including at a public debate held at the Australian Museum in Sydney at which Fullagar faced a number of his professional critics. While making some attempt at a wider analysis of the politics of current archaeological employment practices, in which some researchers are insecurely employed on short-term contracts while others have the luxury of academic tenure, the tone of the article was highly personal. Much of it could be interpreted as a thinly veiled attack on the professional integrity of Fullagar and the rest of the team. In addition, details about Fullagar's age, appearance and personality were discussed in such a way that if the article had been written about a woman there would probably have been complaints to the newspaper about sexist stereotyping.

In broader perspective

Australian press coverage of Jinmium has many of the hallmarks of media attitudes towards archaeology in the United States as described in the late 1980s by Frederick West. West found, for example, that archaeology stories in the *New York Times* and *Science* were frequently not just about the date of early settlement of the Americas (a question which has prompted great public interest) but also about fights between personalities involved in such debates.[18] This sounds all too familiar. According to West, the US press wanted to report controversy in archaeology, with emphasis on 'human content' and simplistic and easy explanations. West, who regards archaeology as being about 'science', argued that the press was a poor place to conduct archaeology, as this too easily compromised its objectivity.

However, a major argument of this book is that archaeological knowledge is rarely objective. The Jinmium case reflects a number of issues already raised in this book, some of which are also discussed by Head. These include the political significance of providing hard scientific evidence for an early date for Indigenous settlement of Australia, which many Indigenous people feel is important in demonstrating to the wider community the legitimacy of their claims to land and culture. Early scientific dates for Indigenous presence in Australia also form a component of Australia's sense of national identity through the non-Indigenous appropriation of such antiquity.[19]

Also important in the Jinmium story is that it was an Australian archaeological find which was significant to world prehistory and therefore of 'common human interest'. Such a find asserts the place of Australian research on the world map and bolsters national pride, although many Indigenous Australians have problems with such ideas. As will be discussed in Chapter 8, answering the question 'How old is settlement?' relies on a mix of scientific and archaeological evidence, the interpretation of which is complex. This research area provides a good forum for those archaeologists who enjoy the cut and thrust of competitive debate, often played out in the media as well as academia, in which there can be only one winner—the person with the oldest date. As discussed by Stephanie Moser (in an Australian context) and Joan Gero (in a North American one), more male than female archaeologists seem to enjoy such competition.[20]

Jinmium media coverage also tapped into undercurrents within the discipline of Australian archaeology itself. Some of this involved disagreement among rock art specialists. It also touched on long-term changes to funding for archaeology in which researchers have come under increasing pressure in recent years to 'publish or perish'. This especially applies to those on short-term employment contracts.[21]

Numerous other stories about Australian archaeology get reported in the newspapers and on television before they get published in peer-reviewed journals, if they ever get published at all. Few if any of these raise any such debate. The main sin committed by the Jinmium team seems to be that they actively courted maximum publicity for their work. They chose to publish in the British-based journal *Antiquity*, which has a wider readership than local Australian journals. And they actively cooperated with a highly glossy, sensationalist and one-sided public presentation of their work by the *Sydney Morning Herald*, which failed to mention, at least initially, that other researchers had serious doubts about their results. Because the Jinmium find was potentially of such great public and scientific significance, some elements of the media made much fuss about the team's 'unethical' behaviour in talking to the press before their work was published. Yet one cannot imagine many newspapers, including the *Australian*, refusing to publish a good story because this would transgress the protocol of scientific publication. In this case it seems the Jinmium researchers fell foul of rivalry between two Australian newspapers owned by competing media interests.

More Australian stories

Other stories about early dates have also attracted media attention but in different ways and with different impacts from Jinmium. In 1998, for example, Mike Morwood and colleagues reported in the respected scientific journal *Nature* on new finds from the site of Mata Menge on the island of Flores, Indonesia.[22] Here stone artefacts and fossilised animal bones had been dated on the basis of stratigraphy and the zircon fission-track method to between 800 000 and 900 000 years ago. The researchers argued the artefacts were made by the hominid species *Homo erectus* who had reached Flores by boat. This claim is even more startling and has greater worldwide significance than early dates for Jinmium. It is generally thought that *H. erectus* did not have the ability to make boats—and that seafaring of this kind, which has also been associated by some researchers with the development of language, was solely a feature of more advanced modern humans. The Flores story was widely reported in the media but with no great drama. In part this was because the research had already been presented in a scientific journal. More significantly, while the finds have some relevance to Australian prehistory, the site is not in Australia, nor is the work about Indigenous Australians, so the wider socio-political implications of the find are very different from Jinmium.

Contrast this with another story which gained media coverage in the late 1990s and early 2000s relating to new research on a human burial at Lake Mungo in the Willandra Lakes region of western New South Wales. The burial (known variously as Mungo 3, Mungo III, WLH3, LM3 and Mungo Man) was first reported by Jim Bowler and excavated by Alan Thorne in 1974. In fact there are several stories here. In 1999 Thorne and his colleagues reported a date of up to 62 000 years for the burial. This was published in the respected international scientific publication *Journal of Human Evolution*. The date was some 20 000 or so years older than the approximate 43 000 years previously reported by Bowler in 1998. Bowler immediately published a paper with John Magee in the next issue of *Journal of Human Evolution* disputing Thorne's new date. A second paper in the same issue by dating specialists Richard Gillespie and Bert Roberts also dismissed the new date as being too old.[23]

In January 2001, a paper was published in the prestigious North American journal *Proceedings of the National Academy of Sciences* by Thorne and a group of Australian molecular geneticists from several research institutions. They described their work in extracting and analysing ancient mitochondrial DNA (mtDNA) from the Mungo 3 skeleton, described in the paper as being around 60 000 years old, and comparing it with mtDNA they had extracted from other ancient skeletons from south-east Australia, ranging in age from around 15 000 to less than 2000 years old.[24] The results were also compared with previous mtDNA samples taken by other researchers from ancient burials in Europe and from living populations across the world, including Indigenous Australians. Among other things, these data were interpreted to suggest that the Mungo 3 skeleton, which is a fully modern *H. sapiens*, possessed genetic material which is now extinct. According to Thorne, this supports the regional continuity rather than the out-of-Africa model for modern human origins. The out-of-Africa model proposes that *H. sapiens* arose only in Africa and spread from there across the world. If this were so, then Mungo 3's genetic material should be like that of other modern human populations. The new study shows it is different.

The research findings were reported as headline news ('DNA clue to man's origin. How Mungo Man has shaken the human family tree') in the *Australian* on 9 January 2001 by science journalist Leigh Dayton. The same edition carried editorial comment, a cartoon by Judy Horacek on the back page, and a colourfully illustrated News Feature article, spread over two pages, also by Dayton ('Mungo Man: The last of his kind?'). Further reports appeared in the *Australian* and in other newspapers over the next week or so by Dayton and others. Many follow-up reports presented differing and dissenting views about the significance of the new research for theories of human evolution. In particular, Bowler, writing in the *Australian* on 10 January 2001, disputed the claimed 60 000-year-old date for Mungo 3.[25] Others argued about the extent to which the DNA analysis really did refute the out-of-Africa model. Many failed to be convinced by Thorne's interpretation. While no one doubted the importance of the DNA analysis, some disputed the Mungo 3 date. Several commented on other possible interpretations of what the DNA results might mean.[26]

Molecular genetics is a specialist area of knowledge. The original research paper in *Proceedings of the National Academy of Sciences* described technical data and consisted of tightly worded arguments primarily aimed at other scientists. For anyone not familiar with the subject matter, the paper is hard to read and evaluate. In presenting this research to a wider audience through her articles for the *Australian*, Dayton translated the results into plain English, interviewed several of the team involved, asked them to explain their work, and sought opinion from other researchers—including those with dissenting views. Colourful diagrams and annotated maps helped explain the major theories of human evolution and genetics. Illustrations were an important element in the *Australian* coverage and elsewhere. Photographs of early human skeletons, including the Mungo 3 burial itself, artists' reconstructions of what our human ancestors may have looked like and photographs of Thorne and DNA specialist Simon Easteal humanised the story. Cartoons in several newspapers added humorous social commentary—poking fun in one case at Australia's middle-class 'coffee drinking set' and in another at 'beer-swilling ockers'. Another cartoon suggested that Biblical Eve was an Australian and another showed a white-coated scientist chopping down the tree of human evolution with an axe.[27]

Another part of this Mungo 3 story concerned the response of Indigenous people, some of whom are highly offended by the display and publication of images of Indigenous human remains. Soon after the story was reported in the *Australian* and other newspapers, Gary Pappin for the Willandra Lakes World Heritage Area Three Traditional Tribal Groups Elders Council issued a press release taking issue with the *Australian* on several counts. Of major concern was the publication of photographs of the Mungo burial:

> The photographic depiction of human remains causes deep and lasting offence to many Aboriginal people who feel it is not appropriate to thus display their ancestors. The use of the photograph of Mungo III in his excavated grave is consequently deeply offensive to us, as it would have been to many other Aboriginal people across Australia. The photograph served no public interest except to fuel European people's morbid fascination with other people's dead and to indicate the media's disrespect for our beliefs.[28]

In the same press release the Elders Council also objected to the published articles, 'including some inane and pointless cartoons (cf. the *Australian* 15/01/01) [which] infer that Mungo III is not one of our ancestors. We refute this suggestion in the strongest possible terms. Mungo Man is one of our forebears and belongs in his traditional country, not in a vault or office in Canberra.'

This echoes sentiments previously reported in May 1999 in the *Sydney Morning Herald* when Thorne announced his earlier research on the early date for the Mungo 3 burial. Under the headline 'Lay ancient Mungo's bones to final rest, say custodians', the article reported the concerns of various Indigenous people from the Willandra Lakes region that burials previously excavated by scientists were still being stored in Canberra. Referring specifically to the Mungo Lady (Mungo 1) and Mungo Man (Mungo 3) burials, Mrs Alice Kelly, an elder of the Mutthi Mutthi people, was quoted as saying, 'We want her to be put right back where she came from . . . I want him brought back and put down in the same place.' One of Mrs Kelly's daughters, Joyce Smith, was also quoted as saying that Mungo Lady, currently stored in a vault at Lake Mungo after the remains were returned to the community by Thorne in 1992, should be reburied. Mutthi Mutthi women particularly wanted to rebury Mungo Lady with appropriate ceremony. According to Smith, 'They just have to take this one more step in putting this very sacred person to rest. She has given so much to our people and she's given the scientific world a hell of a lot, too.'[29]

The 2001 Mungo Man research and media coverage of it are both similar and different from Jinmium. Because the scientists did not commit the 'sin' of breaking this story to the media before it was published in a peer-reviewed journal, this was not relevant here. Major rivalry between the *Sydney Morning Herald* and the *Australian* was not an issue—maybe because in this case the *Australian* got the story first. The initial reportage by Dayton, while strongly promoting Thorne's role in the research, did not suggest that everyone agreed with him about its significance for models of human evolution. The science here is complex. In translating it for a public audience most journalists clearly explained that scientific knowledge is created by carefully balancing evidence.

The story also broke in mid-January, during what is often called the 'silly season', when the Australian parliament is in recess, schools are closed and many Australians are still on summer holidays following the Christmas and New Year break. At that time there was little other news to fill the headlines. This undoubtedly helped promote this story to the front page. While the finds were undoubtedly important and newsworthy, if the story had broken later in the year it would have had to compete with such topics as rising petrol prices, economic issues and an impending Federal election.

Some media coverage reported Indigenous perspectives on the Mungo 3 research in a sympathetic way, but the publication of pictures of an Indigenous human skeleton on the front page of a national newspaper clearly offended many people's sensibilities in this case.

Pre-Cook ships

Other kinds of early dates frequently attract media attention. The Australian public are seemingly very interested in shipwrecks and related finds that suggest that James Cook was not the first European to visit the east coast of Australia. The most famous example of such evidence is the Mahogany Ship, which has taken on almost mythological significance in the Warrnambool area of Victoria. In brief, the remains of an old wooden shipwreck were exposed along the coast between Warrnambool and Port Fairy in 1836 but were reburied and 'lost' again by the 1880s. Many people believe that the Mahogany Ship is a Portuguese caravel known from documentary records to have been wrecked and lost in 1522. If the wreck were the lost Portuguese ship, it would indicate that Europeans were here at least 250 years before Cook's historically documented voyage. The ship has aroused great public interest and features strongly in tourism promotion for the region and for Warrnambool in particular. Such is its appeal that former Victorian Premier Jeff Kennett put up a $250 000 reward for whoever proved its existence. Ian McNiven describes the Mahogany Ship as the 'Lassiter's gold of Australian archaeology'[30] and the ship is seemingly rarely out of the news and the media for long. Local and regional newspaper reports about the ship date back to the 1880s[31] and an Internet search for 'Mahogany Ship' using a popular Australian search engine in early 2001 scored over 175 hits.

The Mahogany Ship was in the news again when long-time shipwreck enthusiast and local resident Des Williams discovered a piece of wood under sand in Armstrong Bay near Warrnambool in 1999. The find was investigated by Williams and by archaeologists from the state's heritage agency, Heritage Victoria, in August 2000. Archaeological excavation exposed a piece of timber about 2 metres long. In a media release, the chair of Victoria's Heritage Council described the new find as being 'possibly the best lead this century to the location of the elusive "ancient wreck"'. This conclusion was based on the location and depth of the wood, its identification by CSIRO scientists as European oak (all other known finds of wood in the area have been native timber species) and the likelihood that the wood was part of a ship—rather than cargo. However, none of this yet proves that the wood is from a sixteenth-century Portuguese vessel and further research is needed. Another ship, *Falls of Halladale*, was wrecked at Peterborough in 1908 and is known to have carried oak in its cargo. The find could derive from this ship or even another wreck.[32]

In 1993 another possible 'pre-Cook' ship attracted great media attention. Archaeologist and environmental scientist Bill Boyd was approached by a group of amateur shipwreck enthusiasts who asked him to radio-carbon date a wooden peg which had previously been collected from the remains of an old wooden shipwreck, now buried once more beneath sand dunes, at Suffolk Park in northern New South Wales. As was the case for Jinmium, Boyd released preliminary dates from the find to the media before publishing his work in a peer-reviewed journal. The wood was identified as yew (*Taxus*), which is native to North America, Europe and China, and the radiocarbon age of 370 years plus or minus 50 could date the peg to the seventeenth century—thus supporting the ship's interpretation as 'pre-Cook'. It could also be much more recent, due to uncertainties in converting a radiocarbon age into exact calendar years. Boyd stressed this in his discussion of the evidence. His own further research into the chemical composition of metal and the construction of a rudder retrieved from the same wreck, oral history and documentary evidence now suggest that the wreck dates to the nineteenth century.[33]

Boyd argues he was under pressure to publicise his preliminary results because the dating work had been commissioned and paid for by members of the public interested in the find. His sponsors wanted him to make the date public, even if it was uncertain, and would have done so anyway without him. The story was first released to a local newspaper, then picked up by a local radio station which conducted a live interview with Boyd. The story was reported by regional radio and television with further interviews, then broadcast on national radio and television on several channels. After the story was reported in the *Sydney Morning Herald* and the *Age* in Melbourne, it was picked up by an international press agency and reported in the *China Daily* (a major English-language paper in mainland China) and by the *Darmstader Echo* (a regional German newspaper), and presumably elsewhere. According to Boyd, apart from some sensationalist headlines, most of the media coverage was favourable and well informed. He attributes this largely to his own actions in taking control of the initial media coverage by preparing an appropriate and carefully thought out press release, and engaging the assistance of a press officer at his university.

Boyd was also much luckier in his dealings with the media than the archaeologists involved in the Jinmium case. His claims were unlikely to upset too many of his professional colleagues. As already noted, while claims for pre-Cook ships are of widespread interest to many members of the Australian public, they are not something which attract the serious attention of most mainstream Australian archaeologists.[34]

Representation in news and current affairs

Many Australian archaeologists are interested in the media and its relationship to them and their work, but few have published on the subject or engaged with theoretical issues identified by media studies researchers.[35] There are many kinds of media outlets. Specialist reporters aim at different audiences. The degree to which a media outlet considers itself local, national or international is important to the way stories are reported. For example, the *Australian* addresses a national audience, while other Australian newspapers are state based. Such factors were relevant to the Jinmium case.[36]

'The media' in Australia and worldwide are currently subject to rapid change brought about by new and convergent technologies, and by forces of government and private enterprise such as state regulation of content, concentration of ownership and globalisation.[37] Such changes have already had an impact on archaeology in the public domain. For example, a noticeable feature in writing this book, which was first conceived in 1996 and finished in 2001, was the degree to which the Internet became an indispensable research tool during this time.

Archaeologists' concern about the media is the way the press, television, radio and film misrepresent archaeologists and their work. Essentially, journalists are on the lookout for a good story. This usually means something new, of interest to people and easily understood. Common ingredients of a good story are conflict, human interest or something connected with a well-known or important person.[38] Media reports can and do represent archaeologists in terms of the stereotypes discussed in Chapter 6, and some archaeologists do indeed want to represent themselves and their work this way, and use the media to do so. Because stories need to be understandable, as we have seen there can be a tendency to favour archaeology which is simplistic and statements which are clear and certain. Stated 'facts' about the past usually have greater news appeal than more cautious, and often more accurate, statements from archaeologists about what their finds could mean. Some media coverage implies that archaeology is primarily about digging up facts.

Controversy, often linked to human interest, manifests itself in media reports about disagreements between archaeologists over the significance of some find or other, and about 'scandals' in the archaeology profession itself. Cases reported in the Australian press in the early 1990s included allegations of a 'Cambridge cabal' in the Department of Prehistory at the Australian National University, and accusations of sexual harassment and professional misconduct at the Centre for Prehistory at the University of Western Australia. Here the proponents wanted their stories reported in the media to embarrass other archaeologists—a case of archaeologists washing their dirty linen in public. Such stories are only incidentally about archaeology, and are the regular substance of media reports in other contexts.[39]

Conflicts between Indigenous Australians and scientists over owner-ship of cultural materials and human remains, and the involvement of archaeology in Indigenous land rights claims and environmental issues, have also been widely reported in the media, as has been apparent throughout this book. The media, and archaeologists themselves, often report that an archaeological find is the 'oldest', 'biggest' or 'best' example of its kind. This satisfies the need for something new, and is also easy for an audience to understand. Archaeology is also often reported in connec-tion with stories about people's own history and heritage, to which they have some sense of personal connection.

Archaeologists frequently argue that they need to communicate better with journalists and other members of the industry to assert greater control over the way they are represented in the media.[40] In her study of the coverage of Australian archaeology in the media, Hilary du Cros found a quite variable picture, depending on the type of archaeology involved and the exact nature of the programme or publication concerned. Science reports on ABC radio and television which actively involved archaeolo-gists in programme content, through on-air interviews for example, produced high-quality reports, particularly when the journalists were knowledgeable about archaeology. Du Cros quotes comments from Sydney-based journalist Geraldine O'Brien, who reports regularly on heritage issues. While noting that archaeology stories rarely made front-page or headline news, O'Brien considered that some archaeologists communicated well and were aware of what makes a good story. As discussed in the context of public education in Chapter 6, many Sydney-based historical archaeologists have made careful use of media coverage to educate the public about their work.[41]

Australian archaeology does not feature often on Australian television—outside news and current affairs programmes. A notable exception was an episode of the popular drama series *Water Rats* based on the activities of water police in and around Sydney Harbour. One episode of the programme called 'Let the Dead' involved a stereotypical clash between archaeologists and Aborigines in Sydney Harbour—but also showed that Australian viewers were able to recognise easily what archaeologists are and do and many of the issues involved.[42]

(Mis)representation is a different issue on the Internet. Here archaeologists can and do represent themselves; and so can everyone else. The quantity of information about archaeology and related topics currently available on the Internet is overwhelming and seemingly growing all the time. However, while the Internet and related industries are perhaps the fastest changing areas of the media with relevance to archaeology, books, magazines, radio and television programmes, films and newspapers continue to be important sources of information, and misinformation, in Australia and beyond. This whole subject invites further research from Australian archaeologists interested in their relationship with the wider public.[43]

8

Archaeology, Indigenous Australia and postcolonialism

Different people explain the past in different ways. In recent years forces inside and outside the academy have challenged and eroded public confidence in the absolute value of archaeological knowledge about Australia's past. This raises interesting problems for archaeologists and heritage managers in their dealings with the public. Modernist thinking of the 1960s and 1970s encouraged archaeologists to promote the validity of their own views of the past (the scientific, the orthodox, the academically respectable), while publicly rejecting others (the romantic, the mystical, the scientifically spurious). This view resonates still. For example, writing in 1996 Peter Hiscock argued that archaeologists should actively oppose New Age and pseudo-scientific claims about Australia's past because they are 'wrong'. To Hiscock, even the silence of archaeologists smacks of implicit support for such views, which he categorises as worrying and postmodern.[1]

But surely here a distinction should be made between the misuse of archaeological evidence in pseudo-science to 'prove' things about the past by reference to 'material evidence' and things people essentially believe about places and objects? People who subscribe to New Age philosophies and connect with places through psychic energy and other mystical forces don't need archaeology to prove what they know. Archaeology is also irrelevant to religious understandings of the world—whether these be Christian, Muslim, Buddhist or any other form of spirituality. In Australia this is particularly relevant to Indigenous people's understanding that they were created in Australia as part of the Dreamtime. Spiritual and religious beliefs about place are social or cultural values (to use cultural heritage management jargon). They are not archaeology. Beliefs can never be 'proven' by archaeology, so why should archaeologists make professional judgements or pronouncements about such things at all—whatever they may think about these matters in private and whatever their own beliefs?[2]

However, when people outside the profession and the discipline appropriate the supposed authority of science and archaeology to authenticate their beliefs and ideas in ways which clearly misrepresent archaeologists and their work, then archaeologists have a right to reject or refute such claims, especially when these could be damaging to them and their profession. As discussed in Chapter 6, such was the case when scientists challenged Allen Roberts' misuse of science to authenticate his beliefs about Noah's Ark. The M2 motorway case is slightly different. Here archaeological and historical evidence was used to refute a claim that a rock formation constructed during the Second World War was a precolonial Indigenous stone alignment. All evidence supported the archaeologist's interpretation of the stones—but despite this some people may still have believed the stones were precolonial or sacred. Should archaeologists argue against this view? In this case someone had to balance these different understandings of the place because the stones were threatened with destruction from a freeway development. Were they significant enough to save? Why? This task fell to cultural heritage managers in a government agency. Should they rely only on archaeological evidence when deciding if a place is significant enough to be conserved? To what extent are other social values also important?

If archaeologists choose to speak out in public against the misuse of archaeology through pseudo-science they must face the consequences. A public fight between Near Eastern archaeologists and some amateur Biblical archaeologists may alienate members of the public on whom Near Eastern archaeologists in Australia rely to support their research. This was a risk that Ian Plimer, as a scientist and geologist, did not have to face when he took Allen Roberts to court over claims about Noah's Ark. Within limits, many members of the public who are interested in archaeology don't especially care whether the work is scientifically correct—they are there for the experience. In challenging the rights of amateurs, archaeologists run the risk of seeming arrogant and elitist, or of operating a vindictive witch hunt, which does not necessarily make for good public relations.

If archaeologists speak out against Indigenous misuse of archaeological evidence, there are different consequences. Colonialism has created a situation in which Indigenous claims to 'sacredness' of land and cultural property are frequently contested by the wider Australian society. Western laws often place Indigenous people in the invidious position of having to provide 'evidence' of their beliefs and rights to land.[3] Archaeology as modernist, processual science has often been offered and accepted by the wider Australian society as a means of providing evidence in assessing various Indigenous claims. If archaeologists choose to enter this arena by speaking out in favour of archaeological evidence (which either supports or refutes Indigenous claims), their message and their motives risk being misunderstood by Indigenous people and by politicians, the media and the wider public.

Political issues surrounding representation and Indigenous identity are of far more than just academic interest in Australia—whether they 'speak out' or 'keep silent' archaeologists are already involved. Lesley Head has commented on this situation, and on the intellectual ambiguities, discordance and uncertainties which at least some Australian archaeologists feel about their personal practice of archaeology involving Indigenous places, and the relationship of their discipline with broader Australian society. She notes that such feelings are grounded in the colonial heritage of archaeological practices in Australia, and current and continuing fracturing and questioning of such practices by the forces of feminism, postmodernity and postcolonialism. Wider issues about research and Indigenous peoples, many of which are relevant to archaeology in Australia, have been discussed from an Indigenous perspective by Linda Tuhiwai Smith.[4]

Feelings of discordance and ambiguity are encountered by Australians in many situations. These have been characterised by several writers as outcomes of a loss of confidence in the absolute value of scientific and related forms of academic knowledge (postmodernity) and changes associated with Australia's growing cultural independence from Britain (postcolonialism or decolonisation).[5] Describing the current state of Australia as postcolonial does not mean that colonialism is somehow over and we can leave all that behind us and move on. The roots of contemporary Australian society are firmly planted in the country's status as a former British colony. While Australia is now entirely independent from Britain in a political sense, we live with the legacy of colonialism. This especially applies to Indigenous people, most of whose country continues to be physically colonised by other Australians.

Colonialism has shaped power balances in Australia. One result of British colonisation was to institutionalise and legitimise Western knowledge traditions (e.g. anthropology, archaeology) and empower non-Indigenous people to study Indigenous culture and its material remains, while excluding Indigenous people and devaluing their knowledge.[6] Since the 1970s Indigenous people have regained more control over some aspects of their culture and places. Archaeologists and anthropologists have less power than they did, and the absolute value of purely Western knowledge traditions (such as archaeology) has been publicly challenged. These and similar changes in Australian society are often discussed in terms of both postcolonialism and postmodernity. Such uncertainties and ambiguities exist for many Australians—not just those involved in the production of academic knowledge.[7]

Nevertheless, Indigenous challenges to the hegemony of Western knowledge, and to white people controlling the study and interpretation of their culture and heritage, have created a great deal of uncertainty for many Australian archaeologists. Archaeologists who are sympathetic to the struggle for Indigenous rights question the role of their profession and the knowledge it produces in the continuing denial of Indigenous rights. In Australia such uncertainty goes beyond a mere sense of unease and intellectual disquiet about whether interpretations of the past are 'equal but different' (which seemingly perplexes some archaeologists in other countries—see 'Speaking out, staying silent', p. 185). In this country Indigenous people have been empowered to have greater control over some kinds of archaeological work. As we have seen, this has resulted in the repatriation and reburial of human skeletal remains and cultural materials, and, in extreme cases, the refusal of excavation and field survey permits for research projects. This situation has come about because at least some Australians support the notion that Indigenous people have special rights in relation to their own culture and heritage which override the interests of all others, including those of archaeologists. Other Australians do not agree that Indigenous people have or should have any special rights. This is about the politics of race, not postmodern intellectualising.

Earlier chapters have outlined changes wrought to Australian archaeology by cultural heritage management, Indigenous involvement and wider public attitudes. Most of this discussion has concerned practice, with less about archaeological knowledge—though the two are linked.

This chapter uses case studies to explore some broader connections between archaeological knowledge and practice given the contexts of postmodernity and postcolonialism in which Australian archaeologists work. The cases also draw together themes which have so far been dealt with largely in isolation from each other.

As we have seen in Chapter 1, archaeological knowledge about Australia's past is essentially modernist or scientific. Archaeologists may disagree about exactly how to explain the past, but they still accept a core set of rules about evidence and explanation. Some kinds of archaeological knowledge are more certain or reliable (in a scientific sense), or less ambiguous, than others. This does not mean that such knowledge is more acceptable to non-archaeologists, easier to understand, or less vulnerable to distortion in the public domain. As the case studies show, this depends on the context in which that knowledge is produced and received. The case studies also demonstrate circumstances where archaeologists choose to 'speak out' or 'stay silent' about the nature of their knowledge—especially when it seemingly contradicts or supports other views of the past which have political or social consequences.

Early dates for human settlement

The date of first human settlement of Australia has vexed scholars for some time. As we have seen, this is not only an important academic research question—early dates produced by radiocarbon and similar geophysical methods also have wider public significance in Australia.[8] In essence, most archaeologists agree that people have lived here for at least 40 000 years based on a large number of scientifically reliable radiocarbon dates from well-stratified and undisturbed archaeological contexts. Many archaeologists are now prepared to accept dates of between 50 000 and 60 000 years based on other kinds of physical dating evidence from a few sites, although others question the reliability of this evidence. Environmental scientists, rather than archaeologists, have made a number of claims for earlier human presence, mostly based on charcoal and pollen evidence considered indicative of human burning of the landscape.

As discussed in earlier chapters, there is clear disagreement among researchers about this question. Individual researchers must base their opinion on their understanding of the archaeological and scientific evidence available in light of their own knowledge and experience as trained archaeologists.[9] Yet the evidence for early dates is not easy to assess. It requires close reading of many data-laden publications, each pushing its own argument, and specialist knowledge of scientific methods, many of which are beyond the immediate expertise of many individual archaeologists. In turn, many of the natural scientists involved in this research must rely on archaeologists to verify the reliability of the samples they analyse, and the archaeological validity of their interpretations. If the 'truth' of this question is really 'out there', finding it requires sifting through large amounts of data, balancing claim and counter-claim.

Currently there *is* no clear and easy answer to the question 'How long have people lived in Australia?' An honest answer would be 'At least 40 000 years, probably longer, but exactly how long we don't really know yet'. Yet this has not stopped at least some archaeologists making definitive pronouncements on the topic and strongly defending their views in the media. Answering such a question on the basis of archaeological evidence alone lies entirely within a modernist academic intellectual framework often described as 'scientific'. Second-guessing the motives of some of the major players, as discussed for the Jinmium case in Chapter 7, is about postmodern deconstruction of archaeological knowledge and the way such knowledge can change in the public domain. Also outside the academic paradigm is the view of some Indigenous people that to ask how long people have lived in Australia is meaningless because they have always been here. Other Indigenous people have publicly claimed that the findings actually support their beliefs. Rather than using science to publicly challenge such claims, archaeologists have chosen to stay silent.

David Frankel provides further interesting comment about the fallout from the Jinmium affair. At the time when claims and counter-claims about the early dates at Jinmium were being widely reported in the media, Frankel and a colleague were conducting archaeological fieldwork in Victoria on Gariwerd sites with Indigenous community representatives. The archaeologists were explaining that while previous research on these sites by archaeologist Peter Coutts had demonstrated that they were only a few thousand years old, their own research now proved that people were living in the area 20 000 years ago. Talk turned to Jinmium and some community members joked, 'The Jinmium team says this, then you say [that date's] too old. Coutts said that, now you say [that date's] too young!

What's going on here? How do we know you are right?!' As Frankel comments, this is about explaining the nature of archaeological inquiry as a continuing and questioning process rather than as a 'truth'.[10]

Knowledge across the boundaries

For some research questions in Australia, archaeological interpretations of the past are not so easily separated from wider public views. Good examples are the differing claims made by archaeologists, Indigenous people and other members of the public about the meaning of the landscape around Lake Condah in the Western District of Victoria. As explained by Josephine Flood, field survey and excavation over a number of years by the Victoria Archaeological Survey (VAS) resulted in the recording of a series of stone circles, alignments and other structures scattered across the region. On the basis of both archaeological and documentary evidence, these have been interpreted as Indigenous cultural sites dated from the last few thousand years and into the time of European settlement.[11]

There are major disagreements about the exact nature and meaning of these structures and the extent to which they were built by Aborigines, by European settlers, or are the result of natural processes. The view that the stones represent the remains of semi-permanent Indigenous 'villages' and extensive traps 'engineered' by Aborigines for catching eels is based on studies of historical documents and archaeological field survey and excavations conducted in the 1970s by Peter Coutts and Jane Wesson. During this time Coutts was the director of VAS, the government heritage organisation in Victoria. Such an interpretation of the archaeology of the region therefore had added authority as an 'official' view sanctioned by an important government employee. Coutts and Wesson's interpretation was also important in Harry Lourandos' arguments for intensification in the mid- to late Holocene period, as mentioned in Chapter 1.

In 1990 Anne Clarke and Giles Hamm conducted further archaeological fieldwork in the region for VAS. This was linked to tourism developments at nearby Lake Condah Mission, which the Victorian government had returned with some land to Gunditjmara people in the late 1980s. Tours to the cultural sites at Lake Condah and the adjoining Allambie property had become an important part of the educational experience offered to Mission visitors.[12] Educational materials about the Lake Condah sites, some of them produced in collaboration with Gunditjmara community representatives, told the story of sedentary populations living in villages composed of closely packed stone-walled houses with flat roofs. Early editions of Josephine Flood's popular book *Archaeology of the Dreamtime* reproduce artist David White's impression of such a village, first published in the *Age* newspaper in 1981.[13]

Clarke is critical of the detail and emphasis of such interpretations. While not denying the Indigenous origin of many of the stone structures, she contends that the process of archaeological interpretation has created a mythical cultural landscape which is not supported by either historical or archaeological evidence.

> The sites of Lake Condah and the surrounding properties have become mythologised within two domains—in the archaeological literature, and as a consequence, in the realm of public knowledge and awareness. The resultant romancing of the stones neither provides an explanation of the regional prehistory based on clearly demonstrated archaeological associations nor does it encourage the implementation of sound management strategies based on well-founded archaeological data.[14]

Clarke and Hamm's new archaeological research demonstrated that many stone features were indeed the remains of eel traps made by Indigenous people. However, there was no evidence for 'villages' or for substantial stone-walled house construction. Instead, Clarke argued, many of the stone circles had probably formed the bases of temporary huts and other structures. Other stone features claimed to be Indigenous cultural sites were more likely to have been produced by the action of tree roots and other natural processes, or to have been built by Europeans as hunting blinds. Clarke took particular exception to the use of the word 'villages' in interpretations of Lake Condah archaeology. This term was first used by nineteenth-century European writers to describe collections of Indigenous hut structures they observed in the region, but not specifically at Lake Condah. Clarke argues that the word 'village', which in modern usage carries with it a range of implicit meanings such as sedentary occupation, property rights, social hierarchy and craft specialisation, is inappropriate here.

In another paper Clarke and Hamm discuss the socio-politics surrounding their 1990 archaeological survey. According to them, an important but unstated undercurrent was a political push by the Victorian government to nominate Lake Condah for World Heritage listing, emphasising the 'unique' nature of this cultural landscape with its 'villages' and associated fish traps. According to Clarke and Hamm, the then 'State Minister thought it important for Victoria to have such a nomination as it did not have any World Heritage localities'.[15]

Some members of the small rural community in the area were suspicious of the archaeologists for being in league with the government and Indigenous people. Presumably fearful of further land rights claims, many of this group dismissed any Indigenous origin for the Lake Condah sites, claiming they were all duck-hunting blinds made by non-Indigenous shooters. Pro-Indigenous members of the community emphasised the size and permanent nature of the Indigenous settlement, even in the face of ambiguous archaeological evidence. Members of the local Indigenous community, with whom the archaeologists were required to work, had their own views about the sites in the area, contingent on community politics.

In a 1996 thesis written for an honours degree in Aboriginal studies at Flinders University, Heather Builth was highly critical of Clarke's reinterpretation of the archaeology of the Lake Condah area, and outlined negative consequences for Gunditjmara people and for archaeologists wishing to conduct future research there. While not arguing for 'villages', Builth preferred to explain the archaeology of the region as the material outcome of the historical development of a sophisticated seasonal fishery for eels by a hierarchical, mainly sedentary society controlled by hereditary chiefs. The production and storage of surplus food is important to the economy and social organisation of hunter-gatherers with a sedentary way of life elsewhere in the world. Citing ethnographic studies of comparable societies in North America, Builth suggested that some of the smaller Lake Condah area stone circles and structures could have functioned as facilities for processing and storing surplus eels.[16]

Builth was especially concerned that Clarke's reclassification of many stone features from cultural to natural had resulted in 83 per cent of previously recorded stone sites in the Allambie survey area being de-registered. This, according to Builth, meant such sites were no longer protected by state heritage legislation, despite continuing threats to the landscape from commercial stone extraction activities.[17] She questioned Clarke's methods for distinguishing between cultural and natural stone features. In discussing the deletion of a previously recorded fish trap from the site register, for example, Builth argued that in case of doubt the structure should be protected until 'future scientific investigation may determine its archaeological significance':

> It could equally well be argued that this structure, if not a fish trap or a
> stone circle, could belong to another cultural category? What is certain
> is that de-registering the sites will quite possibly prevent a re-analysis of
> the material for future generations of archaeologists. This is only a secondary consideration to the possible irretrievable further loss of past
> records to the local people.[18]

David Frankel also comments that differing views of the significance of the stone features have existed for a long time and that Clarke's rejection of some of the stone arrangements as natural features does not really diminish the value of the area as a whole—where there are still many demonstrably artificial stone features. The fish traps are also demonstrably made by people—even if they are not engineered in the way originally suggested by Coutts.[19] Whatever else is demonstrated by research at Lake Condah, the various interpretations placed on the archaeology have been far from objective and value-free, and public perceptions and expectations of archaeology have played a large role in this.

Aborigines and outsiders: Knowledge beyond the fringe?

Currently accepted archaeological theories tend to favour a somewhat isolationist view of Australia's Indigenous past, in which there has been some, but fairly limited, interaction between people living in Australia and people outside the continent at least up to the time of historically documented contact with Macassan fishermen and European explorers and settlers from the seventeenth century onwards.[20] Within a time frame relevant to human evolution and settlement (i.e. the last few hundred thousand years), Australia has always been separated from the South East Asian mainland by sea. All people and many plants and animals had to cross water to get here. This geography has resulted in Australia being relatively, although not totally, isolated from the rest of the world. After the time of initial human colonisation, there is some reliable archaeological evidence for further contacts between outsiders and people already living in Australia. For example, study of early human skeletal remains linked to theories about genetics and demography suggests that there have been successive waves of human migration to Australia. Yet such evidence is ambiguous and researchers disagree on its exact interpretation.

There is good archaeological evidence to prove that the dingo arrived from outside Australia somewhere in the last 4000 years, indicating contact between people already here and people in South East Asia and beyond. There is also reliable evidence that people in north Queensland and Cape York Peninsula maintained regular contact by boat with their neighbours across islands in the Torres Strait and into Papua New Guinea, which is reflected in shared cultural traits in the region.[21] Beyond this, there is no clear and undisputed archaeological evidence for interaction and contact between Aborigines and outsiders before the historic period. Although theories about the ultimate South East Asian origin of various types of Indigenous stone tools have been proposed and debated by certain Australian archaeologists, such ideas have always sat on the fringe of accepted archaeological knowledge and are rejected by many researchers.[22]

Studies of contact between Indigenous Australians and outsiders in the historic period are currently topical with many Australian archaeologists. The first documented interaction between Indigenous people and Europeans was in AD 1606. The antiquity of historically known interaction between visiting Indonesian fishermen from Macassar and Indigenous people in the north of Australia is unclear, but it was independent of subsequent European settlement. James Cook was the first European historically recorded as making direct contact with Indigenous people along Australia's eastern seaboard during his voyage of AD 1770.

Such is the current orthodox view of Indigenous contact with the outside world prior to Cook's voyage, based on verifiable evidence accepted by scientists, archaeologists and historians. Yet ideas about contact between Indigenous people and outsiders based on evidence ranging from the questionable through to the highly doubtful to the totally absurd have long been popular in Australia. Pre-Cook visits to mainland Australia by Polynesians, Indonesians, Portuguese, Spanish, Chinese and Arab explorers and traders are historically possible, but currently unsupported by any reliable evidence.[23] As already discussed, claims for visits and even 'settlement' by such historically known groups are a common feature of 'hidden histories' associated in the public mind with real and imagined shipwrecks, such as the famous Mahogany Ship. This is public knowledge at and beyond the edge of accepted historical and archaeological orthodoxy. Yet such stories have wide popular appeal and 'finds' associated with them have often been reported in the Australian media.

Another common and recurring theme in European interpretations of Australia's past is occupation of the continent by 'pre-Aboriginal' races. Such arguments have been presented in various forms since at least the nineteenth century, and have often been used in the public domain to justify denying present-day Indigenous rights. The argument goes that because the ancestors of today's Indigenous population, in common with Australia's colonial settlers, arrived fairly recently (in some theories 'wiping out' pre-existing populations), Indigenous people are themselves 'invaders' who cannot claim unbroken cultural descendancy from the first people to occupy the continent. They therefore have no more rights to land than other Australians. A less common but linked set of ideas is that Australia was visited before the time of historically known European contact by various outsiders with 'superior' technology and civilisations, who influenced Indigenous culture and beliefs. These contacts and influences are supposedly recorded in rock art and other material evidence.

Such ideas categorise Indigenous societies as essentially primitive and unchanging and suggest that new and innovative elements of Indigenous culture could only have been introduced from outside Australia. The key political issue here is not so much whether such theories are testable against archaeological evidence, but why people think this matters—why is prehistoric genetic ancestry regarded by some Australians as being at all relevant to Indigenous people's claim for their rights in Australia today?

As already discussed, such themes are also very common in pseudoscientific alternative 'archaeologies' of Australia currently doing the rounds in New Age websites and publications. Here the 'pre-Aborigines' are mythical giant ape men, and the outsiders are historically impossible Ancient Egyptians, Phoenicians and Celts. Presumably the predominance of peoples from the ancient world of the northern hemisphere in such explanations is linked to a more general popular interest in overseas archaeology and ancient history, as previously noted. Ancient Egyptians, both real and imagined, have wide popular appeal and feature in similar mystical and improbable explanations in other countries as well.[24]

The predominance of Phoenicians in such Australian mythology may stem in part from the real Phoenicians' famous shipbuilding and seafaring abilities. Macassan ships represented in Indigenous art in northern Australia are presumably the basis of some spurious identifications of Phoenicians and Egyptians, although Egyptians were not especially renowned seafarers. Voyaging skills have been important elements of Polynesian, Macassan and European exploration and settlement in the Asia-Pacific region. However, it also interesting that there are relatively few myths about Polynesians in mainland Australia, although such contacts are the most likely to have occurred.[25]

Most New Age and fringe theories about outside contacts with Indigenous people are quite rightly dismissed by archaeologists and most members of the public as spurious nonsense, with no grounding in fact. Yet, as discussed by Lynette Russell and Ian McNiven, a number of similar claims about the Indigenous past have been made by otherwise respected scholars and researchers throughout Australia's colonial history. For example, Russell and McNiven discuss the case of Indigenous stone circles at Mount Elephant in Victoria, which in the nineteenth century were interpreted by some scholars as having been made by a more 'advanced society' than local Indigenous people. These places were likened to European megaliths, such as Stonehenge, and their Indigenous origins were denied.[26]

Diffusionist explanations of Indigenous prehistory propose that any new elements in the archaeological record of Australia which indicate advances in Indigenous culture, technology or society must ultimately derive from elsewhere. Diffusionism has taken many forms since the nineteenth century, including what McNiven and Russell list as advanced predecessor, advanced successor, and multiple migration models. These form part of a continuing colonialist ideology which has often been used to justify the dispossession of Indigenous people by British settlement and deny them land and cultural rights.[27]

Ideas based on diffusionism and pre-European outside contact are alive and well in the public domain, and not just in New Age websites. Good examples are comments by members of the public in letters to newspapers, and politicians in statements to the media, about the Mabo Native Title decision in the early 1990s. Some people who disagreed with the ruling reiterated a now very outdated and academically untenable theory proposed in 1938 by Joseph Birdsell for a 'tri-hybrid' theory of Indigenous settlement of Australia. This was cited as justification for denying Indigenous Native Title rights.[28]

McNiven and Russell also discuss claims by rock art researcher Graham Walsh, published in 1994, that the Bradshaw paintings found in the Kimberley area of the Northern Territory originated beyond Australia and are not part of Indigenous culture. Walsh's claims attracted much media attention which commented on the political implications of his statements as well as his findings. Walsh, like several other well-known Australians involved in rock art research, has no formal qualifications in the subject but has extensive knowledge. He has spent most of his adult years studying and educating the public about the rock art of remote northern Australia, has worked for the Queensland National Parks and Wildlife Service and has published several popular illustrated books on rock art.[29] His work has made a very valuable contribution to both academic understanding and public awareness of Indigenous rock art.

Walsh's interpretation of the origins of the Bradshaw art style (which was first described in the literature by nineteenth-century explorer Joseph Bradshaw) are based on the style of the motifs, and on the attitude of present-day local Indigenous people to the art. Walsh argues that the 'exquisite form, composition and application' of the Bradshaw art set it apart from other Indigenous art in the region, and that the style and motifs were most similar to those found in rock art from the African Sahara and Tanzania. On this basis he concluded that someone other than Aborigines must have painted the Bradshaw art.[30] While not specifically concluding that people of African origin were responsible, he did suggest the artists may have come from Indonesia or elsewhere. Walsh also divided the rock art of the area into three chronological phases: early 'Archaic Epoch' art styles preceded the 'Erudite Epoch' of the Bradshaw art. Only the more recent 'Aboriginal Epoch' art is attributed by Walsh to Indigenous people. Here, Walsh's terminology is very telling.

McNiven and Russell argue that the Bradshaw case, and Walsh's interpretation, demonstrates the role of Australian archaeology in colonialist discourses and provides an example of the colonial ideology that still frames and constrains the production of archaeological knowledge in Australia. But to what degree do such interpretations of rock art, presented by people with no professional qualifications who are neither employed nor sanctioned by the 'academy' or the government, constitute *archaeological* knowledge at the current time? Although much of Walsh's work has professional credibility in that he has worked with professionals and published articles in highly regarded peer-reviewed academic journals, like several other prominent rock art researchers outside the academy, he is also privately funded.[31]

For reasons already discussed, rock art studies are not subject to the same professional, ethical and government constraints as are other Australian 'archaeologies'. Many views of the past based on rock art originate in the public domain. Some are beyond or largely outside the boundaries of current 'orthodox' archaeological knowledge. To refute Walsh's hypothesis for non-Indigenous origins of the Bradshaw art, Michael Barry conducted extensive statistical analysis of rock art styles from Australia and compared them to 1694 examples of 'similar' art from outside Australia. His results showed that the Bradshaw art was quite distinct from overseas styles, originated in Australia, and shared most common features with other Indigenous art from Arnhem Land. Darrell Lewis has also been critical of Walsh's interpretation of a link between some Bradshaw art styles and the 'Mimi' figures of Arnhem Land, and the relative dates of the two. On these Barry and Lewis have both used a range of scientific evidence and archaeological reasoning to refute Walsh's claims about the origins of the Bradshaw art and their relationship with other Indigenous art styles.[32]

Speaking out, staying silent

These cases demonstrate the complexities of drawing clear and solid boundaries around archaeological knowledge about Australia's Indigenous past. While boundaries do exist, they are permeable, shifting and contingent upon wider social and political factors. Despite this, in all cases archaeology was used to provide concrete evidence about the 'truths' of different pasts. These examples, and others discussed in this book, demonstrate that in doing archaeology and in studying the Australian past, archaeologists must be prepared to play different and even multiple roles.

Such issues are also relevant to the practice of archaeology beyond Australia, where there have been many similar challenges to the theory and practice of modernist, processual archaeology. In English-speaking countries at least, archaeologists writing in the United Kingdom have usually had the loudest voice. To many Australian archaeologists the theoretical revelations of some British post-processual archaeologists about the power relations involved in the practice of archaeology and the relativism of archaeological knowledge come as no great surprise; they have been forced to confront these issues already in a very practical sense while working with Indigenous people under conditions of postcolonialism. This point is well made by Matthew Spriggs in his review of British archaeologist Ian Hodder's book about reflexive archaeological practice, *The Archaeological Process.*[33]

Hodder discusses the impact of postmodernity, and to a much lesser extent postcolonialism, on at least some archaeological practice in terms of the contradictions (ambiguity, uncertainty, diversity and fluidity) which have replaced the 'certainty' and 'closure' of modernist archaeological practice since the 1970s and 1980s. In outlining the development of new, open and self-aware reflexive archaeological practices, he raises interesting and significant points about the social context of his work in excavating and interpreting the prehistoric settlement of Çatalhöyük in Turkey. Among the many stakeholders to whom Hodder feels he has obligations are groups of (Western) Goddess worshippers who espouse New Age views about the significance of Çatalhöyük as a spiritual centre for ecofeminism. Some of these people seemingly want to use material evidence from the site to demonstrate the truths of their beliefs.

Part of the reflexive practices being developed by Hodder and his team at Çatalhöyük entails archaeologists entering into dialogue with this group. This seems to largely involve not dismissing their claims out of hand, defending their right to their beliefs, providing them with site tours, talking to them, and allowing them open access to archaeological data through the Internet. Here dialogue is slightly different from Indigenous community consultation in Australia. Goddess worshippers do not, for example, have the power to stop the excavation or dictate how the archaeologists should do their work or which questions they should address. This is largely up to the Turkish government, from whom the archaeological team must get permits for their excavations.[34]

Making judgements about competing claims to place is complicated in Australia by the relationship between Indigenous identity and some New

Age spirituality. New Agers commonly co-opt elements of Indigenous culture and spirituality. The most obvious Australian example is the spiritual association many non-Indigenous people claim with Uluru (Ayers Rock). Julie Marcus argues that while many New Agers are naive and well meaning, Indigenous people can sometimes regard 'white' appropriation of elements of their culture in this way as inappropriate and offensive, especially when outsiders are seen to be gaining direct economic benefits.[35]

Marcus' point was well illustrated in 1994 when US writer Marlo Morgan published a best-selling book, *Mutant Message Down Under*, about a white woman's supposed travels across Australia with a group of desert Indigenous people in which she takes part in rituals and ceremonies, saves the 'tribe,' and is hailed by them as a 'mutant messenger'. The book, which falls within the category of New Age literature, was originally published as non-fiction, although this was later changed to fiction. Some Indigenous people were angered by the publication and demanded that the US publisher withdraw the book. They were angry that Morgan was marketing herself as an authority on Indigenous culture, spirituality and sacred sites. Robert Eggington of Dumburtung Aboriginal Corporation in Western Australia condemned the book as 'fabricated fantasy' and was concerned that Morgan's false message about Aboriginality would be accepted as 'fact' by naive Americans and Europeans. He noted that if Morgan had done what she claimed to have done, without being initiated, 'it is punishable by death under Aboriginal law'.[36]

In a session on Archaeology and the Goddess held at the third Australian Women in Archaeology conference in Sydney in 1995, Australian ecofeminist Jennifer Hamilton explained the diversity of women's beliefs and practices associated with the Goddess, including co-opting Indigenous beliefs:

> Goddess spirituality is very eclectic, using not only [archaeological resources] but drawing on pre-Christian, European traditions of pagan religions, on sources for the ancient mysteries such as those of Eleusis, on the mythologies of ancient societies and on the traditions of Witchcraft . . . Indigenous religions in each land where the Goddess movement is emerging become important connection points.[37]

Hamilton described ecofeminism as a 'multicultural movement' with great respect for diversity. Yet most likely many Indigenous people would object strongly to ecofeminists appropriating their spirituality. Indigenous identity is not 'multicultural' in the same way as ecofeminism and other New Age movements.

Indigenous cultures are owned by particular people with strict rules about what is appropriate. A further complicating issue is that Indigenous people, especially in south-eastern Australia, sometimes use New Age terminology in describing their own spirituality. Such matters only become a 'problem' for archaeologists if New Age, Indigenous or other groups misuse archaeological evidence to 'prove' their beliefs. Archaeologists need to educate the public about the nature of archaeological knowledge in all its complexities in order to challenge the misuse of archaeological evidence in such circumstances. They need to remind people that while archaeology can provide evidence, it is not about establishing the 'Truth'. New Age claims are not about archaeology, but rather about cultural and social values.

Such issues are a problem for cultural heritage managers rather than the archaeology profession. As discussed elsewhere in this book, archaeologists are certainly stakeholders in cultural places and at times their own interests (in conserving material evidence or investigating it through archaeological and scientific methods) can be incompatible with those of other stakeholders, such as developers who want to destroy Indigenous places or Indigenous people who want to rebury human skeletal remains or re-groove rock engravings. Because the legacy of colonialism gave archaeology and archaeologists primacy in much Australian cultural heritage management of the 1960s and 1970s, archaeologists within government heritage bureaucracies have often been empowered to judge competing claims. But this situation for archaeologists has changed and is changing as Indigenous people have become more empowered within the bureaucracies. Many Australian archaeologists prefer not to sit in judgement of competing knowledge claims about the past. Adjudicating is a task for cultural heritage managers, who can now be traditional owners, as well as Indigenous and non-Indigenous bureaucrats employed by government agencies. It is their job to decide what happens to cultural places.

In an ideal world many Australian archaeologists should aim to explain their work to non-archaeologists, and argue for its value to science and society. They should negotiate with other parties such as Indigenous communities, bottle collectors, development companies and government departments to be allowed to proceed with their research. In an ideal world archaeologists should be able to 'speak up' for their own rights and interests in the material remains of the past, and 'speak out' against pseudo-scientific abuse of archaeological evidence. This is very different from archaeologists sitting in judgement on people's social and cultural values or saying that archaeological values should always come first.

As such an 'ideal world' will never exist, what should or could the role of archaeologists be in Australian society under conditions of postcolonialism? Yannis Hamilakis has discussed similar issues in relation to European archaeology: in the face of postmodernity, what role can or should archaeologists and their profession play in society? He argues that archaeologists should adopt the role of intellectuals in challenging (or speaking out against?) what he describes as 'regimes for the "production of truths"'.[38] As Australian society is sometimes characterised as being 'anti-intellectual', it is not clear how such ideas might translate here, and, as many examples in this book have shown, the contemporary contexts in which archaeologists need to speak out or remain silent are somewhat different.

Archaeologist John Mulvaney is a case in point. Mulvaney has been hailed by many of his colleagues as a public intellectual for his active and open role in the practice of Australian prehistory, history and cultural heritage management over many years. Lesley Head regards Mulvaney's role as emblematic of the ambiguities which many Australian archaeologists face in their professional dealings with Indigenous Australia. She identifies both a 'liberal humanitarian' and a 'postmodern' Mulvaney. As already discussed, John Mulvaney has made many public statements about the scientific value of ancient human skeletal remains which Indigenous people regard as their ancestors—for which he has sometimes been attacked as being anti-Indigenous. At the same time, Mulvaney has publicly supported Indigenous people in their political struggles, and has been praised by anthropologist Deborah Bird Rose for his 'open' and 'postmodern' approach to Australian post-contact settler and Indigenous places in his book *Encounters in Place*. Head notes there are many similar contradictions in Mulvaney's actions, public statements and published work.[39] This book, too, contains many other examples of people (archaeologists and others) speaking out and keeping quiet in seemingly contradictory ways about the nature and practice of archaeology in Australia.

Head suggests that Australian archaeologists should worry less about the tensions and ambiguities inherent in doing archaeology in postcolonial Australia, while being aware that when such archaeology enters the public domain it may be misconstrued and have unpredictable outcomes which are beyond the control of archaeologists themselves. She believes that many Australian archaeologists are already dealing well with the intellectual, practical, political and other challenges of their work, to which they bring a variety of tools, knowledge and approaches based in both the sciences and the humanities, in order to do different types of archaeology. The key is to not insist that what they do need be 'closed' or 'completed' in some way.[40]

Finishing without closure

How then to end a book like this one—which sits firmly in a postmodern or postcolonial framework—without insisting on closure or completion? This book started with the story of another book about Tasmania which never got written. Here my aim has been to explain and explore questions about the recent practice of archaeology and its relation to Indigenous Australia and the wider public. The questions I have discussed are not the same as those which archaeologists frequently ask about Australia's past— about dates and processes and history. This is not an archaeology book— it is rather a book about archaeology in Australia.

My interest here has been in Australian society—its past, present and future—and the role of archaeologists and the public in creating and reflecting elements of Australian identity through the medium of archaeology—however the subject is defined. I present my book as a start to further discussion. There are no right or wrong answers to most of the questions raised here. I know that some people will disagree with my interpretations, while others may be offended. But for those many others who are aware of, and interested in, the kinds of topics discussed here, I hope that my book will encourage people to think about archaeology in new and different ways and to discuss and explore these and related issues in other contexts.

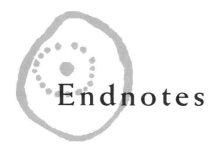

Endnotes

Preface

1 Ryan 1996.
2 For a general overview of the prehistory of Tasmania see Mulvaney & Kamminga 1999:180–189 and 339–356.
3 Allen 1987:9.
4 Griffiths 1991:95. Allen 1983 and 1987 also discuss the case.
5 Mulvaney cited in Griffiths 1991:95.
6 McNiven *et al.* 1993, Allen 1996a.
7 Porch & Allen 1995.
8 Rhys Jones (1977, 1978) discovered bone points and fish bones in the lowest layers of the Rocky Cape site dated before 3500 years ago. More recent upper layers contained neither. These and other patterns in the Tasmanian archaeological record suggested to Jones that the Tasmanians had lost elements of their culture around this time, including eating fish. He saw this as evidence of 'cultural decline' caused by extreme isolation and small population size. His interpretation has since been challenged by other archaeologists (e.g. Pardoe 1991).
9 Bickford 1979, Jones 1992, Ryan 1996:255, 266.
10 Langford 1983:5.
11 Both documentaries are now available on video. *The Last Tasmanian* (video-recording and educational guide). Producer/Director Tom Haydon. North Sydney: Artis Film Productions 1978. *Black Man's Houses* (videorecording). Producers John Moore and Steve Thomas. Written and directed by Steve Thomas. Fitzroy, Victoria. A Steve Thomas/Open Channel Production, 1992.
12 See for example Murray and Allen 1995, TALC 1996, McGowan 1996, Murray 1996a, Allen 1996c, Allen & Cosgrove 1996:10–14.

Chapter 1

1 For histories of archaeology see McBryde 1986, Horton 1991:53–90, Lourandos 1997:98–111, Flood 1995:174–194. For history of collecting see Griffiths 1996:66–85.
2 McBryde 1986:13, Jones 1993.
3 Mulvaney 1969:100–101, Bowdler 1993:123–138.
4 Moser 1994.
5 Papers in Bonyhady & Griffiths 1996a discuss John Mulvaney's career. For history see McBryde 1986:17 and Murray & White 1981.

6 Moser 1995:152, Mulvaney & Kamminga 1999:14–15.

7 Murray & White 1981, White & O'Connell 1982:22–30, McBryde 1986, Flood 1989, Horton 1991, Sullivan 1996 and Griffiths 1996:55–100. See also selected papers in the Special 20th Year Anniversary issue of the journal *Australian Archaeology* 39 (1994). Renfrew & Bahn 1991 discuss the history of archaeology more generally.

8 Davis 1999 discusses the impact of the baby boom culture on media, arts and related areas of Australian intellectual life. Griffiths 1996:92 describes the 1960s as the 'golden years' for Australian archaeology.

9 Mulvaney & Golson 1971.

10 Meehan & Jones 1988a include examples of Australian ethno-archaeology. North American research in Australia includes Gould 1980, Binford 1984 and O'Connell 1987.

11 Radiocarbon determinations from Mungo at first seemed to suggest that people were in the area some time after 32 000 years ago. The 36 000 date was from work by Isabel McBryde at Outer Lake Arumpo in 1974 (cited in Johnston & Clark 1998:109).

12 Willandra Lakes archaeology is described by White & O'Connell 1982:35–39, Webb 1989b, Horton 1991:299–348, Flood 1995:39–55 and H. Allen 1998. Johnston & Clark 1998 provide a useful overview with references of all previous archaeological investigations at Lake Mungo from 1968 to1998.

13 Flood 1995 and Mulvaney & Kamminga 1999 provide general overviews of the significance of this research. John Mulvaney's *Prehistory of Australia* first appeared in 1969, with the second edition in 1975. Other important text books and general overviews include White & O'Connell 1982, Flood 1997 and Lourandos 1997.

14 For Bass Point see Bowdler 1976. For Kurnell see Megaw 1969, J. Allen 1978, Schrire 1972 and Macknight 1976. For women in archaeology and gender studies in archaeology see du Cros & Smith 1993, Balme & Beck 1995 and Casey *et al.* 1998.

15 Lourandos & Ross 1994, Lourandos 1997, Williams 1987, Ross *et al.*1992, Mulvaney & Kamminga 1999:15–17, Hiscock 1986, Head 1987, Rowland 1989, Bird & Frankel 1991, David & Chant 1995.

16 For further information about the history of radiocarbon-dating methods and technical details see Renfrew & Bahn 1991.

17 For further information about dating methods see Renfrew & Bahn 1991.

18 Smith & Sharp 1993 discuss approaches to such sites. Bird & Frankel 1991 discuss why this matters for the Aboriginal archaeology of south-west Victoria.

19 Smith & Sharp 1993:49.

20 Frankel 1991. Examples of such studies can be found in Meehan & Jones 1988a.

21 See Lourandos 1997 and Mulvaney & Kamminga 1999 for overviews of explanations proposed by archaeologists to explain continuity and change in Aboriginal stone tool types.

22 This debate was very topical in the late 1980s as well demonstrated by papers in Meehan & Jones 1988a. Murray's paper (1988) in that volume presents a strong contrary view. See also Murray 1992. Cowlishaw 1992 presents a critical

history of Australian anthropology. Mulvaney & Kamminga 1999:147–171 describe aspects of traditional Indigenous life most relevant to prehistory. See also Cosgrove *et al.* 1990 and papers in Knapp (ed.) 1992.

23 See Frankel 1991:10 and Murray 1992.

24 Such stone tools are described by Mulvaney & Kamminga 1999:234 and 237. Southern uniface points (formerly Pirri points) are found distributed in archaeological contexts across the southern half of the continent. They are small symmetrical, leaf-shaped stone tools. Bondi points are one form of a more general group of stone tools called 'microliths' or 'backed blades'. The particular form known as the Bondi point is widely distributed along the south-east coast. Examples from Bondi Beach were first described in the late nineteenth century. They are small flaked stone tools with a narrow, pointed shape.

25 Jones 1978 and Colley & Jones 1987.

26 Mulvaney & Kamminga 1999:248–249.

27 Harry Lourandos in particular has written about such changes (e.g. Lourandos 1997).

28 See Attwood's Introduction in Attwood & Arnold 1992.

29 Cowlishaw 1992:21.

30 Meehan 1982, 1988.

31 Smith *et al.* 1993 overview studies of Pleistocene Australia. Several papers in the volume (e.g. by Horton, Frankel, Ballard & Pardoe) question the validity or value of subdividing Australian prehistory so sharply into the Pleistocene and the Holocene periods.

32 Wylie 1985.

33 Meehan & Jones 1988b, Murray 1988, Cosgrove *et al.* 1990.

34 See for example Josephine Flood's study of the 'moth hunters' of the Southern Highlands (Flood 1980, 1988). The example of Lake Condah in Victoria is discussed in Chapter 10.

35 Murray 1996a, Colley & Bickford 1996.

36 See Murray & White 1981.

37 For general overviews of Australian historical archaeology with references to these and other important excavations see Connah 1993, Egloff 1994, Jack 1996 and Mulvaney 1997.

38 Pearson & Sullivan 1995 provide details of historic sites legislation in Australia.

39 Connah 1998 and the reply by Mackay & Karskens 1999 are examples of such a debate. Hosty & Stuart 1994 give a history of Australian maritime archaeology. See Jack & Cremin 1994 for more information about industrial archaeology in Australia. Cremin 2001 provides a popular introduction to several Australian historical archaeology projects relevant to the history of Federation—these cover a number of themes.

40 Reynolds 1982:9–11, McGrath 1993:5–120.

41 For example Reynolds 1982 and Baker 1999:159.

42 Mulvaney 1969:26–27, 29, Layton 1992:89–113, Mulvaney & Kamminga 1999:412–419 discuss Macassan archaeology. Torrence & Clarke 2000 and Lilley 2000 describe other examples of Australian and Pacific contact archaeology.

43 Williamson 1998, Torrence & Clarke 2000.

44 For example Stahl 1993.
45 Birmingham 1992.
46 Birmingham 1992, Val Attenbrow, personal communication.
47 Judy Birmingham, personal communication.
48 Renfrew & Bahn 1991 discuss resistivity survey. See also Egloff & Ranson 1988.

Chapter 2
 1 Trigger 1984, 1989.
 2 The 1970 Convention on the Means of Prohibiting and Preventing the Illicit Import, Export and Transfer of Ownership of Cultural Property. For information on World Heritage see United Nations Educational, Scientific and Cultural Organisation, n.d., [WWW document]. http://www.unesco.org (6 February 2002).
 3 Trigger 1984, 1989. Also see for example Kohl & Fawcett 1995 and Graves-Brown et al. 1996. Arnold 1990 and Arnold & Hassmann 1995 discuss Nazi Germany. Shaw 1990 discusses Great Zimbabwe under Rhodesian colonial rule.
 4 For discussion of globalisation see for example Evans 1995, Hamilakis 1999 and Hodder 1999.
 5 Ireland 1996, 2000 and in press, Byrne 1996. Murray 1996b also discusses these issues.
 6 NSW National Parks & Wildlife Service n.d.:4.
 7 Visitors' reactions to Aboriginal rock art sites (including complete misunderstanding and boredom) were described by Jacobs & Gale 1994.
 8 These ideas are further explored by Parrott 1990. Michael Pearson and Sharon Sullivan's book *Looking After Heritage Places* (1995) provides a good general introduction to this whole subject.
 9 Ritchie 1994, Colley 1996a, 2000a, Pearson & Sullivan 1995.
10 Parrott 1990:78–81.
11 Pearson & Sullivan 1995:37.
12 Parrott 1990:76.
13 For more information and detail see Pearson & Sullivan 1995.
14 For general overviews of the role of government in the development and practice of cultural resource management in Australia see Flood 1989, 1993 and Pearson & Sullivan 1995.
15 For further information see Environment Australia, Department of the Environment and Heritage, 2002, [WWW document]. http://www.ea.gov.au/heritage/awh (29 January 2002). The properties and date of listing are: Great Barrier Reef (1981); Kakadu National Park (1981); Willandra Lakes Region (1981); Tasmanian Wilderness (1982); Lord Howe Island Group (1982); Uluru-Kata Tjuta National Park (1987); Central Eastern Rainforest Reserves (Australia) (1987); Wet Tropics of Queensland (1988); Shark Bay, Western Australia (1991); Fraser Island (1992); Australian Fossil Mammal Sites (Riversleigh/Naracoorte) (1994); Heard and McDonald Islands (1997); Macquarie Island (1997); Greater Blue Mountains Area (2000).
16 In early 2001 the Commonwealth government introduced three Bills which would repeal the *Australian Heritage Commission Act 1975* and amend the *Environment*

Protection and Biodiversity Conservation Act 1999. These would establish an Australian Heritage Council, a Commonwealth Heritage List and focus Commonwealth responsibility on a narrower range of national heritage responsibilities. States and territories would be expected to take greater responsibility for places within their own jurisdiction. See Environment Australia, Department of the Environment and Heritage, 2002, [WWW document]. http://www.ea.gov.au (29 January 2002).

17 Bennett 1999:21–24.

18 See Pearson & Sullivan 1995 for further information.

19 See for example Gelder & Jacobs 1997, 1998.

20 The structure, organisation and names of various government portfolios, departments and agencies are subject to change. For further information see the Internet.

21 Further information can be obtained from the Aboriginal and Torres Strait Islander Commission, n.d., [WWW document]. http://www.atsic.gov.au (29 January 2002).

22 Ritchie 1994:230.

23 In the 1980s the *Heritage Act* was used to protect Aboriginal mythological sites until they could be gazetted and protected by the *National Parks and Wildlife Act* (Sullivan 1986). Aboriginal–European 'contact' sites may also be protected by the *Heritage Act* (NSW National Parks & Wildlife Service 1989:24).

24 The most useful sources of up-to-date information about state heritage legislation are the government and relevant community organisation websites.

25 Lowenthal 1985:238–249.

26 Schiffer & Gumerman 1977:2.

27 Bonyhady 1996:144. Lowenthal 1985 discusses why people value places and things from the past. Davison 1991 discusses definitions of 'heritage' in Australia.

28 McNiven & Russell 1995 discuss notions of wilderness and archaeology in World Heritage Areas. Head 1992, 1999 and Griffiths 1996 discuss notions of 'wilderness' in relation to Aborigines.

29 See for example English 2000.

30 H. Allen 1997:147. Cotter *et al.* 2001 discuss heritage landscapes.

31 See for example Appadurai 1986, N. Thomas 1991 and Weiner 1992. Lahn 1996 discusses such concepts in the context of the meanings attached to the Kow Swamp human remains and other Australian Aboriginal heritage items.

32 Bowdler 1984:1.

33 The Burra Charter was first adopted by Australia ICOMOS in 1979 at a meeting held in the town of Burra in South Australia, following review of the Venice Charter, which had previously been adopted by an international ICOMOS conference in Venice in 1966.

34 Further information may be obtained from International Council on Monuments and Sites, Australian National Committee, n.d., [WWW document]. http://www.icomos.org/australia (29 January 2002). Another very important publication, which is primarily for the built environment and historic buildings, is Kerr 1996. See also Marquis-Kyle & Walker 1992.

35 Australian Heritage Commission 1990, NSW Heritage Office 1996.
36 C. Johnston 1992, Byrne, Brayshaw & Ireland 2001.
37 See Sullivan 1993 and the Icomos website, op. cit.
38 Quote is Bowdler 1984:1–2. See also Sullivan & Bowdler 1984, Pearson & Sullivan 1995.
39 McDonald 1996. English 1996 also comments on similar issues.
40 Sullivan 1996, Flood 1989 and L. Smith 1994.
41 Byrne 1991, Mane-Wheoki 1992.
42 Mackay 1996 discusses some of these issues for Australian historical archaeology. Papers in Cooper *et al.* 1995 take a critical perspective on archaeological management in the United Kingdom.
43 See Frankel 1998 for further information about important features and considerations in the practice of archaeology by Australians.
44 Mulvaney 1962.
45 Ramsden 1998, National Board of Employment Education and Training 1994.
46 For more information see Australian Research Council, 2002, [WWW document]. http://www.arc.gov.au (30 January 2002). Collaborative research projects, especially in archaeological science, are also eligible for other sources of government research money such as Australian Institute of Nuclear Science and Engineering (AINSE) grants for physical analysis of archaeological materials.
47 Raab 1984 writes about such ethical problems in a North American case study which is highly pertinent to Australia.
48 Knight 1997 discusses the nature of the archaeological record and Indigenous values of place in the context of consulting archaeology in South Australia.
49 See for example Byrne 1984, Egloff 1984, Hunt 1993, Packard & Dunnett 1994, Blair & Feary 1995 and McConnell n.d.
50 Phil Hunt (New South Wales National Parks and Wildlife Service), personal communication.
51 Egloff 1981.
52 Hope 1995a.
53 Bowdler 1986.
54 See for example Jones 1985, McDonald 1992, Holdaway *et al.* 1998. Much work that gets published from heritage management studies is not identified as such; it is simply published as research findings with no particular comment on its context. These issues have been debated in historical archaeology by Connah 1998 and Mackay & Karskens 1999.
55 Val Attenbrow, personal communication.
56 Article 24. Marquis-Kyle & Walker 1992:63.
57 Denis Byrne (New South Wales National Parks and Wildlife Service), personal communication.
58 Boot & Kuskie 1996 provide an example of a successful collaboration of this kind.
59 Mulvaney 1970:258. Wildesen 1984 provides an insightful overview of the historical development of ethics and professionalism in American archaeology, much of which is relevant to Australia. Moser 1994.
60 For example NSW NPWS n.d. and NSW Heritage Office 1996. See Edgar 1998 for some comments on the NPWS guidelines by a consultant.

61 McGowan 1996:303.

62 Ramsden 1998.

63 This subject received some attention in the Australian archaeological literature in the 1980s (e.g. Frankel 1980). Since then, more has been published about teaching cultural heritage management (including to Aboriginal students) than about teaching Australian archaeology (e.g. Hermes 1992 and Smith *et al.* 1992). See also Feary 1994, Pate 1999 and Colley 2000a.

64 Australian Association of Consulting Archaeologists Incorporated, Register of Consultants 1995, AACAI, PO Box 214, Holme Building, University of Sydney, NSW 2006, Australia.

65 Australian Institute of Professional Archaeologists, GPO Box 5336 BB, Melbourne, Vic. 3001, Australia.

66 For example the North American Register (formerly Society) of Professional Archaeologists, 1999, [WWW document]. http://rpanet.org (30 January 2002) and the British Institute of Field Archaeologists, 2001 [WWW document]. http://www.archaeologists.net (30 January 2002).

67 Davidson 1991, Williams & Johnston 1991.

68 Smith 1994.

Chapter 3

1 Ryan 1996:218–220, 264–266 on Truganini.

2 Griffiths 1996:94–98.

3 See Mulvaney 1991 and Lahn 1996 for Kow Swamp. Chippindale 1985:10 and Webb 1987 discuss the Murray Black collection. McBryde 1995 discusses multiple heritage values of Lake Mungo and the reburial of Mungo Lady (see also Chapter 7). See also Griffiths 1996:94–100. Alan Thorne obtained permission from the relevant Aboriginal community for further work on Lake Mungo skeletal material in the late 1990s (Thorne *et al.* 1999). Murray & Allen 1995 discuss some aspects of the return of cultural materials to Tasmania (*TALC v. La Trobe*).

4 C. Jones 1997.

5 Finkel 1998a and 1998b.

6 Managerialism is the philosophy and practice of applying management theories developed in private industry to areas of the public sector which offer a service to society (e.g. education, welfare, health). Rees & Rodley 1995 are highly critical of such developments. Managerialism has radically changed the way universities and museums have been financed and managed in the 1990s and 2000s. Ramsden 1998, Frankel 1997, White 1998.

7 C. Jones 1997.

8 Pardoe 1992.

9 Davidson *et al.* 1995.

10 Chapters in McGrath 1995 provide a general introduction to Indigenous history in each state and territory. Bennett 1999 and Attwood & Markus 1999 outline recent political history and contemporary social issues.

11 Reynolds 1982, 1989, 1995.

12 For example, in 1937 the Aboriginal Progressive Association was formed as

an Indigenous political organisation campaigning for people's rights. State Records New South Wales May 1998, *A Guide to New South Wales State Archives Relating to Aboriginal People* [WWW document]. http://www.records.nsw.gov.au/publications/aboriginalguide/aboriginalguide-12.htm (30 January 2002).

13 Bennett 1999:21–24.

14 Mudrooroo 1995:197.

15 For more information about Reconciliation see Australasian Legal Information Institute, a joint facility of University of Technology Sydney and University of New South Wales Faculties of Law, n.d., 'Council for Aboriginal Reconciliation Archive', [WWW document]. http://www.austlii.edu.au/au/other/IndigLRes/car (30 January 2002) and Reconciliation Australia, 2001, [WWW document]. http://www.reconciliationaustralia.org/home.html (30 January 2002). Indigenous Australia was a strong symbolic theme in the opening and closing ceremonies of the Sydney 2000 Olympic Games, and Indigenous athlete Cathy Freeman's gold-medal win in the 400 metres race was the highlight of the games for most people in Australia.

16 Ross 1996.

17 Knight 1997:11.

18 Denis Byrne writing in NSW NPWS n.d.:4. English 2000.

19 Ryan 1996:257–262.

20 Ryan 1996:214–217.

21 Pardoe 1991.

22 Cosgrove *et al.* 1990.

23 See for example Cosgrove *et al.* 1990, I. Thomas 1993, Cosgrove *et al.* 1994 and I. Thomas 1995.

24 TALC 1996:296.

25 Interview with Robyne Bancroft in Davidson *et al.* 1995:63.

26 Laila Haglund, personal communication.

27 Schaffer 1995 and McNiven *et al.* 1998 discuss the Eliza Fraser stories in the context of colonial and postcolonial representation. McNiven 1998 discusses archaeology of Fraser Island.

28 H. Allen 1997:147.

29 H. Allen 1997:145.

30 Thorley 1996:11.

31 For example TALC 1996.

32 Tuhiwai Smith 1999:176.

33 For example Strang 1998:25–27 discusses the role of Aboriginal rangers in guiding visitors through the landscape in northern Queensland.

34 See for example Richardson 1989 for an Indigenous Australian perspective and Hubert 1989 for a general overview. Hemming 2000 discusses Ngarrindjeri attitudes to human burials in South Australia.

35 Langford 1983, TALC 1996.

36 Research by Lovell-Jones 1995 is relevant here.

37 McKay 1993. The origins and history of the AAA code of ethics and its relationship to the WAC code are described by Davidson 1991, Williams & Johnston 1991 and McBryde 1992.

38 Griffiths 1996:87.
39 Such claims have been made in print by, for example, R. Jones 1990, Mulvaney 1991a, Stone 1992, J. Allen 1995b and Murray 1996c. McBryde 1992 discusses the political implications of such claims.
40 Langford 1983, TALC 1996.
41 Gelder & Jacobs 1998:88–89.
42 Murray 1996b, 1996c.
43 Byrne 1998.
44 Colley & Jack 1996, Menage 1998.
45 NSW Heritage Office 1998.
46 Proudfoot *et al.* 1991.
47 Bickford 1996.
48 See papers in Historic Houses Trust of NSW 1996, particularly Flanagan 1996.
49 Tuhiwai Smith 1999, writing from the perspective of an Indigenous researcher in New Zealand, discusses a range of issues about research and Indigenous people in the context of imperialism and colonialism, most of which are highly pertinent to the current situation in Australia.
50 McKay 1993:51.
51 Extract from a letter to Pamela Gait from the TALC quoted in Gait 1995.
52 Wright 1995.
53 Hope 1995b, Mansell 1995.
54 Birmingham 1992 presented her archaeological research at the contact site of Wybalenna, Flinders Island, Tasmania, in the form of an investigation of Aboriginal resistance to European colonialism.
55 TALC 1996:296.
56 Fagan 1996.
57 Janke 1998.
58 The correct name is the Australian Archaeological Association. The accurate and full title is the 'Code of Ethics of the Australian Archaeological Association (Members' obligations to Australian Aboriginal and Torres Strait Islander people)'. The code is published in *Australian Archaeology* 39:129 (1994).

Chapter 4

1 Pardoe 1992, Field *et al.* 2000. Davidson *et al.* 1995 discuss many examples of collaboration between archaeologists and Indigenous community members.
2 For example Firth 1998 describes amicable working relations between Aborigines and anthropologists in the 1930s.
3 Several Indigenous people have expressed such sentiments to me in the course of my own work and teaching. Hemming 2000:63 discusses voiced disagreement amongst Ngarrindjeri people in South Australia over this topic in the 1940s.
4 Peters-Little 2000.
5 Thorley 1996.
6 Thorley 1996:11.
7 Lovell-Jones 1992, 1995.
8 Pardoe 1990.
9 TALC 1996.

10 These comments apply to a lesser extent to researchers based in museums, who are funded in a different way and who do not have the same teaching responsibilities as university academics.

11 Although, as discussed in Chapter 2, recent changes in Department of Education, Science and Training policy favouring more applied research should encourage more academics to get involved in cultural heritage management projects, which until recently counted far less in funding formulas than 'pure' research.

12 See for example the Editorial in the journal *Australian Archaeology* by Feary & Smith 1995.

13 Dodson *et al.* 1993, Field & Dodson 1999.

14 For example, Mulvaney & Kamminga 1999:121–129 discuss the Australian megafauna evidence.

15 Finkel 1998a.

16 Field *et al.* 2000.

17 Finkel 1998a:1342.

18 Finkel 1998a:1343.

19 Clarke 1995, Greer 1996.

20 See for example papers in Lilley 2000 by Fullagar & Head, Harrison, McDonald and Veth.

21 Davidson *et al.* 1995.

22 David Frankel, personal communication. Research results are described by Bird & Frankel 1998b and Bird, Frankel & van Waarden 1998. The context of the project is described by Bird & Frankel 1998a.

Chapter 5

1 See Pearson & Sullivan 1995 for more detail on how the planning system and heritage legislation can be used to conserve cultural places.

2 The best sources of up-to-date information about legislation are the government and other relevant websites.

3 James 1995, Ah Kit 1995, English 1996.

4 e.g. Gollan 1992.

5 The provisions of 'relics' legislation and the NSW *National Parks and Wildlife Act* are discussed in Chapter 4.

6 The following information is based on Corkill 1995a and 1995b and on comments on an earlier draft of this section of the book provided to the author by Tessa Corkill and Laila Haglund.

7 Arguments and protests against the M2 by a range of groups (including the Nature Conservation Council of NSW Inc. and the Total Environment Centre Inc., Freeway Busters and the Coalition of Transport Action Groups) are documented on several websites including Nature Conservation Council of New South Wales, Urban Bushland Program, 2001, [WWW document]. http://nccnsw.org.au/bushland (30 January 2002).

8 See Allison 1995 and other reports in the *Sydney Morning Herald* (Sacred site and relics challenge to tollway thwarted, 29 October, p. 7 and M2 action halted, 9 May).

9 Paul Taçon, personal communication.

10 *AACAI Newsletter* 63, June 1995, p.4.

11 Tessa Corkill, personal communication.

12 Corkill 1995a:4.

13 Corkill 1995b:19.

14 Tessa Corkill, personal communication.

15 See for example Ross 1996, Holdaway *et al.* 1998.

16 Tessa Corkill, personal communication.

17 Attenbrow in press and Val Attenbrow, personal communication.

18 Limitations of the 'salvage' process for archaeology are discussed in Chapter 2.

19 Egloff 1981.

20 In the mid-1990s the Commonwealth government's nature conservation agency, ANCA, entered into consultation with Aboriginal organisations in all states to consider ways of protecting Indigenous values of place by setting up Indigenous Protected Areas (Davies 1999). Information about NSW from Phil Hunt (NPWS), personal communication.

21 Examples from Tasmania are discussed in the Preface. NSW examples include Egloff 1981 (Mumbulla Mountain), McDonald & Ross 1990 (Angophora Reserve) and Gollan 1992 (Ballina). Boyd *et al.* 1996 discuss some general issues.

22 Szpak 1997.

23 Paul Taçon, personal communication.

24 But see David & Wilson 1999.

25 The best known recent cases are the Hindmarsh Island bridge development in South Australia and the dispute over mining at Coronation Hill in Kakadu National Park (NT). Both cases are discussed by Gelder & Jacobs 1998.

26 Tessa Corkill, personal communication.

27 See for example papers in Birckhead *et al.* 1992. Bradshaw 2000 describes agreements made between Hamersley Iron Pty Ltd and traditional land owners in Western Australia. See also Howitt 1998 and Strang 1998. Murphy 1996 discusses the benefits and limitations for Aboriginal people of joint management agreements. Strang 1998 discusses Aboriginal-controlled heritage management in Queensland. See also Models of Aboriginal Involvement in Birckhead *et al.* 1992. Blair & Feary 1995 discuss broader community and Aboriginal participation in regional assessment of heritage values in East Gippsland, Victoria.

28 Bennett 1999:127–128, Howitt 1998:29–30.

29 Howitt 1998 describes the RTZ-CRA Ltd case. Bradshaw 2000 discusses Hamersley Iron Pty Ltd.

30 Bennett 1999:166–168 discusses how Indigenous people of the south-east have been effectively dispossessed of their Native Title.

31 Byrne in NSW National Parks & Wildlife Service n.d.: 8.

32 Byrne in NSW National Parks & Wildlife Service n.d.: 5.

33 McNiven 1998.

34 Denis Byrne, personal communication.

35 Comments on Jervis Bay were expressed to me personally. Brockwell *et al.* 1989, and papers by Fullagar & Head, Harrison, McDonald and Veth in Lilley (ed.) 2000 discuss the way archaeology has been used in recent Native Title claims.

36 Ian McNiven, personal communication.
37 Langford 1983:2.
38 McKenzie 2000.
39 C. Smith *et al.* 2000.

Chapter 6

1 Du Cros 1999. There are few published studies of public attitudes towards archaeology in Australia, although some students have written undergraduate honours and postgraduate theses on the topic.
2 Whitten & Brooks 1972:191.
3 Robinson 1984 is highly critical of the politics of *Raiders of the Lost Ark*.
4 Weissensteiner 1993, cited in du Cros 1999.
5 S. Clarke 1999.
6 Wheeler n.d.
7 Australian archaeologist Louise Zarmati 1995 discusses the 'archaeologist as hero' myth implied by Indiana Jones.
8 Carman 1997.
9 J. Thomas 1991.
10 See Langford 1983.
11 Pardoe 1992, who describes himself as a scientist, discusses some of these issues.
12 Westwood 1987.
13 Westwood 1987:6.
14 Cole 1980:2.
15 Hiscock 1996:152–154.
16 Meskell 1998, Hodder 1998, J. Hamilton 1998.
17 Chippindale *et al.* 1990.
18 In the highly popular 'X-Files' series, FBI agents investigate cases relating to the supernatural and extraterrestrial. Conspiracy theories abound. Someone (we are never quite sure who) is trying to hide 'the truth' about extraterrestrials which the government wants to keep secret from the people. Alternative archaeology sometimes features in the programme. Such ideas are commonly expressed by 'alternative archaeologists'. See Hiscock 1996.
19 For example, Russell & McNiven 1998 discuss nineteenth-century speculation about the 'pre-Aboriginal' or 'non-Aboriginal' origins of a stone circle at Mount Elephant in Victoria.
20 See links to alternative archaeology pages from the Australian National University's Department of Archaeology and Anthropology website page, for example Hiscock, Peter, 2001, 'Archaeology World', [WWW document]. http://arts.anu.edu.au/arcworld/arcworld.htm (30 January 2002).
21 See Awareness Quest, 2001, [WWW document]. http://www.awarenessquest.com (5 February 2002).
22 Very large stone tools (usually called waisted blades or axes) are in fact found in some early sites in Australia and New Guinea.
23 The latter must refer to orthodox archaeological research by Kris Courtney and Ian McNiven reported in the journal *Australian Archaeology* (Courtney & McNiven 1998).

24 Trigger 1989:14.

25 Colley 1996a.

26 Lowenthal 1985.

27 David Frankel, personal communication.

28 Earthwatch Institute, n.d., [WWW document]. http://www.earthwatch.org
(6 February 2002). Other examples are the Whitsunday Island Project in
Queensland (B. Barker) and the Garua Island Project in West New Britain,
Papua New Guinea (R. Torrence).

29 See Near Eastern Archaeology Foundation, University of Sydney, 1998,
[WWW document]. http://www.archaeology.usyd.edu.au/neaf (6 February
2002).

30 In rare cases, slaves were used for excavation. Charles Orser & Brian Fagan
(1995:1–2) describe one of the first excavations in Virginia in the United States
in AD 1781 by Thomas Jefferson, who ordered his slaves to dig a trench
through a Native American burial mound. Slave labour was also used in early
excavations at Pompeii (Estelle Lazer, personal communication).

31 Colley 2000a:174.

32 P. Fowler 1987 discusses Thatcherite policies towards heritage in the United
Kingdom.

33 McNiven 1998:39.

34 The Australian Associated Press Mawson's Huts Foundation, 1997, [WWW
document]. http://www.mawsons-huts.com.au (30 January 2002). Anon 1997,
and Mulvaney cited in Dayton 1997b.

35 Dayton 1997b discusses the issues.

36 Hamilakis 1999:73–74, Hodder 1999.

37 See for example Central Land Council, Pitjantjatara Council, Mutitjulu Community 1987 in relation to Uluru.

38 Rothwell 1996a.

39 Rothwell 1996a.

40 For Quinkan art and the contribution of Trezise, see Flood 1997.

41 AASV 1996 and Presland 1998.

42 Mulvaney 1988:4.

43 Presland 1998.

44 Wright 1971:57.

45 Mulvaney 1998.

46 Renfrew & Bahn 1991:63.

47 Digging up the Past Foundation, n.d., [WWW document]. http://www.argonet.
co.uk/education/diggings (30 January 2002).

48 Down 1999.

49 The case was widely reported in the *Sydney Morning Herald*, the *Australian*, the
Sun Herald and other Australian newspapers in mid- to late 1992. See for
example Hills 1992 and Pockley 1992. See also Colley 1992.

50 Australian Skeptics Inc., 2001, [WWW document]. http://www.skeptics.com.au
(5 February 2002).

51 Hills 1992:32.

52 Ronald Sackville talking on ABC Radio National's *Religion Report*, Wednesday

4 June 1997, transcript at http://www.abc.net.au/rn/talks/8.30/relrept/trr9723.htm. See also Curtin 1997, Curtin & Dayton 1997, Dayton 1997a and Moloney 1997. The case was also reported overseas through Reuter.

53 Griffiths 1996.

54 For example Vitelli 1996:29–110.

55 See McKenzie 2000 for bottle collectors. For further information on legislation for historic shipwrecks see Australian Institute for Maritime Archaeology, n.d., [WWW document]. http://www.aima.net.au (5 February 2002).

56 This section is based on Colley 2000a.

57 Feary 1994a.

58 Connah 1998, Anon. 1998, Mackay & Karskens 1999, Colley 2000a. Teaching workshop on maritime and historical archaeology held at the 2000 Conference of the Australasian Society of Historical Archaeology, Flinders University, Adelaide.

59 Cited in Colley 2000a:172–173.

60 Zarmati & Cremin 1998.

61 Helen Nicholson, cited in Colley 2000a. David Frankel, personal communication.

62 Val Attenbrow, cited in Colley 2000a. For further information about the Australian Museum, see Australian Museum, Sydney, 2001, [WWW document]. http://www.amonline.net.au (5 February 2002).

63 Historic Houses Trust of NSW 1996.

64 Flanagan 1996.

65 Wayne Johnson, cited in Colley 2000a:176.

66 New South Wales Heritage Office 1998.

67 Nadia Iacono and Matthew Kelly, cited in Colley 2000a:175. Estelle Lazer, personal communication.

68 Colley 2000a:175.

Chapter 7

1 See for example Baker & Thomas 1990.

2 Fullagar, Price & Head 1996.

3 For an overview of other current evidence for the possible date of first human settlement of Australia, see Mulvaney & Kamminga 1999:130–146.

4 See Mulvaney & Kamminga 1999:148. The implications of these different theories are actually more complicated, as they imply things about the boat-building and cognitive abilities of whoever were the first humans or hominids to reach Australia, who had to cross water to get here.

5 Paul Taçon and Lesley Head, personal communications.

6 Roberts et al. 1998, Spooner 1998, Watchman et al. 2000.

7 Head 1996:738.

8 See Woodford 1996a and 1996b. Jinmium attracted huge media attention. Key newspaper reports about Jinmium have generally been listed in full in the text and are also included in the bibliography. This list is not comprehensive—even of Australian media coverage.

9 Chippindale 1996:729.

10 Leech 1996a, 1996b, C. Smith 1996, Morwood 1996.
11 Chippindale 1996:730.
12 Rothwell 1996b, Blair 1996, Taçon & Fullagar 1996.
13 Anon. 1996.
14 Ceresa 1996, Ellicott 1996.
15 Cullen 1996.
16 C. Jones 1996a, 1996b.
17 Leech 1997.
18 West 1990.
19 Head 1996, 1998. Byrne 1996 also discusses archaeology and Australian nationalism.
20 Moser 1996, Gero 1993.
21 Davis 1999.
22 Morwood *et al.* 1998.
23 Thorne *et al.* 1999, Bowler & Magee 2000, Gillespie & Roberts 2000.
24 Adcock *et al.* 2001.
25 Bowler 2001.
26 The following list of media reports is not comprehensive: Dayton 2001a, 2001b, Harris 2001, C. Jones 2001, Jones & Dixon 2001, O'Malley 2001, O'Neill 2001, Vince 2001, Walker 2001.
27 Horacek 2001 shows two women in a café drinking coffee and discussing the find. Woman 1: 'Analysis of Mungo Man's DNA has provided us with more pieces of the puzzle of where we've come from'. Woman 2: 'If only someone could work out what to analyse to tell us where we're going'. Rowen (in Walker 2001) shows an 'Aussie bloke' wearing shorts, thongs and colourful shirt, beer can in hand, described as 'Mambo Man' (in reference to the Australian clothing company), standing next to a statue of his ancestor 'Mungo Man', who has identical physical features and is also wearing thongs. McNeilly (in Jones & Dixon 2001) shows a naked woman plucking an apple from a tree while holding a koala in her arms. Tiedemann (in Bowler 2001) shows a scientist with axe.
28 Pappin for Willandra Lakes World Heritage Area Three Traditional Tribal Groups Elders Council 2001.
29 Quoted in Jopson 1999.
30 Ian McNiven, personal communication.
31 South West Institute of Technical and Further Education, Victoria 2000.
32 Heritage Victoria 2000, Adams 2000.
33 Boyd 1995, Boyd, Charter & Lancaster 1994.
34 Du Cros 1992 also discusses the case of the Mahogany Ship. See also du Cros 1999.
35 See for example Cunningham & Turner 1997, Boyd-Barrett & Newbold 1995, R. Fowler 1991.
36 Leigh Dayton, personal communication.
37 Turner & Cunningham 1997:4.
38 Masterton & Patching 1990.
39 For example Whittaker 1990, Poprzeczny 1992.
40 West 1990, Boyd 1995.

41 Du Cros 1999.

42 David Frankel, personal communication.

43 See Champion & Chippendale 1997 for an introduction to a special section of the journal *Antiquity* devoted to electronic archaeology. Hodder 1999 also provides much relevant discussion.

Chapter 8

1 Hiscock 1996.

2 Chippindale *et al.* 1990.

3 Gelder & Jacobs 1998.

4 Head 1998, Tuhiwai Smith 1999.

5 Hodder 1999 and Hamilakis 1999 both discuss meanings of postmodernism in relation to archaeology. Murray 1996b and 1996c discusses the notion of 'decolonising' Australian archaeology.

6 Tuhiwai Smith 1999.

7 For example, Ken Gelder and Jane Jacobs discuss elements of what they call 'Uncanny Australia' created by Australian society's attempts to deal with Indigenous 'sacredness' under conditions of postcolonialism. In her discussion of postmodernity and Australian archaeology, Lesley Head 1998 also cites work by anthropologist Deborah Bird Rose in describing a postcolonial world in which social and ecological systems are ruptured, broken and wounded by colonialism, yet where people strive for what she calls 'wholeness'. Gelder & Jacobs 1998, Rose 1996.

8 Mulvaney & Kamminga 1999 provide a good summary of data and arguments. Head 1998 discusses wider public implications.

9 This is an assumption. No one has done any research on how individual Australian archaeologists decide which view of the past they will accept.

10 Bird & Frankel 1998b, David Frankel, personal communication 2000.

11 Flood 1995:240–245.

12 A. Clarke 1994, Clarke & Hamm 1996.

13 See for example Video Education Australasia *et al.* 1990. Clarke 1994 discusses artists' illustrations of such houses and other public interpretations. See the original 1983 and revised 1989 Collins editions of Flood's *Archaeology of the Dreamtime*. The illustration has been removed from later editions.

14 Clarke 1994:1.

15 Clarke & Hamm 1996:81. About the same time South Australia was also concerned that it did not have any World Heritage listings either and proposed parts of the Nullarbor Plain be nominated.

16 Builth 1996:135, Builth 2000.

17 Builth 1996:85.

18 Builth 1996:86.

19 David Frankel, personal communication 2000.

20 Bowdler 1993:133–134 discusses this issue.

21 Mulvaney & Kamminga 1999 discuss these data and their interpretation.

22 Discussed by Veth *et al.* 1998.

23 Mulvaney & Kamminga 1999:419–423.
24 Meskell 1997.
25 I am grateful to John Clegg for his comments on voyaging and Phoenicians. Stanbury & Clegg 1990:92 also give an example of Indigenous rock engravings being ascribed to holy Indian hares carved by Maoris on a migration voyage to New Zealand.
26 Russell & McNiven 1998.
27 McNiven & Russell 1997.
28 Mulvaney 1969:50–53 and Prentis 1995 discuss Birdsell's and related tri-hybrid theories. Bennett 1999:164–169 overviews the Mabo case. Letters to the *Sydney Morning Herald* include Plowman 1993, Trebeck 1993. See also reply by White 1993.
29 Takarakka Rock Art Australia, 1999, [WWW document]. http://www.kilpatha.com/info.html (5 February 2002).
30 Walsh 1994:74.
31 See for example Walsh & Morwood 1999 and further references contained within it.
32 Barry 1997, Lewis 1997.
33 Spriggs 1998.
34 Hodder 1998, 1999.
35 Marcus 1988. Similar issues have been discussed for New Zealand by Tuhiwai Smith 1999:102.
36 Dropulich 1996, Janke 1998:23.
37 Hamilton 1998:170.
38 Hamilakis 1999:60.
39 Head 1998:2–3, Mulvaney 1993, Bonyhady & Griffiths 1996b.
40 Head 1998:2–3.

Bibliography

Aboriginal and Torres Strait Islander Commission. www.atsic.gov.au (29 January 2002).

Adams, D. 2000. Dig raises fresh Mahogany ship hopes. In *The Age*. 15 August. www.theage.com.au/news/20000816/A6374–2000Aug15.htm (1 September 2001).

Adcock, G.I., S. Dennis, S. Eastel, G.A. Huttley, L.S. Jermiin, W.J. Peacock & A. Thorne 2001. Mitochondrial DNA sequences in ancient Australians: Implications for modern human origins. *Proceedings of the National Academy of Sciences of the United States of America* 98(2): 537–542.

Ah Kit, J. 1995. Aboriginal aspirations for heritage conservation. *Historic Environment* 11:34–36.

Allen, H. 1997. Conceptions of time in the interpretation of the Kakadu landscape. In D.B. Rose & A. Clarke (eds). *Tracking Knowledge in Northern Australian Landscapes*. Casuarina, NT: North Australia Research Unit. Pages 141–154.

——1998. Reinterpreting the 1969–1972 Willandra Lakes archaeological surveys. *Archaeology in Oceania* 33:207–220.

Allen, J. 1978. The archaeology of nineteenth century British imperialism: An Australian case study. In R.L. Schuyler (ed.). *Historical Archaeology: A Guide to Substantive and Theoretical Contributions*. Farmingdale, NY: Baywood. Pages 139–148.

——1983. Aborigines and archaeologists in Tasmania, 1983. *Australian Archaeology* 16:7–10.

——1987. The Politics of the Past. Inaugural Address, La Trobe University. Melbourne: La Trobe University.

——1995a. A short history of the Tasmanian affair. *Australian Archaeology* 41:43–48.

——1995b. We find that what's theirs is theirs—but what's ours? Letter to the editor. *Australian* 2–3 September.

——1996a (ed.). *Report of the Southern Forests Archaeological Project*. Volume 1. Melbourne: School of Archaeology, La Trobe University.

——1996b. Warreen Cave. In J. Allen (ed.). *Report of the Southern Forests Archaeological Project*. Volume 1. Melbourne: School of Archaeology, La Trobe University. Pages 135–167.

——1996c. Letter to the editors. *Australian Archaeology* 42:66–67.

Allen, J. & R. Cosgrove 1996. Background history of the Southern Forests Archaeological Project. In J. Allen (ed.). *Report of the Southern Forests Archaeological Project*. Volume 1. Melbourne: School of Archaeology, La Trobe University. Pages 3–17.

Allison, C. 1995. The road that ate Sydney. *Sydney Morning Herald*. News Review. 11 November. Page 27.

Anon. 1996. Jinmium find calls for caution. *Australian*. Editorial. 24 September.

——1997. PM backs foundation. The AAP Mawson's Huts Foundation. A special advertising report. *Weekend Australian*. 10–11 May. Page 8.

——1998. The Disappearing Historical Archaeologist. *Australian Archaeology* 46:47–48.

Appadurai, A. 1986. *The Social Life of Things*. Cambridge: Cambridge University Press.

Archaeological and Anthropological Society of Victoria Inc., 1996, www.home.vicnet.net.au/~aasv/aasvhom.htm (1 September 2001).

Arnold, B. 1990. The past as propaganda: Totalitarian archaeology in Nazi Germany. *Antiquity* 64(244):464–478.

Arnold, B. & H. Hassmann 1995. Archaeology in Nazi Germany: The legacy of the Faustian bargain. In P.L. Kohl & C. Fawcett (eds). *Nationalism, Politics and the Practice of Archaeology*. Cambridge: Cambridge University Press. Pages 70–81.

Attenbrow, V. in press. *Sydney's Aboriginal Past*. Sydney: University of New South Wales Press.

Attwood, B. & J. Arnold (eds) 1992. *Power, Knowledge and Aborigines*. Melbourne: La Trobe University Press.

Attwood, B. & A. Markus 1999. *The Struggle for Aboriginal Rights*. Sydney: Allen & Unwin.

Australian Associated Press, 1997, Mawson's Huts Foundation. www.mawsons-huts.com.au (5 February 2002).

Australian Department of Communications, Information Technology and the Arts. www.dcita.gov.au (29 January 2002).

Australian Heritage Commission 1989. *Protecting Australia's National Estate: The Power and Roles of Federal, State, Local Government and Voluntary Organisations Involved in Heritage Conservation in Australia.* Canberra: Australian Heritage Commission.

——1990. *Criteria for the Register of the National Estate.* Canberra: Australian Heritage Commission.

Australian Institute for Maritime Archaeology. www.aima.iinet.au (5 February 2002).

Australian Museum, Sydney, 2001. www.amonline.net.au (5 February 2002).

Australian Research Council 1998. *Knowing Ourselves and Others: The Humanities in Australia into the 21st Century.* Prepared by a Reference Group for the Australian Academy of the Humanities. 4 volumes. Canberra: Department of Employment, Education, Training and Youth Affairs.

——2002. www.arc.gov.au (30 January 2002).

Australian Skeptics Inc. 2001. www.skeptics.com.au (5 February 2002).

Awareness Quest, 2001. www.awarenessquest.com (5 February 2002).

Baker, F. & J. Thomas 1990. *Writing the Past in the Present.* Lampeter, Wales: St David's University College.

Baker, R. 1999. *Land is Life: From Bush to Town: The Story of the Yanyuwa people.* Sydney: Allen & Unwin.

Balme, J. & W. Beck (eds) 1995. *Gendered Archaeology. The Second Australian Women in Archaeology Conference.* Canberra: ANH Publications, Research School of Pacific and Asian Studies, Australian National University.

Barry, M. 1997. I would sooner not call them Bradshaws. BA (Hons) thesis. Sydney: School of Archaeology, University of Sydney.

Bennett, S. 1999. *White Politics and Black Australians.* Sydney: Allen & Unwin.

Bickford, A. 1979. 'The Last Tasmanian': Superb documentary or racist fantasy? *Filmnews.* January 1979. Pages 11–14.

——1996. The archaeological project 1983–1990. In Historic Houses Trust of NSW. *Sites: Nailing the Debate: Archaeology and Interpretation in Museums, Seminar, 7–9 April 1995.* Edited by S. Hunt & J. Lydon. Sydney: HHT. Pages 65–74.

Binford, L.R. 1984. An Alyawara day: Flour, spinifex, gum and shifting perspectives. *Journal of Anthropological Research* 40:157–182.

Birckhead, J., T. de Lacy & L. Smith (eds) 1992. *Aboriginal Involvement in Parks and Protected Areas*. Canberra: Aboriginal Studies Press.

Bird, C. & D. Frankel 1991. Chronology and explanation in western Victoria and south-east South Australia. *Archaeology in Oceania* 26:1–16.

——1998a. University, community and government: Developing a collaborative archaeological research project in western Victoria. *Australian Aboriginal Studies* 1998(1):35–39.

——1998b. Pleistocene and Early Holocene archaeology in Victoria. A view from Gariwerd. *The Artefact* 21:48–62.

Bird, C., D. Frankel & N. van Waarden 1998. New radiocarbon determinations from the Grampians-Gariwerd region, western Victoria. *Archaeology in Oceania* 33:31–36.

Birmingham, J. 1992. *Wybalenna: The Archaeology of Cultural Accommodation in Nineteenth Century Tasmania*. Sydney: Australian Society for Historical Archaeology.

Blair, R. 1996. Letter to the editor. *Australian*. 30 September.

Blair, S. & S. Feary 1995. Regional assessment of cultural heritage: A new approach based on community and expert partnerships. *Historic Environment* 11:15–21.

Bonyhady, T. 1996. The stuff of heritage. In T. Bonyhady & T. Griffiths (eds). *Prehistory to Politics: John Mulvaney, the Humanities and the Public Intellectual*. Melbourne: Melbourne University Press. Pages 144–162.

Bonyhady, T. & T. Griffiths (eds) 1996a. *Prehistory to Politics: John Mulvaney, the Humanities and the Public Intellectual*. Melbourne: Melbourne University Press.

——1996b. The making of a public intellectual. In T. Bonyhady & T. Griffiths (eds). *Prehistory to Politics: John Mulvaney, the Humanities and the Public Intellectual*. Melbourne: Melbourne University Press. Pages 1–19.

Boot, P. & P. Kuskie 1996. Consultancy and thesis: What's the difference? Two approaches to archaeological survey of Jumping Creek Valley, Queanbeyan. *Australian Archaeology* 43:23–27.

Bowdler, S. 1976. Hook, line and dilly bag: An interpretation of an Australian coastal shell midden. *Mankind* 10:248–258.

——1984. Archaeological significance as a mutable quality. In S. Sullivan & S. Bowdler (eds). *Site Surveys and Significance Assessment in Australian Archaeology*. Canberra: Department of Prehistory, Research School of Pacific Studies, Australian National University. Pages 1–9.

——1986. Recent directions in Tasmanian prehistory and the role of cultural resource management. *Australian Archaeology* 23:3–10.

——1993. Views of the past in Australian prehistory. In M. Spriggs, D.E. Yen, W. Ambrose, R. Jones, A. Thorne & A. Andrews (eds). *A Community of Culture: The People and Prehistory of the Pacific*. Canberra: Department of Prehistory, Research School of Pacific Studies, Australian National University. Pages 123–138.

Bowler, J. 2001. Mungo dates out of kilter. *Australian*. Opinion. 10 January. Page 11.

Bowler, J.M. & J.W. Magee 2000. Redating Australia's oldest human remains: A sceptic's view. *Journal of Human Evolution* 38:719–726.

Boyd, B. 1995. Media coverage of an archaeological issue: Lessons from the press release of initial radiocarbon dating results of a possible pre-Cook European ship at Suffolk Park, northern New South Wales. *Australian Archaeology* 40:50–55.

Boyd, B., C. Charter & G. Lancaster 1994. The Suffolk Park shipwreck, Northern NSW: Pre-Cook explorers or 19th century trader? *Archaeology in Oceania* 29:91–94.

Boyd, B., M. Cotter, W. O'Connor & D. Sattler 1996. Cognitive ownership of heritage places: Social construction and cultural heritage management. In S. Ulm, S. Lilley & A. Ross (eds). *Australian Archaeology '95: Proceedings of the 1995 Australian Archaeological Association Annual Conference*. Tempus 6. St Lucia, Qld: Anthropology Museum, University of Queensland. Pages 123–140.

Boyd-Barrett, O. & C. Newbold 1995. *Approaches to Media: A Reader*. London: Arnold.

Bradshaw, E. 2000. Mining and cultural heritage management: The Hamersley Iron experience. In I. Lilley (ed.). *Native Title and the Transformation of Archaeology in the Postcolonial World*. Sydney: University of Sydney, Oceania Monographs 50. Pages 10–23.

Brockwell, S., T. Gara, S. Colley & S. Cane 1989. The history and archaeology of Ooldea Soak and Mission. *Australian Archaeology* 28:55–79.

Builth, H. 1996. Lake Condah revisited: Archaeological constructions of a cultural landscape. BA (Hons) thesis, Aboriginal studies. Adelaide: Flinders University of South Australia.

——2000. The connection between Gunditjamara Aboriginal people and their environment: The case for complex hunter-gatherers in

Australia. In G. Moore, J. Hunt and L. Trevillan (eds). *Environment-Behaviour Research on the Pacific Rim*. Sydney: University of Sydney, Faculty of Architecture. Pages 197–210.

Byrne, D. 1984. A survey strategy for a coastal forest. In S. Sullivan & S. Bowdler (eds). *Site Surveys and Significance Assessment in Australian Archaeology*. Canberra: Department of Prehistory, Research School of Pacific Studies, Australian National University. Pages 61–70.

——1991. Western hegemony in archaeological heritage management. *History and Anthropology* 5:269–276.

——1996. Deep nation: Australia's acquisition of an indigenous past. *Aboriginal History* 20:82–107.

——1998. *In Sad but Loving Memory: Aboriginal Burials and Cemeteries of the Last 200 years in NSW*. Sydney: NSW National Parks and Wildlife Service.

Byrne, D., H. Brayshaw & T. Ireland 2001. *Social Significance. A Discussion Paper*. Sydney: NSW National Parks and Wildlife Service.

Carman, J. 1997. *Material harm: Archaeological Studies of War and Violence*. Glasgow: Cruithne Press.

Casey, M., D. Donlon, J. Hope & S. Wellfare (eds) 1998. *Redefining Archaeology: Feminist Perspectives*. Canberra: ANH Publications, Research School of Pacific & Asian Studies, Australian National University.

Central Land Council, Pitjantjatara Community, Muṯitjulu Community 1987. *Sharing the Park. Anangu Initiatives in Ayers Rock Tourism*. Alice Springs: Institute for Aboriginal Development.

Ceresa, M. 1996. Rock that holds fingerprints of life. *Australian*. 25 September. Page 1.

Champion, S. & C. Chippendale 1997. Introduction. Special review section: Electronic archaeology. *Antiquity* 71:1026.

Chippindale, C. 1985. Skeletons rattle down under. *New Scientist*. 14 March. Pages 10–11.

——1996. Editorial. *Antiquity* 70:729–739.

Chippindale, C., P. Devereux, P. Fowler, R. Jones & T. Sebastian 1990. *Who Owns Stonehenge?* London: B.T. Batsford Ltd.

Chippindale, C. & P.S.C. Taçon (eds) 1998. *The Archaeology of Rock-art*. Cambridge: Cambridge University Press.

Clark, J. 1983. *The Aboriginal People of Tasmania*. Hobart: Tasmanian Museum & Art Gallery.

Clarke, A. 1994. Romancing the Stones. The cultural construction of an archaeological landscape in the Western District of Victoria. *Archae-ology in Oceania* 29(1):1–15.

——1995. Archaeology on Groote Eylandt. In I. Davidson, C. Lovell-Jones & R. Bancroft (eds). *Archaeologists and Aborigines Working Together.* Armidale, NSW: University of New England Press. Pages 13–15.

Clarke, A. & G. Hamm 1996. Stumbling over stones: Site management at Lake Condah. In L. Smith & A. Clarke (eds). *Issues in Management Archae-ology.* Tempus 5. St Lucia, Qld: Anthropology Museum, University of Queensland. Pages 79–84.

Clarke, S. 1999. Tell Lara we love her. *Sydney Morning Herald.* ICON. 23–29 October. Pages 4–5.

Cleere, H. (ed) 1984. *Approaches to the Archaeological Heritage: A Comparative Study of World Cultural Resource Management Systems.* Cambridge & New York: Cambridge University Press.

——(ed) 1989. *Archaeological Heritage Management in the Modern World.* London & Boston: Unwin Hyman.

Cole, J.R. 1980. Cult archaeology and unscientific method and theory. *Advances in Archaeological Method and Theory* 3:1–33.

Colley, S. 1992. Noah's Ark, archaeology, professionalism and the public. *Australian Association of Consulting Archaeologists Incorporated Newsletter* 52:11–12.

——1996. Caught in the web: Cultural policy, cultural places and Australian archaeology. *Culture and Policy* 7(2):141–154.

——1997. A pre- and post-contact Aboriginal shell midden at Disaster Bay, New South Wales south coast. *Australian Archaeology* 45:1–19.

——2000a. Archaeology and education in Australia. *Antiquity* 74:171–177.

——2000b. Mass higher education, university funding, student numbers and historical archaeology at Sydney University. *Australasian Society for Historical Archaeology Newsletter* 30(1):9–10.

Colley, S. & A. Bickford 1996. 'Real' Aborigines and 'Real' Archaeology: Aboriginal places and Australian historical archaeology. *World Archaeo-logical Bulletin* 7:5–21.

Colley, S. & R.I. Jack 1996. Australian heritage places. In International Council on Monuments and Sites. *Monuments and Sites Australia.* Colombo, Sri Lanka: ICOMOS. Pages 15–28.

Colley, S. & R. Jones 1987. New fish bone data from Rocky Cape, north west Tasmania. *Archaeology in Oceania* 22:67–71.

Collis, J. 2000. Towards a national training scheme for England and the United Kingdom. *Antiquity* 74:208–214.

Connah, G. 1993. *The Archaeology of Australia's History*. Cambridge: Cambridge University Press.

——1998. Pattern and purpose in historical archaeology. *Australasian Historical Archaeology* 16:3–7.

Cooper, M.A., A. Firth, J. Carman & D. Wheatley 1995. *Managing Archaeology*. London: Routledge.

Corkill, T. 1995a. M2 mayhem—or nightmare on the superhighway to nowhere. *Australian Association of Consulting Archaeologists Incorporated Newsletter* 63:4.

——1995b. Meanwhile, back to real life on the M2. *Australian Association of Consulting Archaeologists Incorporated Newsletter* 64:19.

Cosgrove, R., J. Allen & B. Marshall 1990. Palaeoecology and pleistocene human occupation in south central Tasmania. *Antiquity* 64:59–78.

——1994. Late Pleistocene human occupation in Tasmania: A reply to Thomas. *Australian Archaeology* 38:28–35.

Cotter, M., R. Boyd & J. Gardiner (eds.) 2001. *Heritage Landscapes: Understanding place and communities*. Lismore, NSW: Southern Cross University Press.

Council for Aboriginal Reconciliation. www.reconciliation.org.au/council (5 February 2002).

Courtney, K. & I. McNiven 1998. Clay tobacco pipes from Aboriginal middens on Fraser Island, Queensland. *Australian Archaeology* 47:44–53.

Cowlishaw, G. 1992. Studying Aborigines: Changing canons in anthropology and history. In B. Attwood & J. Arnold (eds). *Power, Knowledge and Aborigines*. Melbourne: La Trobe University Press. Pages 20–31.

Cremin, A. (ed.) 2001. *1901. Australian Life at Federation: An Illustrated Chronicle*. Sydney: University of New South Wales Press.

Cullen, J. 1996. The first man was an Aussie. *Sun Herald*. 22 September.

Cunningham, S. & G. Turner (eds) 1997. *The Media in Australia: Industries, Texts, Audiences*. Sydney: Allen & Unwin.

Curtin, J. 1997. Ark case judge asks if court should get involved. *Sydney Morning Herald*. 18 April. Page 3.

Curtin, J. & L. Dayton 1997. The man who put the Loch Ness monster into the Ark. *Sydney Morning Herald*. 11 April. Pages 1 & 6.

David, B. & D. Chant 1995. Rock art and regionalization in north Queensland prehistory. *Memoirs of the Queensland Museum* 37:357–528.

David, B., I. McNiven, V. Attenbrow, J. Flood & J. Collins 1994. Of Lightning Brothers and white cockatoos: Dating the antiquity of signifying systems in the Northern Territory, Australia. *Antiquity* 68:241–251.

David, B. & M. Wilson 1999. Re-reading the landscape: Place and identity in NE Australia during the late Holocene. *Cambridge Archaeological Journal* 9(2):163–188.

Davidson, I. 1991. Notes for a code of ethics for Australian archaeologists working with Aboriginal and Torres Strait Islander heritage. *Australian Archaeology* 32:61–64.

Davidson, I., C. Lovell-Jones & R. Bancroft (eds) 1995. *Archaeologists and Aborigines Working Together*. Armidale, NSW: University of New England Press.

Davies, J. 1999. *Indigenous protected areas*. www.waite.adelaide.edu.au/AME/jdavies/B6.html (1 October 2001).

Davis, M. 1999. *Gangland: Cultural Elites and the New Generationalism*. Second edition. Sydney: Allen & Unwin.

Davison, G. 1991a. A brief history of the Australian heritage movement. In G. Davison & C. McConville (eds). *A Heritage Handbook*. Sydney: Allen & Unwin. Pages 14–27.

——1991b. The meanings of 'heritage'. In G. Davison & C. McConville (eds). *A Heritage Handbook*. Sydney: Allen & Unwin. Pages 1–13.

Dayton, L. 1997a. Ark or no ark, what were the golf tees doing there? *Sydney Morning Herald*. 11 April. Page 6.

——1997b. Huts in heritage storm. *Sydney Morning Herald*. Opinion. 5 August.

——2001a. DNA clue to man's origin. *Australian*. 9 January. Page 1.

——2001b. Mungo Man: The last of his kind? *Australian*. News Feature. 9 January. Pages 8–9.

——2001c. All in the family? *Australian*. Features. 10 January. Page 13.

Department of Archaeology and Anthropology, Australian National University, 1999. www.anu.edu.au/AandA (6 February 2002).

Digging up the Past Foundation. www.argonet.co.uk/education/diggings (30 January 2002).

Dodson, J.R., R. Fullagar, J.H. Furby, R. Jones & I. Prosser 1993. Humans and megafauna in a Late Pleistocene environment from Cuddie

Springs, north western New South Wales. *Archaeology in Oceania* 28:94–99.

Down, D. 1999. Has the ark of the covenant been found? *Archaeological Diggings* 6(4), August–September 1999:23.

Dropulich, S. 1996. Outraged Aborigines seek ban on 'mutant' bestseller. *ANU Reporter* (31 January) 27(1):1.

du Cros, H. 1992. To see ourselves as others see us: Australian archaeology's value to Australian contemporary culture. Paper presented at Archaeology in the Early 1990s research seminar. 22–24 August. Reproduced in an unpublished collection of papers of the same name. Armidale, NSW: Department of Archaeology & Palaeoanthropology, University of New England.

——1999. Popular notions of Australian archaeology. *Journal of Australian Studies* 62:190–197; 260–261.

du Cros, H. & L. Smith (eds) 1993. *Women in Archaeology: A Feminist Critique.* Canberra: Department of Prehistory, Research School of Pacific Studies, Australian National University.

Earthwatch Institute. www.earthwatch.org (6 February 2002).

Edgar, J. 1998. NSW NPWS—Aboriginal Cultural Heritage Standards & Guidelines Kit, Appendix 4: Some Comments. *Australian Association of Consulting Archaeologists Incorporated Newsletter* 76:6–8.

Egloff, B. 1981. *Mumbulla Mountain: An Anthropological and Archaeological Investigation.* National Parks and Wildlife Service Occasional Paper 4. Sydney: NSW NPWS.

——1984. Sampling the five forests. In S. Sullivan & S. Bowdler (eds). *Site Surveys and Significance Assessment in Australian Archaeology.* Canberra: Department of Prehistory, Research School of Pacific Studies, Australian National University. Pages 71–78.

——1994. From Swiss Family Robinson to Sir Russell Drysdale: Towards changing the tone of historical archaeology in Australia. *Australian Archaeology* 39:1–8.

——1997. 'Sea long stretched between': Perspectives of Aboriginal fishing on the south coast of New South Wales in light of *Mason v. Triton.* Paper presented at the Aboriginality in South-East Australia Conference. Canberra: Centre for Cross-Cultural Research, Australian National University.

Egloff, B. & D. Ranson 1988. The application of earth resistivity surveys to

Australian archaeological sites. *Journal of the Australian Society for Historical Archaeology* 6:57–73.

Ellicott, J. 1996. More dating tests for Jinmium rocks. *Australian*. 25 September. Page 2.

Ellis, B. 1994. *Rethinking the Paradigm: Cultural Heritage Management in Queensland*. Ngulaig 10. Brisbane: University of Queensland Aboriginal and Torres Strait Islander Studies Unit.

English, A. 1996. Legislative and policy frameworks for indigenous involvement in cultural heritage management in New Zealand and New South Wales. *Environmental and Planning Law Journal* 13:103–119.

English, A.J. 2000. An emu in the hole. Exploring the link between biodiversity and Aboriginal cultural heritage in New South Wales, Australia. *Parks* 10(2):13–25. Gland, Switzerland: IUCN, the World Conservation Union.

Environment Australia, Department of the Environment and Heritage, 2002, 'Australian and World Heritage', www.ea.gov.au/heritage/awh (29 January 2002).

Evans, C. 1995. Archaeology against the state. Roots of internationalism. In P.J. Ucko (ed.). *Theory in Archaeology: A World Perspective*. London: Routledge. Pages 312–326.

Fagan, B. 1996. Archaeology's dirty secret. In K.D. Vitelli (ed.). *Archaeological Ethics: Readings from Archaeology Magazine*. Walnut Creek, London, New Delhi: Altamira Press. Pages 247–251.

Feary, S. 1994a. Teaching and research in archaeology: Some statistics. *Australian Archaeology* 39:130–132.

——1994b. Assessing the cultural values of forests. In M. Sullivan, S. Brockwell & A. Webb (eds). *Archaeology in the North: Proceedings of the 1993 Australian Archaeological Association Conference*. Darwin: North Australia Research Unit, Australian National University. Pages 294–318.

Feary, S. & M. Smith 1995. Editorial. *Australian Archaeology* 41:iii.

Field, J., J. Barker, R. Barker, E. Coffey, L. Coffey, E. Crawford, L. Darcy, T. Fields, G. Lord, B. Steadman & S. Colley 2000. Coming back: Aborigines and archaeologists at Cuddie Springs. *Public Archaeology* 1:35–48.

Field, J.R. & J. Dodson 1999. Late Pleistocene megafauna and archaeology from Cuddie Springs, south-eastern Australia. *Proceedings of the Prehistoric Society* 65:275–302.

Finkel, E. 1998a. Aboriginal groups warm to studies of early Australians. *Science* 280 (29 May):1342–1343.

——1998b. University funding feels big chill. *Science* 280 (29 May): 1342–1343.

Firth, R. 1998. Anthropologists and Aborigines 65 years ago. *Australian Aboriginal Studies* 1998(1):40–42.

Flanagan, R. 1996. Anti-museum: The case of the Strahan Wharf Centre. In Historic Houses Trust of NSW. *Sites: Nailing the debate: Archaeology and Interpretation in Museums, Seminar, 7–9 April 1995.* Edited by S. Hunt & J. Lydon. Sydney: HHT. Pages 179–198.

Flood, J. 1980. *The Moth Hunters: Aboriginal Prehistory of the Australian Alps.* Canberra: Australian Institute of Aboriginal Studies.

——1988. No ethnography, no moth hunters. In B. Meehan & R. Jones (eds). *Archaeology with Ethnography: An Australian Perspective.* Canberra: Department of Prehistory, Research School of Pacific Studies, Australian National University. Pages 270–276.

——1989. 'Tread softly, for you tread on my bones': The development of cultural resource management in Australia. In H.F. Cleere (ed.). *Archaeological Heritage Management in the Modern World.* London: Unwin Hyman. Pages 79–101.

——1993. Cultural resource management in Australia: The last three decades. In M. Spriggs, D.E. Yen, W. Ambrose, R. Jones, A. Thorne & A. Andrews (eds). *A Community of Culture: The People and Prehistory of the Pacific.* Canberra: Department of Prehistory, Research School of Pacific Studies, Australian National University. Pages 259–265.

——1995. *Archaeology of the Dreamtime.* Revised Edition. Sydney: Angus & Robertson.

——1997. *Rock Art of the Dreamtime.* Sydney: Angus & Robertson.

——1999. *Archaeology of the Dreamtime.* Revised Edition. Sydney: Harper Collins.

Flood, J., I. Johnson & S. Sullivan 1989. *Sites and Bytes: Recording Aboriginal Places in Australia.* Australian Heritage Commission Special Australian Heritage Publication Series, No. 8. Canberra: Australian Government Publishing Service.

Fowler, D.D. 1982. Cultural Resources Management. *Advances in Archaeological Method and Theory* 5:1–50.

Fowler, P. 1987. What price the man-made heritage? *Antiquity* 61: 409–423.

Fowler, R. 1991. *Language in the News: Discourse and Ideology in the Press*. London & New York: Routledge.

Frankel, D. (ed.) 1980. Education and Training in Prehistory and Archaeology in Australia. *Australian Archaeology* 11:69–184.

——1991. *Remains to be Seen: Archaeological Insights into Australian Prehistory*. Melbourne: Longman Cheshire.

——1995. The Australian transition: Real and perceived boundaries. *Antiquity* 69:649–655.

——1997. The Australian Research Council and archaeology. *Australian Archaeology* 45:45–47.

——1998. Archaeology. In Australian Research Council. *Knowing Ourselves and Others: The Humanities in Australia into the 21st Century*. Prepared by a Reference Group for the Australian Academy of the Humanities. Volume 2. Canberra: Department of Employment, Education, Training and Youth Affairs. Pages 17–28.

Fullagar, R.L.K., D.M. Price & L.M. Head 1996. Early human occupation of northern Australia: Archaeology and thermoluminescence dating of Jinmium rock-shelter, Northern Territory. *Antiquity* 70:751–773.

Gait, P. 1995. Excavating under an enforced agenda. Letter to the editor. *Australian*. 16–17 September.

Geering, K. & C. Roberts 1992. Current limitations on Aboriginal involvement in Aboriginal site management in centralwest and north-west New South Wales. In J. Birckhead, T. de Lacy & L. Smith (eds). *Aboriginal Involvement in Parks and Protected Areas*. Canberra: Aboriginal Studies Press. Pages 207–214.

Gelder, K. & J.M. Jacobs 1997. Promiscuous sacred sites: Reflections on secrecy and scepticism in the Hindmarsh Island Affair. *Australian Humanities Review*, Issue 6, June–July 1997. www.lib.latrobe.edu.au/AHR/archive/Issue-June–1997/gelder.html (6 February 2002).

——1998. *Uncanny Australia: Sacredness and Identity in a Postcolonial Nation*. Melbourne: Melbourne University Press.

Gero, J.M. 1993. The social world of prehistoric facts: Gender and power in Paleoindian research. In H. du Cros & L. Smith (eds). *Women in Archaeology: A Feminist Critique*. Canberra: Department of Prehistory, Research School of Pacific Studies, Australian National University. Pages 31–40.

Gillespie, R. 1997. Alternative timescales: A critical review of Willandra Lakes dating. *Archaeology in Oceania* 33:169–182.

Gillespie, R. & R.G. Roberts 2000. On the reliability of age estimates for human remains at Lake Mungo. *Journal of Human Evolution* 38:727–732.

Gollan, K. 1992. Ballina: A story about conservation process and outcomes. Paper presented at Archaeology in the Early 1990s research seminar. 22–24 August. Reproduced in an unpublished collection of papers of the same name. Armidale, NSW: Department of Archaeology & Palaeoanthropology, University of New England.

Gould, R. 1980. *Living Archaeology*. Cambridge: Cambridge University Press.

Graves-Brown, P., S. Jones & C. Gamble (eds) 1996. *Cultural Identity and Archaeology: The Construction of European Communities*. London: Routledge.

Greer, S. 1996. Archaeology, heritage and identity in Northern Cape York Peninsula. In S. Ulm, I. Lilley & A. Ross (eds). *Australian Archaeology '95: Proceedings of the 1995 Australian Archaeological Association Annual Conference*. Tempus 6. St Lucia, Qld: Anthropology Museum, University of Queensland. Pages 103–106.

Griffiths, T. 1991. History and natural history: Conservation movements in conflict? In D.J. Mulvaney (ed.). *The Humanities and the Australian Environment: Papers from the Australian Academy of the Humanities Symposium, 1990*. Canberra: Australian Academy of the Humanities. Pages 87–110.

——1996. *Hunters and Collectors: The Antiquarian Imagination in Australia*. Cambridge: Cambridge University Press.

Grose, S. 1999. Mungo 3 time frame dates to 68,000 years. *Canberra Times*. 21 May.

Hall, J. & I.J. McNiven (eds) 1999. *Australian Coastal Archaeology*. Canberra: ANH Publications, Research School of Pacific and Asian Studies, Australian National University.

Hamilakis, Y. 1999. La trahison des archéologues? Archaeological practice as intellectual activity in postmodernity. *Journal of Mediterranean Archaeology* 12(1):60–79.

Hamilton, J. 1998. Reclaiming the goddess: Feminist spirituality and the use of symbols. In M. Casey *et al.* (eds). *Redefining Archaeology: Feminist Perspectives*. Canberra: ANH Publications, Research School of Pacific and Asian Studies, Australian National University. Pages 168–172.

Harris, T. 2001. Extinct gene gives debate a new life. *Australian*. 10 January. Page 1.

Haydon, T. 1978. *The Last Tasmanian* (videorecording and educational guide). North Sydney: Artis Film Productions.

Head, L. 1987. The Holocene prehistory of a coastal wetland system: Discovery Bay, southeastern Australia. *Human Ecology* 15:435–462.

——1992. Australian Aborigines and a changing environment: Views of the past and implications for the future. In J. Birckhead, T. de Lacey & L. Smith (eds). *Aboriginal Involvement in Parks and Protected Areas.* Canberra: Aboriginal Studies Press. Pages 47–63.

——1996. Headlines and songlines. *Meanjin* 55(4):736–743.

——1998. Risky representations: The 'seduction of wholeness' and the public face of Australian archaeology. *Australian Archaeology* 46:1–4.

——1999. *Second Nature: The History and Implications of Australia as Aboriginal Landscape.* Syracuse, New York: Syracuse University Press.

Head, L., C. Gosden & J.P. White (eds) 1994. Social Landscapes. *Archaeology in Oceania* 29(3).

Hemming, S. 2000. Ngarrindjeri burials as cultural sites: Indigenous heritage issues in Australia. *World Archaeological Bulletin* 11:58–66.

Heritage Victoria. Possible link to mahogany ship. Media release, 18 August. www.heritage.vic.gov.au/media_ancient1.html (6 February 2002).

Hermes, M. 1992. Developing a course in Australian prehistory and cultural resources management for tertiary Aboriginal students at Bachelor College. *Australian Archaeology* 35:66.

Hills, B. 1992. The boat people. *Good Weekend* magazine. 15 August. Pages 29–34.

Hiscock, P. 1986. Technological change in the Hunter Valley and its implications for the interpretation of late Holocene change in Australia. *Archaeology in Oceania* 21:40–50.

——1996. The New Age of alternative archaeology in Australia. *Archaeology in Oceania* 31:152–164.

Hiscock, P. & S. Mitchell 1993. *Stone Artefact Quarries and Reduction Sites in Australia: Towards a Type Profile.* Australian Heritage Commission Technical Publications Series 4. Canberra: Australian Government Publishing Service.

Historic Houses Trust of NSW, 1996. *Sites: Nailing the Debate: Archaeology and Interpretation in Museums, Seminar, 7–9 April 1995.* Edited by S. Hunt & J. Lydon. Sydney: HHT.

Hodder, I. 1992. *Theory and Practice in Archaeology.* London: Routledge.

——1998. The goddess and the leopard's den: Conflicting interpretations at Çatalhöyük. In M. Casey *et al.* (eds). *Redefining Archaeology: Feminist Perspectives*. Canberra: ANH Publications, Research School of Pacific and Asian Studies, Australian National University. Pages 165–171.

——1999. *The Archaeological Process*. Oxford: Blackwell Publishers.

Holdaway, S., D. Witter, P. Fanning, R. Musgrave, G. Cochrane, T. Doelman, S. Greenwood, D. Pigdon & J. Reeves 1998. New approaches to open site spatial archaeology in Sturt National Park, New South Wales, Australia. *Archaeology in Oceania* 33:1–19.

Hope, J. 1995a. Aboriginal burial conservation in the Murray-Darling Basin. *Historic Environment* 11:57–60.

——1995b. *Realpolitik* in archaeology. Letter to the editor. *Australian*. 4 October.

Horacek, J. 2001. *Australian*. 4 January. Page 16.

Horton, D. 1991. *Recovering the Tracks: The Story of Australian Archaeology*. Canberra: Aboriginal Studies Press.

Hosty, K. & I. Stuart 1994. Maritime archaeology over the last twenty years. *Australian Archaeology* 39:9–18.

Howitt, R. 1998. Recognition, respect and reconciliation: Steps towards decolonisation? *Australian Aboriginal Studies* (1):28–34.

Hubert, J. 1989. A proper place for the dead: A critical review of the 'reburial' issue. In R. Layton (ed.). *Conflict in the Archaeology of Living Traditions*. London: Unwin Hyman. Pages 131–166.

Hunt, P. 1993. Hinterland forests of East Gippsland: An archaeological survey of the far East Gippsland Forest Management Area. Unpublished report to the Department of Conservation and Natural Resources, Victoria, and the Australian Heritage Commission.

Institute of Field Archaeologists (UK), 2001. www.archaeologists.net (30 January 2002).

International Council on Monuments and Sites 1996. *Monuments and Sites Australia*. General editor K. Proust. Colombo, Sri Lanka: ICOMOS.

International Council on Monuments and Sites, Australian National Committee. www.icomos.org/australia (6 February 2002).

Ireland, T. 1996. Excavating national identity. In Historic Houses Trust of NSW. *Sites: Nailing the Debate: Archaeology and Interpretation in Museums, Seminar, 7–9 April 1995*. Edited by S. Hunt & J. Lydon. Sydney: HHT. Pages 85–106.

——2000. The archaeology of nation in Australia. *World Archaeological Bulletin* 11:67–93.

——in press. 'The absence of ghosts': Landscape and identity in the archaeology of Australia's settler culture. *Historical Archaeology*.

Jack, R.I. 1996. Historical archaeology in Australia. *World Archaeological Bulletin* 7:22–31.

Jack, R.I. & A. Cremin 1994. *Australia's Age of Iron: History and Archaeology*. Melbourne & Sydney: Oxford University Press.

Jacobs, J.M. & F. Gale 1994. *Tourism and the Protection of Aboriginal Cultural Sites*. Australian Heritage Commission Special Australian Heritage Publication Series No. 10. Canberra: Australian Government Publishing Service.

James, P.C. 1995. Anglo-Australian law and the Aboriginal cultural heritage. *Historic Environment* 11:52–56.

Janke, T. 1998. *Our Culture: Our Future. Report on Australian Indigenous Cultural and Intellectual Property Rights*. Canberra: Australian Institute of Aboriginal and Torres Strait Islander Studies and the Aboriginal and Torres Strait Islander Commission.

Johnston, C. 1992. *What is Social Value? A Discussion Paper*. Australian Heritage Commission Technical Publication Series No. 3. Canberra: Australian Government Publishing Service.

Johnston, H. & P. Clark 1998. Willandra Lakes archaeological investigations 1968–98. *Archaeology in Oceania* 33:105–119.

Johnston, H., P. Clark & J.P. White (eds) 1998. Willandra Lakes: People and Palaeoenvironments. *Archaeology in Oceania* 33(3).

Jones, C. 1996a. Scientific breakthrough or debacle? *Canberra Times*. 28 September.

——1996b. ACT settlement could predate NT site. *Canberra Times*. 29 September.

——1997. Between a rock and a hard place. *Bulletin*. 6 May. Pages 24–25.

——2001. DNA casts doubt on 'out-of-Africa' human origin. *Canberra Times*. 10 January. Page 3.

Jones, C. & J. Dixon 2001. Who was Mungo's Mum? *Canberra Times*. 11 January. Page 5.

Jones, R. 1977. The Tasmanian paradox. In R.S.V. Wright (ed.). *Stone Tools as Cultural Markers: Change, Evolution and Complexity*. Canberra: Australian Institute of Aboriginal Studies. Pages 189–204.

——1978. Why did the Tasmanians stop eating fish? In R.A. Gould (ed.). *Explorations in Ethnoarchaeology*. Alberquerque: University of New Mexico Press. Pages 11–48.

——(ed.) 1985. *Archaeological Research in Kakadu National Park*. Canberra: Department of Prehistory, Research School of Pacific and Asian Studies, Australian National University and Australian National Parks and Wildlife Service.

——1990. Sylwadau cynfrodor ar Gôr y Cewri; or a British Aboriginal's land claim to Stonehenge. In C. Chippindale *et al.* (eds).*Who Owns Stonehenge?* London: B.T. Batsford Ltd. Pages 62–87.

——1992. Tom Haydon 1938–1991: Film interpreter of Australian archaeology. *Australian Archaeology* 35:51–64.

Jopson, D. 1999. Lay ancient Mungo's bones to final rest, say custodians. *Sydney Morning Herald*. 31 May. Page 5.

Knapp, A.B. (ed.) 1992. *Archaeology, Annales and Ethnohistory*. Cambridge: Cambridge University Press.

Knight, J. 1997. Perceptions of the archaeological record. *Australian Association of Consulting Archaeologists Incorporated Newsletter* 72:11–13.

Kociumbas, J. (ed.) 1998. *Maps, Dreams, History: Race and Representation in Australia*. Sydney Studies in History No. 8. Sydney: Department of History, University of Sydney.

Kohl, P.L. & C. Fawcett (eds) 1995. *Nationalism, Politics and the Practice of Archaeology*. Cambridge: Cambridge University Press.

Lahn, J. 1996. Dressing up the dead: Archaeology, the Kow Swamp remains and some related problems with heritage management. In L. Smith & A. Clarke (eds). *Issues in Management Archaeology*. Tempus 5. St Lucia, Qld: Anthropology Museum, University of Queensland. Pages 25–31.

Langford, R. 1983. Our heritage—Your playground. *Australian Archaeology* 16:1–6.

Layton, R. 1992. *Australian Rock Art: A New Synthesis*. Cambridge: Cambridge University Press.

Leech, G. 1996a. Challenge to the origin of man. Scientists split over rock find's implications for evolution. *Australian*. 23 September. Page 1.

——1996b. Scientists query dating methods in historic rock find. *Australian*. 24 September. Page 1.

——1997. The dating game. *Australian*. 21 February.

Lewis, D. 1997. Bradshaws: The view from Arnhem Land. *Australian Archaeology* 44:1–16.

Lilley, I. (ed.) 2000. *Native Title and the Transformation of Archaeology in the Postcolonial World*. Sydney: University of Sydney Oceania Monographs 50.

Lourandos, H. 1997. *Continent of Hunter-Gatherers: New Perspectives in Australian Prehistory*. Cambridge: Cambridge University Press.

Lourandos, H. & A. Ross 1994. The great 'intensification debate': Its history and place in Australian archaeology. *Australian Archaeology* 39:54–62.

Lovell-Jones, C. 1992. Observer and observed: A comparative study of Aboriginal participation in archaeological research. Paper presented at Archaeology in the Early 1990s research seminar. 22–24 August. Reproduced in an unpublished collection of papers of the same name. Armidale, NSW: Department of Archaeology & Palaeoanthropology, University of New England.

——1995. Observer and observed: Aboriginal consultation in New South Wales and Queensland. In I. Davidson, C. Lovell-Jones & R. Bancroft (eds). *Archaeologists and Aborigines Working Together*. Armidale, NSW: University of New England Press. Page 12.

Lowenthal, D. 1985. *The Past is a Foreign Country*. Reprinted 1990. Cambridge: Cambridge University Press.

Mackay, R. 1996. Political, pictorial, physical and philosophical plans: Realising archaeological research potential in urban Sydney. In Historic Houses Trust of NSW. *Sites: Nailing the Debate: Archaeology and Interpretation in Museums, Seminar, 7–9 April 1995*. Edited by S. Hunt & J. Lydon. Sydney: HHT. Pages 125–138.

Mackay, R. & G. Karskens 1999. Historical archaeology in Australia: Historical or hysterical? Crisis or creating awakening? *Australasian Historical Archaeology* 17:110–115.

Macknight, C.C. 1976. *The Voyage to Marege: Macassan Trepangers in Northern Australia*. Melbourne: Oxford University Press.

Mane-Wheoki, J. 1992. Sacred sites, heritage and conservation: Differing perspectives on cultural significance in the South Pacific. *Historic Environment* 9:32–36.

Mansell, M. 1995. *Realpolitik* in archaeology. Letter to the editor. *Australian*. 4 October.

Marcus, J. 1988. The journey out to the centre. The cultural appropriation of Ayers Rock. In A. Rutherford (ed.). *Aboriginal Culture Today*. Special issue of *Kunapipi* X (1&2). Sydney: Dangaroo Press. Pages 254–274.

Marquis-Kyle, P. & M. Walker 1992. *The Illustrated Burra Charter*. Canberra: International Council on Monuments and Sites Australia.

Masterton, M. & R. Patching 1990. *Now the News in Detail: A Guide to Broadcast Journalism in Australia*. Geelong, Vic.: Deakin University Press.

McBryde, I. 1986. Australia's once and future archaeology. *Archaeology in Oceania* 21:13–28.

——1992. The past as a symbol of identity. *Antiquity* 66:260–266.

——1995. Dream the impossible dream? Shared heritage, shared values or shared understanding of disparate values? *Historic Environment* 11(2&3):8–14.

McConell, A. n.d. *Forest Archaeology Manual*. Hobart: Forestry Commission Tasmania.

McDonald, J. 1992a. *The Archaeology of the Angophora Reserve Rock Shelter*. Environmental Heritage Monograph Series 1. Sydney: NSW National Parks and Wildlife Service.

——1996. The conservation of landscapes: A strategic approach to cultural heritage management. In S. Ulm, I. Lilley & A. Ross (eds). *Australian Archaeology '95: Proceedings of the 1995 Australian Archaeological Association Annual Conference*. Tempus 6. St Lucia, Qld: Anthropology Museum, University of Queensland. Pages 113–121.

McDonald, J. & A. Ross 1990. Helping the police with their enquiries: Archaeology and politics at Angophora Reserve rockshelter, NSW. *Archaeology in Oceania* 25:114–121.

McGowan, A. 1996. A view from the castle: Administering Aboriginal heritage legislation in a changing policy environment. In S. Ulm, I. Lilley & A. Ross (eds). *Australian Archaeology '95: Proceedings of the 1995 Australian Archaeological Association Annual Conference*. Tempus 6. St Lucia, Qld: Anthropology Museum, University of Queensland. Pages 301–310.

McGrath, A. 1995. *Contested Ground: Australian Aborigines under the British Crown*. Sydney: Allen & Unwin.

McKay, M. 1993. A comment on the WAC code of ethics. *Australian Archaeology* 37:50–53.

McKenzie, L. 2000. Bottle collectors—vandals or amateur archaeologists? A challenge for archaeologists. Paper presented at the Australasian

Society for Historical Archaeology Conference, Flinders University, Adelaide, December.

McNiven, I., B. Marshall, J. Allen, N. Stern & R. Cosgrove 1993. The Southern Forests Archaeological Project: An overview. In M.A. Smith, M. Spriggs & B. Frankhauser (eds). *Sahul in Review: Pleistocene Archaeology in Australia, New Guinea and Island Melanesia*. Canberra: Department of Prehistory, Research School of Pacific Studies, Australian National University. Pages 213–224.

McNiven, I.J. & L. Russell 1995. Place with a past: Reconciling wilderness and the Aboriginal past in World Heritage areas. *Journal of the Royal Historical Society of Queensland* XV(11):505–519.

McNiven, I.J. 1994. 'Relics of a by-gone race?': Managing Aboriginal sites in the Great Sandy region. *Ngulaig Monograph Series* 12. St Lucia, Qld: Aboriginal and Torres Strait Islander Unit, University of Queensland.

——1998. Shipwreck saga as archaeological text: Reconstructing Fraser Island's Aboriginal past. In I.J. McNiven, L. Russell & K. Schaffer (eds). *Constructions of Colonialism*. London & New York: Leicester University Press. Pages 37–50.

McNiven, I.J. & L. Russell 1997. 'Strange paintings' and 'mystery races': Kimberley rock-art, diffusionism and colonialist constructions of Australia's Aboriginal past. *Antiquity* 71:801–809.

McNiven, I.J., L. Russell & K. Schaffer (eds) 1998. *Constructions of Colonialism*. London & New York: Leicester University Press.

Meehan, B. 1982. *Shell Bed to Shell Midden*. Canberra: Australian Institute of Aboriginal Studies Press.

——1988. The 'dinnertime camp'. In B. Meehan & R. Jones (eds). *Archaeology with Ethnography: An Australian Perspective*. Canberra: Department of Prehistory, Research School of Pacific Studies, Australian National University. Pages 171–181.

Meehan, B. & R. Jones (eds) 1988a. *Archaeology with Ethnography: An Australian Perspective*. Canberra: Department of Prehistory, Research School of Pacific Studies, Australian National University.

——1988b. Preface. In B. Meehan & R. Jones (eds). *Archaeology with Ethnography: An Australian Perspective*. Canberra: Department of Prehistory, Research School of Pacific Studies, Australian National University. Pages vii–ix.

Megaw, J.V.S. 1969. Captain Cook and bone barbs at Botany Bay. *Antiquity* 43:213–216.

Menage, G. 1998. Contested spaces, contested times: The 'Day of mourning and protest' site. *Public History Review* 7:119–139.

Meskell, L. 1998. That's capital M, capital G. In M. Casey *et al.* (eds). *Redefining Archaeology: Feminist Perspectives.* Canberra: ANH Publications, Research School of Pacific and Asian Studies, Australian National University. Pages 147–153.

Moloney, F.J. 1997. Believing between the lines. *Sydney Morning Herald.* 10 April. Page 17.

Morwood, M. 1996. Jinmium and the dilemmas of dating. *Australian.* 24 September. Page 13.

Morwood, M.J., P.B. O'Sullivan, F. Aziz & A. Raza 1998. Fission-track ages of stone tools and fossils on the east Indonesian island of Flores. *Nature* 392:173–176.

Moser, S. 1994. Building the discipline of Australian archaeology. In M. Sullivan, S. Brockwell & A. Webb (eds). *Archaeology in the North: Proceedings of the 1993 Australian Archaeological Association Conference.* Darwin: North Australia Research Unit, Australian National University. Pages 17–29.

——1995. The 'Aboriginalization' of Australian archaeology. The contribution of the Australian Institute of Aboriginal Studies to the indigenous transformation of the discipline. In P.J. Ucko (ed.). *Theory in Archaeology: A World Perspective.* London & New York: Routledge. Pages 150–177.

——1996. Science, stratigraphy and the deep sequence: Excavation vs regional survey and the question of gendered practice in archaeology. *Antiquity* 70:813–823.

Mudrooroo 1995. *Us Mob: History, Culture, Struggle: An Introduction to Indigenous Australia.* Sydney: Angus & Robertson.

Mulvaney, D.J. 1962. Advancing frontiers in Australian archaeology. *Oceania* XXXIII(2):135–138.

——1969. *The Prehistory of Australia.* London: Thames & Hudson.

——1970. Human factors in the deterioration and destruction of antiquities and their remedy. In *Prehistory and Heritage: The Writings of John Mulvaney.* Occasional Papers in Prehistory 17. Canberra: Department of Prehistory, Research School of Pacific Studies, Australian National University. Pages 258–261.

——1989. *Encounters in Place: Outsiders and Aboriginal Australians 1606–1985.* Brisbane: University of Queensland Press.

——1990. Afterword: The view from the window. In S. Janson & S. MacIntyre (eds). *Through White Eyes.* Sydney: Allen & Unwin. Pages 155–167.

——(ed.) 1991a. *The Humanities and the Australian Environment: Papers from the Australian Academy of the Humanities Symposium, 1990.* Australian Academy of the Humanities Occasional Paper No. 11. Canberra: Australian Academy of the Humanities.

——1991b. Past regained, future lost: The Kow Swamp Pleistocene burials. *Antiquity* 65:12–21.

——1997. 'Musing amidst the ruins . . .' *Australasian Historical Archaeology* 14:3–8.

——1998. Dr Gallus and Australian Archaeology. *The Artefact* 21:4–8.

Mulvaney, D.J. & J. Golson 1971. *Aboriginal Man and Environment in Australia.* Canberra: Australian National University Press.

Mulvaney, D.J. & J. Kamminga 1999. *Prehistory of Australia.* Sydney: Allen & Unwin.

Murphy, L. 1996. The political application of cultural heritage management: Indigenous participation or indigenous control? In S. Ulm, I. Lilley & A. Ross (eds). *Australian Archaeology '95: Proceedings of the 1995 Australian Archaeological Association Annual Conference.* Tempus 6. St Lucia, Qld: Anthropology Museum, University of Queensland. Pages 141–146.

Murray, T. 1988. Ethnoarchaeology or palaeoethnology? In B. Meehan & R. Jones (eds). *Archaeology with Ethnography: An Australian Perspective.* Canberra: Department of Prehistory, Research School of Pacific Studies, Australian National University. Pages 1–16.

——1992. Aboriginal (pre)history and Australian archaeology: The discourse of Australian prehistoric archaeology. In B. Attwood & J. Arnold (eds). *Power, Knowledge and Aborigines.* Melbourne: La Trobe University Press. Pages 1–19.

——1993a. Communication and the importance of disciplinary communities: Who owns the past? In N. Yoffee & A. Sherratt (eds). *Archaeological Theory: Who Sets the Agenda?* Cambridge: Cambridge University Press. Pages 105–116.

——1993b. The childhood of William Lanne: Contact archaeology and Aboriginality in Tasmania. *Antiquity* 67:504–519.

———1996a. Contact archaeology: Shared histories? Shared identities? In Historic Houses Trust of NSW. *Sites: Nailing the Debate: Archaeology and Interpretation in Museums, Seminar, 7–9 April 1995.* Edited by S. Hunt & J. Lydon. Sydney: HHT. Pages 199–213.

———1996b. Creating a post-Mabo archaeology of Australia. In B. Attwood (ed.). *In the Age of Mabo.* Sydney: Allen & Unwin. Pages 73–86.

———1996c. Aborigines, archaeology and Australian heritage. *Meanjin* 55(4):725–735.

Murray, T. & J. Allen 1995. The forced repatriation of cultural properties to Tasmania. *Antiquity* 69:871–874.

Murray, T. & J.P. White 1981. Cambridge in the bush? Archaeology in Australia and New Guinea. *World Archaeology* 13(2):255–263.

National Board of Employment, Education and Training 1994. *Review of Grant Outcomes No. 15: Classics, Classical Archaeology and Prehistory 1986–1990.* Australian Research Council Evaluation Programme. Canberra: Australian Government Publishing Service.

New South Wales Heritage Office 1996. *NSW Heritage Manual.* Sydney: Department of Urban Affairs and Planning.

———1998. *Skeletal Remains: Guidelines for the Management of Human Skeletal Remains under the* Heritage Act 1977. Sydney: NSW Heritage Office.

———March 1999, 'Newsletter'. www.heritage.nsw.gov.au/pub/newslet/mar99 (6 February 2002).

New South Wales National Parks and Wildlife Service 1989. *Report of New South Wales Ministerial Task Force on Aboriginal Heritage and Culture 1989.* Sydney: NSW National Parks and Wildlife Service.

———n.d. *Aboriginal Cultural Heritage Standards and Guidelines Kit.* Sydney: NSW NPWS.

O'Connell, J. 1987. Alyawara site structure and its archaeological implications. *American Antiquity* 52(1):74–108.

O'Malley, B. 2001. Bones of contention. *Courier Mail.* 12 January.

O'Neill, G. 2001. The destruction of Eve. *Bulletin.* 16 January. Pages 28–31.

Orser, C.E. & B.M. Fagan 1995. *Historical Archaeology.* New York: Harper Collins.

Packard, P. & G. Dunnett 1994 (eds). *Cultural Values in Forests: Proceedings of a Workshop Conducted by the Australian Heritage Commission and the National Forest Inventory 11–12 May 1992.* Australian Heritage Commission Technical Publication 5. Canberra: Australian Government Publishing Service.

Pappin, G. for Willandra Lakes World Heritage Area Three Traditional Tribal Groups Elders Council 2001. Press release. January.

Pardoe, C. 1990. Sharing the past: Aboriginal influence on archaeological practice, a case study from New South Wales. *Aboriginal History* 14(1–2):208–223.

——1991. Isolation and evolution in Tasmania. *Current Anthropology* 32(1):1–21.

——1992. Arches of radii, corridors of power: Reflections on current archaeological practice. In B. Attwood & J. Arnold (eds). *Power, Knowledge and Aborigines*. Melbourne: La Trobe University Press. Pages 132–141.

——1995. Riverine, biological and cultural evolution in southeastern Australia. *Antiquity* 69:696–713.

Parrott, H. 1990. Legislating to protect Australia's material cultural heritage: Guidelines for cultural resources professionals. *Australian Archaeology* 31:75–82.

Pate, F. D. 1999. The graduate certificate in tertiary education at Flinders University: Improving teaching and learning in undergraduate archaeology. *Australian Archaeology* 49:60–62.

Pearson, M. & S. Sullivan 1995. *Looking After Heritage Places: The Basics of Heritage Planning for Managers, Landowners and Administrators*. Melbourne: Melbourne University Press.

Peters-Little, F. 2000. The community game: Aboriginal self-definition at the local level. AIATSIS Research Discussion Papers Series 10. Canberra: Australian Institute of Aboriginal and Torres Strait Islander Studies.

Plowman, S. 1993. Letter to the editor. *Sydney Morning Herald*. 10 June.

Pockley, P. 1992. Outcry over Noah's Ark claim. *Sun Herald*. 31 May. Page 48.

Poprzeczny, J. 1992. Prehistory may soon be history. *Australian*. 1 April. Page 23.

Porch, N. & J. Allen 1995. Tasmania: Archaeological and palaeoecological perspectives. *Antiquity* 69:714–732.

Prentis, M.D. 1995. From Lemuria to Kow Swamp: The rise and fall of tri-hybrid theories of Aboriginal origins. *Journal of Australian Studies* 45:79–91.

Presland, G. 1998. A. S. Gallus and the Archaeological Society of Victoria. *The Artefact* 21:9–13.

Proudfoot, H., A. Bickford, B. Egloff & R. Stocks 1991. *Australia's First Government House*. Sydney: Allen & Unwin in conjunction with the NSW Department of Planning.

Raab, L.M. 1984. Achieving professionalism through ethical fragmentation: Warnings from client-oriented archaeology. In E.L. Green (ed.). *Ethics and Values in Archaeology*. New York & London: The Free Press. Page 51.

Ramsden, P. 1998. *Learning to Lead in Higher Education*. London & New York: Routledge.

Rees, S. & G. Rodley 1995. *The Human Costs of Managerialism: Advocating the Recovery of Humanity*. Sydney: Pluto Press.

Register (formerly Society) of Professional Archaeologists, 1999. www.rpanet.org (30 January 2002).

Renfrew, C. & P. Bahn 1991. *Archaeology: Theories, Methods and Practice*. London: Thames & Hudson.

Reynolds, H. 1982. *The Other Side of the Frontier: Aboriginal Resistance to the European Invasion of Australia*. Melbourne: Penguin.

——1989. *Dispossession: Black Australians and White Invaders*. Sydney: Allen & Unwin.

——1995. *Fate of a Free People*. Melbourne: Penguin.

Richardson, L. 1989. The acquisition, storage and handling of Aboriginal skeletal remains in museums: An indigenous perspective. In R. Layton (ed.). *Conflict in the Archaeology of Living Traditions*. London: Unwin Hyman. Pages 105–186.

Ritchie, D. 1994. Principles and practice of site protection laws in Australia. In D.L. Carmichael, J. Hubert, B. Reeves & A. Schande (eds). *Sacred Sites, Sacred Places*. London: Routledge. Pages 227–244.

Roberts, R., M. Bird, J. Olley, R. Galbraith, E. Lawson, G. Haslett, H. Yoshida, R. Jones, R. Fullagar, G. Jacobsen & Q. Hua 1998. Optical and radiocarbon dating at Jinmium rock shelter, northern Australia. *Nature* 393:358–362.

Robinson, C. 1984. *Indiana Jones*, the Third World and American foreign policy: A review article. *Race and Class* XXVI(2):83–91.

Rose, D.B. 1996. Rupture and the ethics of care in colonized space. In T. Bonyhady & T. Griffiths (eds). *Prehistory to Politics. John Mulvaney, the Humanities and the Public Intellectual*. Melbourne: Melbourne University Press. Pages 190–215.

Ross, A. 1996. Landscape as heritage. In L. Smith & A. Clarke (eds). *Issues in Management Archaeology*. Tempus 5. St Lucia, Qld: Anthropology Museum, University of Queensland. Pages 7–17.

Ross, A. & members of the Quandamooka Aboriginal Land Council 1996. Aboriginal approaches to cultural heritage management: A Quandamooka case study. In S. Ulm, I. Lilley & A. Ross (eds). *Australian Archaeology '95: Proceedings of the 1995 Australian Archaeological Association Annual Conference.* Tempus 6. St Lucia, Qld: Anthropology Museum, University of Queensland. Pages 107–112.

Ross, A.C., T.H. Donnelly & R.J. Wasson 1992. The peopling of the arid zone: Human–environment interactions. In J.R. Dodson (ed.). *The Naïve Lands: Prehistory and Environmental Change in Australia and the Southwest Pacific.* Sydney: Longman Cheshire. Pages 76–114.

Rothwell, N. 1996a. Renegade of Rock. *Weekend Australian*. Review. 14–16 September. Page 3.

——1996b. Politics etched in stone. *Australian*. 23 September. Page 1.

Rowland, M.J. 1989. Population increase, intensification or a result of preservation? Explaining site distribution patterns on the coast of Queensland. *Australian Aboriginal Studies* 2:32–42.

Russell, L. & I.J. McNiven 1998. Monumental colonialism. Megaliths and the appropriation of Australia's Aboriginal past. *Journal of Material Culture* 3(3):283–299.

Ryan, L. 1996. *The Aboriginal Tasmanians.* Sydney: Allen & Unwin.

Schaffer, K. 1995. *In the Wake of First Contact: The Eliza Fraser Stories.* Cambridge: Cambridge University Press.

Schiffer, M.B. & G.J. Gumerman (eds) 1977. *Conservation Archaeology: A Guide for Cultural Resource Management Studies.* New York: Academic Press.

Schrire, C. 1972. Ethnoarchaeological models and subsistence behaviour in Arnhem Land. In D.L. Clarke (ed.). *Models in Archaeology.* London: Methuen. Pages 653–670.

Schultz, J. 1997. The press. In S. Cunningham & G. Turner (eds). *The Media in Australia: Industries, Texts, Audiences.* Sydney: Allen & Unwin. Pages 23–46.

Shaw, T. 1990. Bones in Africa. Presidential Address 1989. *Proceedings of the Prehistoric Society* 56:1–10.

Smith, C. 1996. Why caution is the best technique. *Australian*. 24 September. Page 13.

——1997. Editorial. *Australian Archaeology* 44:iii–iv.

Smith, C., P. Birt, P. Saeki, C. de Leuien, J. Steele, T. Owen, M. Wright, C. Wilson, P. Keller & J. James 2000. Burra Community Archaeology

Project. wwwehlt.flinders.edu.au/archaeology/*smith/burraweb/project front.htm (6 February 2002).

Smith, L. 1994. Heritage management as postprocessual archaeology? *Antiquity* 68:300–309.

Smith, L., A. Clarke & A. Alcock 1992. Teaching cultural tourism: Some comments from the classroom. *Australian Archaeology* 34:43–47.

Smith, M.A. & N. Sharp 1993. Pleistocene sites in Australia, New Guinea and Island Melanesia: Geographic and temporal structure of the archaeological record. In M.A. Smith, M. Spriggs & B. Frankhauser (eds). *Sahul in Review: Pleistocene Archaeology in Australia, New Guinea and Island Melanesia*. Canberra: Department of Prehistory, Research School of Pacific Studies, Australian National University. Pages 37–59.

Smith, M.A., M. Spriggs & B. Frankhauser (eds) 1993. *Sahul in Review: Pleistocene Archaeology in Australia, New Guinea and Island Melanesia*. Canberra: Department of Prehistory, Research School of Pacific Studies, Australian National University.

South West Institute of Technical and Further Education, Victoria, Learning Resource Centre Collections, 2000, 'Mahogany Ship Articles'. www.swtafe.vic.edu.au/lrc/collections/mahoganyship/tableof contents.htm (6 February 2002).

Spooner, N. 1998. Human occupation at Jinmium, northern Australia: 116,000 years old or much less? *Antiquity* 71:173–178.

Spriggs, M. 1998. Review of 'The Archaeological Process by Ian Hodder. Oxford: Blackwell. 1999'. *Australasian Historical Archaeology Journal* 16:100–101.

Stahl, A.B. 1993. Concepts of time and approaches to analogical reasoning in historical perspective. *American Antiquity* 58(2):235–260.

Stanbury, P. & J. Clegg 1990. *A Field Guide to Aboriginal Rock Engravings with Special Reference to Those Around Sydney*. Sydney: Sydney University Press.

State Records New South Wales, May 1998, 'A Guide to the New South Wales State Archives relating to Aboriginal People'. www.records. nsw.gov.au/publications/aboriginalguide/aboriginalguide-12.htm (30 January 2002).

Stone, J. 1992. The ownership of culture: Reconciling our common and separate heritages. *Archaeology in Oceania* 27:161–167.

Strang, V. 1998. The strong arm of the law: Aboriginal rangers, anthropology and archaeology. *Australian Archaeology* 47:20–29.

Sullivan, S. 1985. The custodianship of Aboriginal sites in southeastern Australia. In I. McBryde (ed.). *Who Owns the Past?* Melbourne: Oxford University Press. Pages 139–156.

——1986. Aboriginal sites and the law. In A. Ross (ed.). *Planning for Aboriginal Site Management: A Handbook for Local Government Planners.* Sydney: NSW National Parks and Wildlife Service. Pages 52–60.

——1993. Cultural values and cultural imperialism. *Historic Environment* 10:54–62.

——1996. Reflexions of 27 Years. In S. Ulm, I. Lilley & A. Ross (eds). *Australian Archaeology '95: Proceedings of the 1995 Australian Archaeological Association Annual Conference.* Tempus 6. St Lucia, Qld: Anthropology Museum, University of Queensland. Pages 1–14.

Sullivan, S. & S. Bowdler (eds) 1984. *Site Surveys and Significance Assessment in Australian Archaeology.* Canberra: Department of Prehistory, Research School of Pacific Studies, Australian National University.

Szpak, C. 1997. But . . . has it been used? An analysis of the attributes of shelters with evidence of use and shelters with evidence of the potential for use. Diploma of Arts thesis, Prehistoric and Historical Archaeology, University of Sydney.

Taçon, P.S.C. & R. Fullagar 1996. Living with the past. *Sydney Morning Herald.* 24 September.

Takarakka Rock Art Australia, 1998. www.kilpatha.com/info.html (5 February 2002).

Tasmanian Aboriginal Land Council 1996. Will you take the next step? In S. Ulm, I. Lilley & A. Ross (eds). *Australian Archaeology '95: Proceedings of the 1995 Australian Archaeological Association Annual Conference.* Tempus 6. St Lucia, Qld: Anthropology Museum, University of Queensland. Pages 293–300.

Thomas, I. 1993. Late Pleistocene environments and Aboriginal settlement patterns in Tasmania. *Australian Archaeology* 36:1–13.

——1995. Models and prima-donnas in southwest Tasmania. *Australian Archaeology* 41:21–23.

Thomas, J. 1991. Science versus anti-science? *Archaeological Review from Cambridge* 10(1):27–36.

Thomas, N. 1991. *Entangled Objects: Exchange, Material Culture, and Colonialism in the Pacific.* Cambridge, Mass.: Harvard University Press.

Thomas, S. 1992. *Black Man's Houses* (videorecording). Fitzroy, Vic.: A Steve Thomas/Open Channel Production.

Thorley, P. 1996. Self-representation and Aboriginal communities in the Northern Territory: Implications for archaeological research. *Australian Archaeology* 43:7–12.

Thorne, A. 1971. Mungo and Kow Swamp: Morphological variation in Pleistocene Australians. *Mankind* 8:85–89.

Thorne, A., R. Grün, G. Mortimer, N.A. Spooner, J.J. Simpson, M. McCulloch, L. Taylor & D. Curnoe 1999. Australia's oldest human remains: Age of the Lake Mungo 3 skeleton. *Journal of Human Evolution* 36:591–612.

Thorne, A. & P. Macumber 1972. Discoveries of late Pleistocene man at Kow Swamp, Australia. *Nature* 238:316–319.

Torrence, R. & A. Clarke (eds) 2000. *The Archaeology of Difference: Negotiating Cross-cultural Engagements in Oceania*. London: Routledge.

Trebeck, M. 1993. Letter to the editor. *Sydney Morning Herald*. 10 June.

Trigger, B.G. 1984. Alternative archaeologies: Nationalist, colonialist, imperialist. *Man* 19:355–370.

——1989. *A History of Archaeological Thought*. Cambridge: Cambridge University Press.

Tuhiwai Smith, L. 1999. *Decolonizing Methodologies. Research and Indigenous Peoples*. Dunedin: University of Otago Press.

Turner, G. & S. Cunningham 1997. The media in Australia today. In S. Cunningham & G. Turner (eds). *The Media in Australia: Industries, Texts, Audiences*. Sydney: Allen & Unwin. Pages 3–19.

Ulm, S., I. Lilley & A. Ross (eds) 1996. *Australian Archaeology '95: Proceedings of the 1995 Australian Archaeological Association Annual Conference*. Tempus 6. St Lucia, Qld: Anthropology Museum, University of Queensland.

United Nations Educational, Scientific and Cultural Organisation. www.unesco.org (6 February 2002).

Veth, P., P. Hiscock, S. O'Connor & M. Spriggs 1998. Gallus on the crossroads: Diffusionist models for Asian artefact 'traditions' in Australia and the last hurrah for cultural evolution. *The Artefact* 21:14–18.

Video Education Australasia, Film Victoria, the Department of Conservation and Environment, Museum of Victoria & Cambridge University Press 1990. *Living Aboriginal History* and *People of the Lake*. Videocassette and educational booklet.

Vince, G. 2001. Aboriginal ancestry descends into robust debate. *Australian*. 10 January. Page 4.

Vitelli, K.D. (ed.) 1996. *Archaeological Ethics: Readings from* Archaeology *Magazine*. Walnut Creek, London, New Delhi: Altamira Press.

von Daniken, E. 1971. *Chariots of the Gods*. Corgi: London.

——1972. *Return to the Stars*. Corgi: London.

Walker, F. 2001. When it comes to the bare bones, we're fair dinkum. *Sun-Herald*. 14 January. Page 41.

Walsh, G.L. 1994. *Bradshaws: Ancient Rock Paintings of North-west Australia*. Geneva: Bradshaw Foundation.

Walsh, G.L. & M.J. Morwood 1999. Spear and spearthrower evolution in the Kimberley region, NW Australia: Evidence from rock art. *Archaeology in Oceania* 43(2):45–58.

Watchman, A., P. Taçon, R. Fullagar & L. Head 2000. Minimum ages for pecked rock markings from Jinmium, north western Australia. *Archaeology in Oceania* 35:1–10.

Webb, S. 1987. Reburying Australian skeletons. *Antiquity* 61:292–296.

——1989a. *Prehistoric stress in Australian Aborigines: A Palaeopathological Study of a Hunter-gatherer Population*. Oxford: British Archaeological Reports, International Series 490.

——1989b. *The Willandra Lakes Hominids*. Canberra: Department of Prehistory, Research School of Pacific Studies, Australian National University.

Weiner, A.B. 1992. *Inalienable Possessions: The Paradox of Keeping-While-Giving*. Berkeley: University of California Press.

Weissensteiner, R. 1993. Indiana Jones Fantasy vs. Archaeological Reality: Examining the Portrayal of Archaeology in Popular Film. BA (Hons) thesis. Canberra: Australian National University.

West, F.H. 1990. Archaeology in the press: Science misserved? *Review of Archaeology* 11(2):25–32.

Westwood, J. (ed.) 1987. *The Atlas of Mysterious Places*. London: Weidenfeld & Nicolson.

Wheeler, Robert, 2000, *The Tomb Raider Archive: Lara Croft*. www.trarchive.ctimes.net/laracroft.html (1 November 2000).

White, J.P. 1974. *The Past is Human*. London: Angus & Robertson.

——1993. Letter to the editor. *Sydney Morning Herald*. 18 June. Page 14.

——1998. Money, journals and universities. *Archaeology in Oceania* 33:83.

White, J.P. & J.F. O'Connell 1982. *A Prehistory of Australia, New Guinea and Sahul*. Sydney: Academic Press.

Whittaker, M. 1990. 'Cambridge cabal' claim in academia. *Australian*. 18 April.

——1998. Stirring the mega-possum. *Australian Magazine*. 8–9 August. Pages 14–19.

Whitten, D.G.A. & J.R.V. Brooks 1972. *The Penguin Dictionary of Geology*. London: Penguin.

Wildesen, L.E. 1984. The search for an ethic in archaeology: An historical perspective. In E.L. Green (ed.). *Ethics and Values in Archaeology*. New York: The Free Press. Pages 3–12.

Williams, E. 1987. Complex hunter-gatherers: A view from Australia. *Antiquity* 61:310–21.

Williams, E. & D. Johnston 1991. The World Archaeological Congress (WAC) and the WAC First Code of Ethics. *Australian Archaeology* 32:64–67.

Williamson, C. 1998. Late Holocene Australia and the writing of Aboriginal history. In T. Murray (ed.). *Archaeology of Aboriginal Australia: A Reader*. Sydney: Allen & Unwin. Pages 141–148.

Woodford, J. 1996a. Unveiled: Outback Stonehenge that will rewrite our history. *Sydney Morning Herald*. 21 September. Page 1.

——1996b. The dating game. *Sydney Morning Herald*. News Review. 28 September. Page 33.

——1999. It's a date: Our Mungo Man was here 56,000 years ago. *Sydney Morning Herald*. 21 May.

Wright, R. 1971. *Archaeology of the Gallus Site, Koonalda Cave*. Canberra: Australian Institute of Aboriginal Studies.

——1995. They don't dig it here. Letter to the editor. *Australian*. 20 September.

Wylie, A. 1985. The reaction against analogy. *Advances in Archaeological Method and Theory* 8:63–111.

Yelland, P. 2000. Fed's policy brings offshore on. *Sydney Morning Herald*. IT Jobs. 1 February. Page 6c.

Zarmati, L. 1995. Popular archaeology and the archaeologist as hero. In J. Balme & W. Beck (eds). *Gendered Archaeology: The Second Australian Women in Archaeology Conference*. Canberra: ANH Publications, Research School of Pacific & Asian Studies, Australian National University. Pages 43–50.

Zarmati, L. & A. Cremin 1998. *Experience Archaeology*. Cambridge: Cambridge University Press.

Index

industrial archaeology, 16, 18
intellectual property, 49, 87–8; see also
    Indigenous rights
intensification see Australian archaeology
Internet and archaeology, 133, 168,
    170
Ireland, Tracy, 23
Irrawang (NSW), 17
isolation see Australian archaeology

Jacobs, Jane, 80
Janke, Terri, 88
Jervis Bay (NSW), 123
Jinmium (NT), 154–61, 176
Johnson, Wayne, 152
Jones, Cheryl, 60–1, 159
Jones, Indiana, 128,129
Jones, Rhys, xi, 12, 15, 155, 157

Kakadu National Park (NT), 73–4
Kalkadoon people (Qld), 124
Kamminga, Johan, x, 155
Keating, Paul, 136
Keep River (NT), 154
keeping places see repatriation and
    reburial
Keilor (Vic), 144
Kelly, Alice, 165
Kennett, Jeff, 166
Kenniff Cave (Qld), 4
Knight, James, 67
Koonalda Cave (SA), 144
Kow Swamp (Vic), 59–60, 80, 195; see
    also repatriation and reburial
Kurnell (NSW), 6
Kutikina Cave (Tas), x–xi, 71

Lake Condah (Vic), 123, 177
Lake George (ACT), 159
Lake Mungo (NSW), 5, 6, 136, 162–5
    Mungo Lady, 60, 165
    Mungo Man, 162–5 passim
Land and Environment Court (NSW),
    109
landscapes see cultural landscapes;
    cultural places
Langford, Ros, xii, 77, 79, 124
Lapstone Creek (NSW), 2

Lara Croft, 129
The Last Tasmanian, xi–xii, 68
La Trobe University, xi, xii, 103–4
Lauer, Peter, 72–3, 139
Leech, Graeme, 157
legislation see also consulting archaeology,
    cultural heritage management,
        Environmental Impact Assessment
    and ethical behaviour, 56
    forms of heritage legislation, 25, 29, 90
    relationship with policy and
        administration, 24–6, 90
    role in defining professionalism, 50
    role of Commonwealth, states and
        territories, 24–5, 26–30
Lewis, Darrell, 185
ley lines see alternative archaeologies
Lightning Brothers see rock art
looting see antiquities trade
lost civilisations see alternative
    archaeologies
Lourandos, Harry, 7, 177
Lovell-Jones, Christine, 62, 94, 102
Lowenthal, David, 136

M2 motorway, 107–112, 114, 116,
    118–9, 172; see also Environmental
    Impact Assessment
Mabo, Eddie, 65–6
Mabo, High Court of Australia ruling,
    66, 106, 183; see also Native Title
Macassans see Australian archaeology
Macknight, Campbell, 6–7
Magee, John, 162
Mahogany Ship, 166, 182
Malakunanja II (NT), 155
managerialism, 61, 197
Mana-Wheoki, Jonathon, 38
Mansell, Michael, 85
Maori (New Zealand), 38
Marcus, Julie, 187
maritime archaeology see Australian
    archaeology
Marquis-Kyle, Peter, 34
Marshall, Brendan, 70
Mata Menge, Flores (Indonesia), 162
material evidence see also Australian
    archaeology; rock art; stone tools